RIDING THE WAVES OF THE NEVER NORMAL

the
UNCERTAINTY
principle

Peter Hinssen

Lannoo
Campus

Contents

Dedication 9

1

The Never Normal 11

2

Are We Making Any Progress? 21
The Most Dangerous Time 22
You Have Been Here Before 23
What Goes Up Must Come Down 24
Cycles And Waves 27
Rise And Fall 29
The Constructal Law 33
Looking At The Stars 35
Positive In The Long Term 36

3

WTF? (What Is The Future?) 41
Palantíri And Mutually Assured Destruction 42
THE Think Tank 43
Shell And The 1973 Oil Crisis 45
The Discontinuity Case 46
Blinded By Beliefs 47
Preparing For Uncertainty 48
Great, But Not Perfect 49
The Living Company 50
Run Like Machines 51
The Memory Of The Future 54
Lack Of Imagination 55
Tools For Foresight 57
Remarkable People 57

4

Game-changers: The Good, The Bad And The Ugly **61**

The Silicon Valley Of The 14th Century 62

In Search of Excellence 67

Built To Last 73

The Zoo 74

The Zipper Effect 81

Unleashing The Tiger 83

Thrive, Not Survive 84

5

Risk, The Root Of All Progress **103**

The Ubiquity Of Risk 105

Be Prepared 110

Risk Is A Spectrum 112

The Unthinkable 116

The Greatest Risk To Us Is Us 120

Reality Distortion 123

Fake It Till You Make It 128

The Uncertainty Principle 133

The Courage To Lead 136

6

For Progress, There Is No Cure **149**

The Super Martian 150

DeepMind And Omni-Use Technologies 153

The Flood 157

The Gorilla Problem 160

The Need For Speed 163

7

A New Age Of Work **171**

Motivational Coffee Mugs And Circumnavigation 172

Learned Resilience And Active Hope 178

The Post-Industrial Hustle 181

Artificial Intelligence And Bullshit Jobs 185

The 15-Hour Work Week 190

Liminality 193

The Shadow Dream 194

Mind-Wandering, Door Handles And Rebalancing 198

8

Builders And Thinkers **203**

Why We Need Engineers 204

The Disastrous Darien Scheme 207

French Engineering FTW 209

The Dream That Became A Nightmare 211

Uncle Sam's Panama Power Play 214

Beep, Beep, Beep 217

An Advocate For Technological Acceleration 220

Protopia 226

Rational Optimism 229

9

Still Hope To See **237**

Quantum Wonderland 240

The Omni-Bot 247

Artificial General Intelligence 254

Rewriting Ourselves 262

OUTRO

Uncertainty Is A Feature, Not A Bug **271**

Endnotes 275

About Peter Hinssen 284

Other Books by Peter Hinssen 285

Thank You 286

Dedication

This book is dedicated to my four grandparents—the people who shaped me into who I am today. I am the combination of all four, and for that, I am deeply grateful.

To Rene Vermandel, who left this world far too soon. Though I never had the chance to know you, the stories about your kindness, your loving nature, your warmth, and your endless curiosity have always stayed with me. Your spirit lives on in the values I cherish most.

To Margriet Labat, who raised me as a young boy. My early childhood is filled with memories of your care, and that warmth still lingers with me today. Thank you for giving me such a strong foundation of love and security.

To Betty Backers, whose infectious joy for life has always been an inspiration. Your ability to embrace life with such positivity and energy continues to remind me of what truly matters.

To Theo Hinssen, who had a profound influence on my life. Your dedication, passion, and unwavering work ethic were a powerful example for me. I had the privilege of truly connecting with you as I was starting my journey, and those conversations meant the world to me. How you delighted in my passion for technology and entrepreneurship is something I'll never forget. I can only hope to pass on your mindset and values to the next generation.

This book stands as a tribute to their influence, their love, and their lasting legacy.

1

The Never Normal

If you're always trying to be normal, you will never know how truly amazing you can be. —MAYA ANGELOU

I have a deeply complex relationship with the word 'normal'.

Back in 2010, when I published my first mainstream business book, *The New Normal*, I was quite pleased with myself for coining the concept; not least because of that neat little alliteration that rolled so smoothly off the tongue. At the time, I was obsessed with the idea that digital—still seen as a kind of 'magic'—would one day become the norm. So I wrote an entire book to persuade the world of this inevitable transformation.

Years of experience as a tech entrepreneur had taught me that this is simply how technological innovation works. It follows an S-curve: it starts as something 'special', then, as adoption accelerates, it flips into the second phase where it becomes 'ordinary'. And, looking back, that's exactly what happened with digital. No one even uses that word anymore. That's how run-of-the-mill it has become.

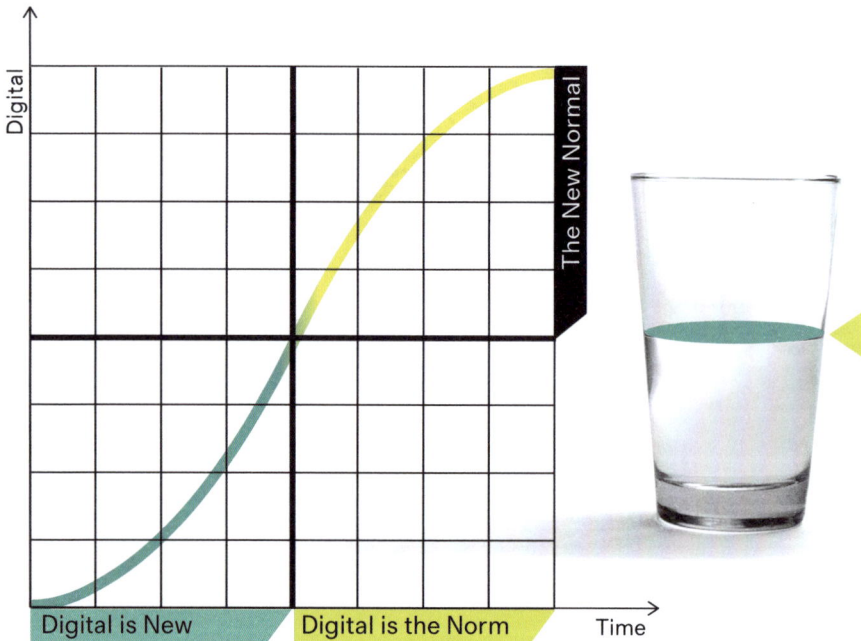

Over the years, I also came to recognize a fascinating disconnect between the technological S-curve and our expectation-curve. They rarely align. Roy Amara captured this dynamic best in his eponymous law: 'We tend to overestimate the effect of a technology in the short run and underestimate the effect in the long run.'

The contrast between the two plays out something like this:

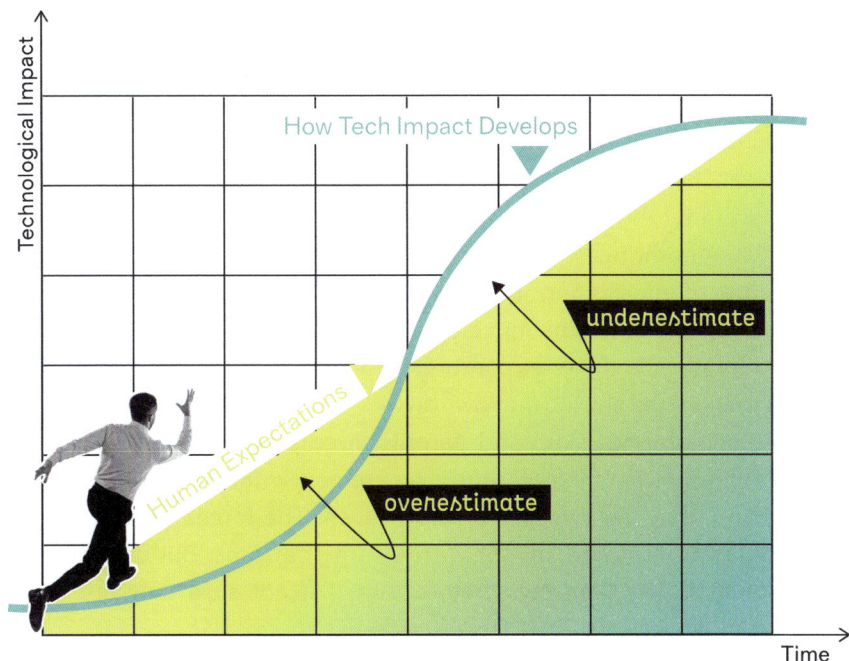

After that, I became truly passionate about finding the Next Normal: identifying the next big thing still simmering beneath the surface, ready to reshape our lives before inevitably evolving into just another commodity. But as I dug deeper, I realized something had changed. There wasn't just one singular next big thing, there were many.

So I introduced a new term: New Normals, plural.

Belgian designer and researcher Thomas Lommée perfectly captured that idea when he wrote 'The next big thing will be a lot of small things' on the facade of one of the Ghent University buildings in 2015. I came to understand that rather than one 'Big' New Normal, we were dealing with several 'Little' New Normals—like Big Data, AI, quantum computing, the metaverse and many more. In some ways, it was as if we were observing a quantum state that had yet to collapse, existing in multiple possibilities and scenarios at once.

After the pandemic, however, I grew to loathe the term New Normal. It had become inextricably linked to the impact of COVID—synonymous with lockdowns, restrictions, and all the challenges that came with them. What was once a term of progress and transformation had taken on a darker, more limiting connotation. As I said, my relationship with 'normal' has always been complicated.

Then came another curveball (see what I did there?).

The pattern of consecutive S-curves replacing one another still held true, just as the brilliant Carlota Perez—one of my personal heroes—once described: 'The Industrial Revolution gave way to the Age of Steam, which was followed by the Age of Steel, Electricity, and Engineering, then the Age of Oil, Automobiles, and Mass Production, eventually leading to our current Age of Information'. But the real shift wasn't in *what* was happening, it was in how fast. What once took 20 to 30 years to fully play out was now accelerating, with cycles compressing into just a decade. The pace of transformation had shifted into overdrive.

While our grandparents and parents largely experienced *one* major wave of innovation in their lifetimes, we are now witnessing three or four. Our children may see five, six, or even seven. The forces of creative destruction and disruption still follow the same patterns. But now, they're accelerating faster than ever before. And I'm not sure they are 'little' changes any longer...

One of the most profound consequences of this acceleration is how we *perceive* the forces of change. Think of a tree. To most of us, trees appear steadfast and unchanging. But if you were to speed up their growth—from seed to sapling to towering oak—and then watch their seasonal transformations over years, the sheer scale of change would be staggering. In the same way, technological S-curves are no longer distant, abstract phenomena. For the first time, we can actually *see* several of them unfold within our own lifetimes. That acceleration, that dynamic of continuous change is what I have come to call the Never Normal.

The Never Normal makes many of us extremely uncomfortable. It also fuels the belief that we are experiencing the most volatile and uncertain period in human history. I'm pretty sure that someone living through the fall of Roman Empire, the Great Depression or the Chinese Cultural Revolution might disagree. A big reason for this perception is chronocentrism: our innate tendency to see our own era as uniquely significant and to assume that the events shaping our world are more valuable than those of the past. Every generation believes they are witnessing unprecedented times and that history is shifting in ways never seen before. And, of course, we are no different.

But the only truly unprecedented thing right now is the speed. Not the uncertainty. In many ways, things have always been volatile, uncertain, complex and ambiguous (good old VUCA) or brittle, anxious, non-linear, and incomprehensible (BANI). Unexpected things have always happened. 'It [was always] difficult to make predictions, especially about the future,' to use Nobel prize-winning quantum physicist Niels Bohr's quip. Just ask Xerox, Blackberry, Blockbuster or even Louis XVI.

But I have come to believe that this Never Normal 'Uncertainty' is not necessarily a bad thing.

In the 1949 classic *The Third Man*, a character called Harry Lime (played by Orson Welles) tells the protagonist Holly Martins a story about a cuckoo clock he purchased in Switzerland. He says: 'In Italy, for 30 years under the Borgias, they had warfare, terror, murder and bloodshed, but they produced Michelangelo, Leonardo da Vinci and the Renaissance. But in Switzerland, they had brotherly love, they had 500 years of democracy and peace—and what did that produce? The cuckoo clock.'

As cynical as it may sound, limitations often force the imagination to work harder than in 'easy' conditions. That is why hard times often breed more radical, long-lasting innovations. Look at what the Cold War forced DARPA to come up with, as I'll explain later. Just like that, the current seismic shocks—be they technological, geopolitical, biological, social or economic—force us to look for solutions that are exceptionally useful. Which is why I, as a pathological optimist, believe that the Never Normal is an opportunity more than a challenge. It is ripe with untapped raw potential.

We just need a little imagination to be able to thrive.

Werner Karl Heisenberg was a German theoretical physicist, one of the main pioneers of the theory of quantum mechanics and, of course, the originator of 'The Uncertainty Principle', also the title of this book. Heisenberg taught us that 'Not only is the Universe stranger than we think, it is stranger than we *can* think.' You could say the same about the future in uncertain times: it is often stranger than we *can* think. It is filled with 'unknown unknowns' as Donald Rumsfeld loved to say.

These unknowns are why prediction is such a powerful tool, but also one with clear limitations. We can never control the future by forecasting it, but we *can* control how we respond to it—and how fast. The key is not to be paralyzed by fear when faced with the Never Normal. American futurist Alvin Toffler captured this phenomenon perfectly with the term 'future shock'—the 'physical and psychological distress suffered by those unable to cope with the rapid pace of social and technological change'. That's probably why we've been experiencing some kind of weird dichotomy these past few years: between those of us—like me—who are really excited about the potential of the Never Normal and then the others who are uncomfortable, anxious and would love to return to the slower pace of the Old Normal.

But I could not have formulated it any better than that other famous Heisenberg, the alias of *Breaking Bad*'s anti-hero Walter White: 'What I came to realize is that fear, that's the worst of it, that's the real enemy. So, get up, get out in the real world and you kick that bastard as hard as you can, right in the teeth.' Okay, I would have perhaps put it a little less aggressively, but you get the point, I'm sure.

At the beginning of 2025, DeepSeek sent a shock wave through the Western world. It was completely overhyped (I'm almost wondering who will remember it when this book comes out), but it's also the perfect example of how China fearlessly kicked its limitations 'right in the teeth'. This was probably not what Biden had in mind when he made the protectionist move to restrict the export of advanced chips to China. Many believed with him that the chip limitations would set back the Chinese AI industry for many years. But if there is one thing the Chinese love, it's a good challenge. Out of that emerged an obscure (well, out here in the West anyhow) company that was able to turn these constraints around and transform them into an advantage: it trained a model that was pretty much on par with those of OpenAI or Google but—and this is the impressive part—which took just two months to train, at minimal cost, using Nvidia's less-advanced H800 chips (at least that's what it claimed). And, in a power move, it even made the model Open Source. It was glorious and terrifying, depending on who you were talking to. Marc Andreessen called this the Sputnik moment of AI.

That right there. That's exactly how the Never Normal works: if you accept its pressure and use it right, you'll make diamonds out of coal.

In fact, when faced with the disruption of the Never Normal, companies have two fundamental choices: Robustness or Resilience. Robustness is about strength and resistance: the ability to withstand disruptions without being significantly affected. It's a defensive strategy, built on stability and durability. The application for organizations is typically all about 'hedging': the use of deflective mechanisms to mitigate risks.

Resilience, on the other hand, is about agility and adaptation: the capacity to recover, evolve, and even flourish in the face of change. Robustness is about survival; resilience is about thriving. It means that companies can apply a 'leverage mechanism' to not just face the Never Normal, but to use its power to unlock potential.

DeepSeek clearly chose resilience. It did not just bounce 'back'. It absorbed the disruptive energy, and used it to bounce 'forward', Aikido-style.[1] And I believe that you can too, which is why I wrote this book.

That's where The Uncertainty Principle comes in.

As mentioned earlier, The Uncertainty Principle was introduced by physicist Werner Heisenberg in 1927 as a fundamental concept in quantum mechanics. It states that it is impossible to simultaneously know both the exact position and exact momentum of a particle with perfect precision. The more accurately one of these properties is measured, the less accurately the other can be known. This principle is not due to flaws in measurement instruments. It is a fundamental property of nature.

And of business.

Just as quantum particles are governed by inherent uncertainties, business decisions are filled with unpredictable risks. When a company embarks on a new venture or innovation, it must always embrace a certain level of uncertainty about the outcome. Paradoxically, the more a company tries to control and mitigate every aspect of a new project—much like attempting to measure both position and momentum with absolute precision—the more rigid and less adaptable it becomes. And this over-emphasis on control can stifle innovation, slow decision making, and lead to missed opportunities.

The key to navigating uncertainty is actually quite simple. It lies not in control but in acceptance. We must teach our brains that uncertainty isn't something to fear. It simply means that countless possibilities lie ahead—in a quantum state, if you will—waiting to take shape until the moment you decide to act. And for those with an entrepreneurial mindset, that isn't daunting. It's absolutely thrilling.

I vigorously hope that you, dear reader, will come to share my enthusiasm about the Never Normal in the coming pages. Enjoy!

▼ Endnotes on p. 275

It has been my philosophy of life that

difficulties vanish
when faced boldly. —ISAAC ASIMOV

Are We Making Any Progress?

When you invent the ship, you also invent the shipwreck; when you invent the plane you also invent the plane crash; and when you invent electricity, you invent electrocution... Every technology carries its own negativity, which is invented at the same time as technical progress. —PAUL VIRILIO

The Most Dangerous Time

When I was a young boy and started reading the newspaper, probably around the age of 10 or 11, I remember becoming incredibly depressed. All the stories I read were grim and dark, tragedies from across the globe, from famine to war, from terrorism to genocide. My most naïve idea was to think that 'By the time I am older, this will all have been resolved.' On the contrary.

I stopped watching the news altogether years ago. I found it to be a relentless stream of predominantly negative narrative, which was dragging me down more than lifting me up.

Not long before he passed away, the British physicist Stephen Hawking wrote a brilliant op-ed piece in *The Guardian* called **'This is the most dangerous time for our planet.'**[2]

Hawking reflects on the transformative and often turbulent impacts of globalization and technological advancements on society. He recognizes a growing disconnect and discontent among the general population, manifestations of a broader, global frustration over widening economic disparities and the perceived failures of leadership to address such issues effectively. He discusses the inevitable and sometimes destructive consequences of rapid technological change, such as job losses in manufacturing and potential future impacts on middle-class professions due to artificial intelligence.

But the main message of his column is that we run the risk that these evolutions will enrich a small group while leaving behind the majority. This visibility of inequality, amplified by social media and global connectivity, fuels discontent and drives mass migration, as people seek better opportunities, often leading to further social and political strain.

The crux of Hawking's argument is a call for a profound shift in how global leaders and elites respond to these challenges. He urges a move towards greater humility, cooperation, and a rethinking of how resources are distributed and managed. Hawking's final plea is for unity and collaborative effort to address some of the most pressing challenges facing humanity, such as climate change, overpopulation, and environmental degradation, stressing that our survival depends on our ability to work together and transcend our differences.

Clearly, he was not the most optimistic chap towards the end of his life.

I am a perennial optimist and have been my entire life. My choice to study to become an engineer was absolutely in line with that fundamental philosophy. I did and still do believe in a world that can be designed, built and constructed. And that innovation and technology can help us build a better world. For all.

You Have Been Here Before

At odd and unpredictable times, we cling in fright to the past. —ISAAC ASIMOV

I also grew up on an overdose of science fiction. Perhaps one of the greatest thinkers and writers of the past century was Isaac Asimov. He was certainly seen as one of the 'Big Three' science fiction writers of his age (together with Arthur C. Clarke and Robert Heinlein). But he was not just a writer, he was a man of science, a professor of biochemistry at Boston University.

He was also an incredibly prolific writer. During his lifetime he wrote or edited more than 500 books, as well as an estimated 90,000 letters and postcards.

Perhaps his most famous work is the *Foundation* series, an absolute masterpiece. It was deemed impossible to portray on screen, until Apple TV developed the series for streaming. It was released in 2021, starring the brilliant Jared Harris as the protagonist Hari Seldon, a professor of mathematics at Streeling University on the planet Trantor, the capital of the first Galactic Empire.

Seldon develops a new field called 'psychohistory', a fictional algorithmic science that combines history, sociology, and statistical mathematics to help predict the future behavior of very large groups of people. This predictive tool operates on the premise that while individual actions can be highly unpredictable, the behavior of large masses of people can be more reliably forecast through the analysis of historical patterns and psychological data.

Psychohistory works only when dealing with vast populations and it requires that the population under study remains ignorant of the psychohistorical analysis to prevent their behavior from changing in reaction to the predictions. In other words, it has to be kept secret, in order not to influence the outcome.

The core concept of the *Foundation* series is that professor Seldon used psychohistory to predict that the Galactic Empire would eventually fall. This would result in a subsequent 30,000 years of barbarism, before the galaxy would eventually aggregate again into a Second Empire. It was possible, however, to use psychohistory to influence future events in such a way that this 'Great Interregnum' was shortened from 30,000 years to a mere 1,000.

I always found that concept utterly upsetting and dispiriting: the Great Empire had to fall, before a new Empire could rise out of the ashes.

But of course, psychohistory was just a fictional idea, a figment of the imagination of the great Isaac Asimov. Or was it?

While psychohistory remains a fictional concept, its underlying idea— that large-scale human behavior can be modeled and predicted if enough data is available—does resonate with current trends in data analytics, artificial intelligence, and predictive modeling.

What Goes Up Must Come Down

In fact, that's pretty much what Peter Turchin does.

Peter's father Valentin Turchin[3] is considered one of the fathers of cybernetics and artificial intelligence. He had a career both in Russia and in the US. He was born in the Soviet Union in 1931.

Turchin graduated from Moscow State University, where he studied theoretical physics. He quickly became involved in cybernetics and computer science, but his career in the Soviet Union was marred by political challenges, particularly due to his advocacy for democratic reforms and his criticisms of the Soviet regime. Due to his political views, Turchin faced professional ostracism and was eventually forced to emigrate. After emigrating to the United States in the late 1970s, Turchin continued his work in cybernetics and computer science, as he took a faculty position at the City College of New York. His work remains influential in discussions about the philosophy of computer science, cybernetics, and the broader implications of technology on society.

He is also the father of Peter Turchin,[4] who is about as close to a real human version of Hari Seldon as you will find.

Peter Turchin was born in Russia, but moved to the US when his father was exiled from the Soviet Union in 1977. He studied evolutionary biology and zoology, and was eventually one of the founding fathers of the concept of

'Cliodynamics' which is a real-life attempt to make Asimov's concept of psychohistory come to life.

Named after Clio, the ancient Greek muse of history, Cliodynamics aims to apply a data-driven scientific approach to understanding history and social dynamics. Turchin developed the concept to demonstrate the idea that historical and social phenomena follow certain predictable patterns that can be scientifically analyzed and used to make predictions about future societal trends. This involved the development of equations and algorithms that can describe how societies evolve, how empires rise and fall, and how economic changes can affect social stability.

Cliodynamics relies heavily on quantitative data gathered from historical records. This data includes demographic, economic, and military records which are used to test hypotheses about social behavior and historical events. Turchin and his team have fed all the known data from previous societies, empires and civilizations into a huge database, and tried to model and predict patterns and the mechanisms behind social cohesion, conflict, and other dynamic social phenomena.

It also tries to predict the patterns of political stability and instability, understanding the dynamics of empire formation and decline, and analyzing the factors that drive societal-scale changes over centuries. One significant application has been the study of cycles of violence, such as internal wars, and how economic conditions, such as income inequality and resource scarcity, influence these cycles.

Turchin junior wrote up his findings in the book *War and Peace and War: The Rise and Fall of Empires*. And that must be one of the most depressing works I have ever read. It basically follows the great quote from Isaac Newton, when describing the force of gravity: 'What goes up must come down.' In other words, every empire, every civilization follows predictable transitions. From war to greatness, chaos to order. Peace, however, never lasts. In the end, tensions rise, cracks grow, war rages again and societies crumble. In that process, the dawn of a new civilization is nurtured.

Not everyone agrees that Cliodynamics is really useful. *The Economist* criticized the work of Peter Turchin by comparing it to seismology: sure, you can predict that 'eventually' an earthquake could happen, but if you can't say exactly when the ground will tremble, it significantly reduces the effectiveness.

But the evidence seems to be there: what goes up, eventually comes down.

Mark Twain, who often was a more light-hearted narrator, said something very similar in his book *The Gilded Age: A Tale of Today*:

> Every civilization carries the seeds of its own destruction, and the same cycle shows in them all. The Republic is born, flourishes, decays into plutocracy, and is captured by the shoemaker whom the mercenaries and millionaires make into a king. The people invent their oppressors, and the oppressors serve the function for which they are invented.

In his essay: *The Fate of Empires and Search for Survival*, Sir John Glubb, a British soldier, scholar, and author, examines the life cycles of empires and identifies common patterns in their rise and fall.

Glubb identifies six stages in the life cycle of an empire: the age of pioneers, the age of conquests, the age of commerce, the age of affluence, the age of intellect, and the age of decadence.

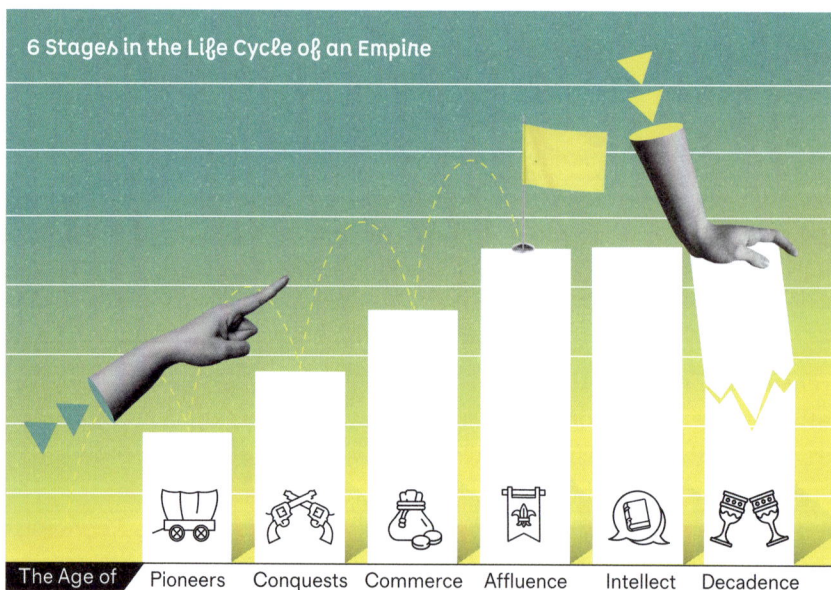

6 Stages in the Life Cycle of an Empire

The Age of — Pioneers — Conquests — Commerce — Affluence — Intellect — Decadence

He argues that empires go through these stages in a very predictable pattern, and that the age of decadence is usually marked by a decline in moral values, a lack of purpose, and an overemphasis on individualism.

Furthermore, Glubb observes that empires generally sustain a lifespan of 250 to 300 years and that their downfall is often precipitated by internal degradation, economic downturns, and military overextensions. He suggests that the survival of an empire depends on its ability to adapt to changing circumstances, maintain a sense of purpose, and foster a sense of loyalty and service among its citizens.

Let's unpack that: a sense of purpose, loyalty, and adapting to a constantly changing environment. Starts to look a lot like a recipe for the Never Normal...

Cycles And Waves

So far, I'm not sure that I've been doing such a great job in getting your spirits up...

Let me recap: the world is constantly changing, faster and faster. Nothing you can really do about that. And when you compile the history of all the world's civilizations, there is one absolute guarantee: eventually you will fail.

And then I haven't even mentioned the eventual entropic heat death[5] of the Universe yet...

So yes, if you look at the life cycle of the entire Universe: not positive. When you look at the life cycle of an entire civilization: questionable. But there are plenty of volatilities inside these larger time windows where extremely interesting things can happen, and where you can absolutely make the difference.

I talked about my fascination with S-curves in the first chapter, and the brilliance of those studying them, like Carlota Perez. But there is actually a whole set of waves and cycles that have been studied which provide longer term patterns of rise and fall, growth and decline.

The Kondratiev wave, named after the Russian economist Nikolai Kondratiev, is a theory that suggests economic development progresses in long-term cycles of approximately 50 to 60 years. These cycles, also known as 'long waves', consist of alternating periods of high sectoral growth and periods of relatively slow growth. Kondratiev initially identified these patterns through an extensive study of price data in nineteenth-century England, and since then, the concept has been expanded to include a broader range of economic indicators.

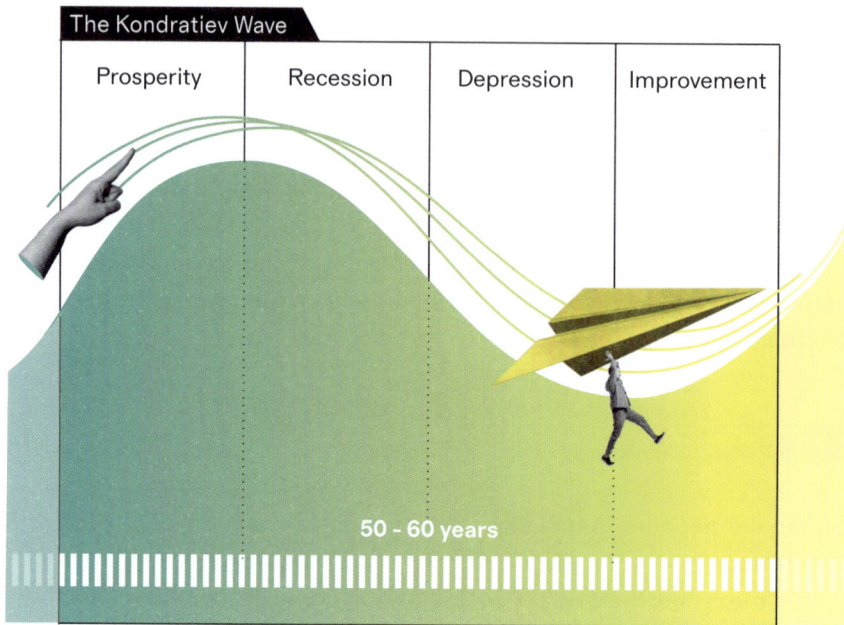

The Kondratiev Wave

| Prosperity | Recession | Depression | Improvement |

50 - 60 years

According to the theory, each wave arises from technological innovations that significantly boost productivity and economic output, leading to an upswing in the economy. This prosperous phase is characterized by an increase in investment and expansion across various sectors. Over time, however, the initial advantages of these innovations diminish, and economic growth slows down, leading to a downturn or a depressive phase in the cycle. This downturn is marked by reduced capital investment, higher unemployment, and a slower pace of economic activity.

Economists and historians who have studied Kondratiev waves argue that these cycles can be seen in the Industrial Revolution's mechanization, the rise of steel and heavy engineering, the diffusion of information technology, and other key historical developments. These waves are influential in shaping economic policy and business strategy, as understanding the phase of the cycle can lead to better decision making regarding investment, production, and innovation. Despite some skepticism in academic circles regarding its predictive power, the concept of Kondratiev waves continues to be a useful tool for analyzing long-term trends.

Rise And Fall

I believe it is absolutely vital that organizations that want to thrive in the Never Normal need to understand the bigger picture. You need to sense the long waves, be conscious of the shifting cycles, and use the force of change to rise to the occasion.

But even as a company, it is not easy to stay out of the negative spiral of entropic decay. There, we have fundamental patterns and laws as well. And that brings us to arguably the most influential political thinker of the Renaissance period.

If I had a time machine, and could only use it five (well yes, you would at least need that number)[6] times, then I'm sure I would pay Machiavelli a visit in the 15th century.

Born in 1469, the Florentine diplomat, author, philosopher, and historian Niccolò di Bernardo dei Machiavelli was the absolute rock star of political thought during the Renaissance. Best known for *Il Principe* (*The Prince*), Machiavelli's name has become synonymous with cunning political tactics and the use of deceit in business and governance. The term 'Machiavellian' itself has come to denote a form of political manipulation that is often considered unscrupulous. *The Prince* is a pragmatic exploration of power dynamics and statecraft, drawing from Machiavelli's extensive experience as a diplomat and observer of great leaders.

Machiavelli's life was steeped in the tumultuous political landscape of Florence. Starting his career in the Florentine Republic as a banker's assistant, he quickly rose to become the chancellor and chief executive officer of the government. His tenure coincided with a period of constant upheaval, marked by the invasions of Italy by foreign powers like France, Spain, and Austria, which profoundly influenced his political theories. It was his hope that the fragmented Italian city-states would unify under a strong leadership to repel these foreign invaders effectively.

➤ I really do assume that you are reading the endnotes as well, otherwise it is going to be very difficult to follow my narrative.

Apart from his political writings, Machiavelli's interactions with other contemporary giants were significant. His collaboration with Leonardo da Vinci, who served briefly as Florence's military engineer, likely influenced his thoughts on war and politics. Despite a promising start, Machiavelli found himself at odds with the powerful Medici family, who dominated Florentine political affairs. After the Medicis regained control of Florence, Machiavelli was dismissed from his position and subjected to imprisonment and torture, accused of conspiring against them.

In the aftermath of his political downfall, Machiavelli penned *The Prince* as a means to regain favor with the Medici rulers, dedicating it to Lorenzo di Piero de' Medici. Although he never saw his work published or reaped its benefits—Machiavelli died in 1527, five years before its publication—the book immortalized him as the father of modern political science.

My favorite set of ideas from the vast body of work is the concept of Machiavellian forces, as it relates to startups, companies, countries, and empires.

It outlines four stages of organizational and political development that reflect the rise and fall of such entities through cycles of growth, dominance, decline, and renewal or collapse.

The Rise

(Foundation and Growth)—In the initial stage, the focus is on building the foundation. For a startup or empire, this involves innovative strategies, strong leadership, and a clear vision that differentiates the entity from its competitors or predecessors. This period is characterized by rapid growth, enthusiasm, and the aggressive pursuit of goals. The leaders at this stage are often visionary, risk-takers, and highly motivated to establish their mark on the world.

The Peak

(Stability and Dominance)—At this stage, the entity has established a significant presence and influence in its market or region. There is a shift from aggressive expansion to managing, maintaining, and capitalizing on the achieved positions. Processes become standardized, and the focus is on efficiency and consolidation of power. Leadership may become more conservative, focusing on sustaining success rather than pushing boundaries.

The Decline

(Complacency and Challenges)—This phase begins when an entity fails to adapt to changes or underestimates new competitors or evolving situations. Complacency from prolonged success might lead to missed opportunities for innovation or ignoring potential threats. Leadership may struggle with bureaucracy, internal conflicts, and a disconnect from the foundational strategies that led to initial success.

The Renewal or Collapse

(Transformation or Dissolution)—Faced with potential failure, an entity must either transform itself or risk collapse. This involves significant changes in strategy, leadership, or operations—essentially a reinvention of the organization or state. Some manage to innovate and adapt, finding new paths to success, while others fail to overcome challenges, leading to their dissolution or absorption by rivals.

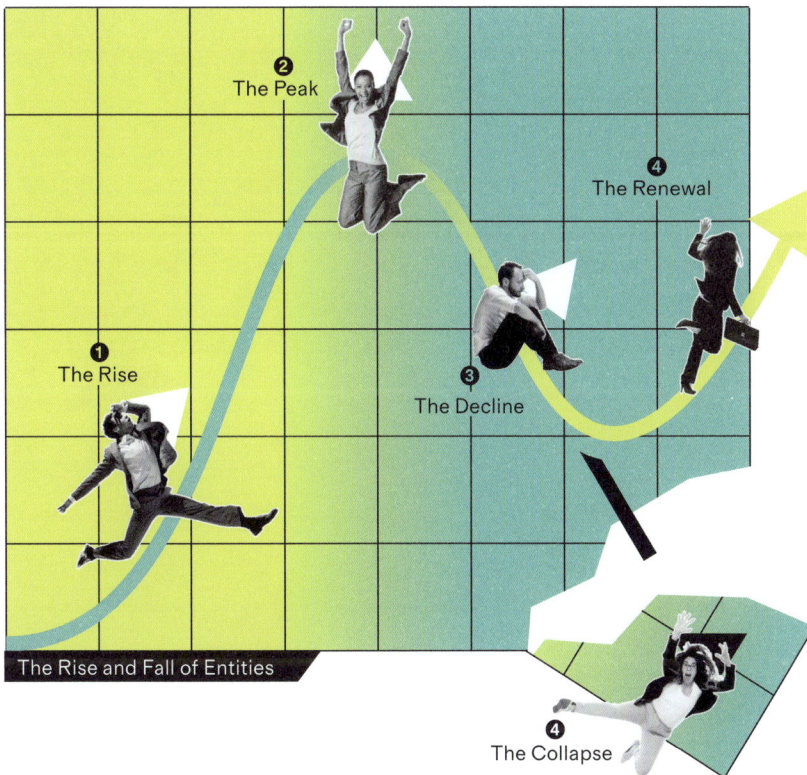

The Peak ❷

The Renewal ❹

The Rise ❶

The Decline ❸

The Rise and Fall of Entities

The Collapse ❹

These stages are reflective of the natural cycle of growth and decay that Machiavelli observed in political states, but you'll recognize that they are equally applicable to modern organizations and businesses, small and large. Rather than seeing these phases of up and down as inevitabilities, leaders can learn from these patterns to recognize their own position and how they can strengthen or change it.

A slightly more cynical view of the four Machiavellian stages is this:

Machiavellian Forces

Startups, companies, countries and empires usually go through four stages:

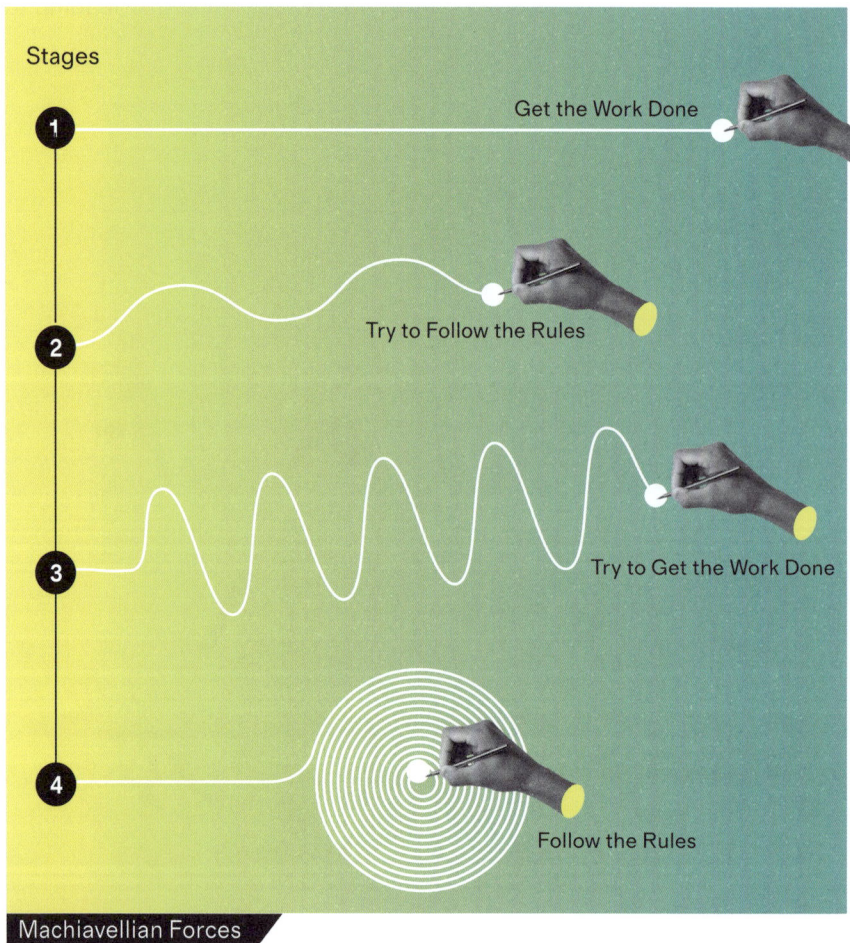

Stages

1 — Get the Work Done

2 — Try to Follow the Rules

3 — Try to Get the Work Done

4 — Follow the Rules

Machiavellian Forces

First stage

GET THE WORK DONE, without worrying about other factors.

Second stage

GET THE WORK DONE, try to follow rules, and minimize casualties.

Third stage

TRY TO GET THE WORK DONE, while trying harder to follow rules and minimizing casualties in accordance with new internal rules and procedures.

Fourth stage

Follow all the internal rules and procedures, and also the external ones. It does not matter whether the job is done or not.

I'm sure Niccolò would have loved that last version.

The Constructal Law

Understanding the bigger picture, the relentless patterns of rise and fall, the cycles and waves, the Never Normal can seem quite daunting. But as Professor Jon Kabat-Zinn—best known for developing Mindfulness-Based Stress Reduction (MBSR)—said: 'You can't stop the waves, but you can learn to surf.' If you want to excel at surfing, you'll need to sense, pick up, understand and leverage the **flow** that you are in. because standing still in the Never Normal is lethal.

We have arrived at the wonderful theory of thermodynamics.[7,8] It is one of the most fascinating areas of science, which has a rich and long history, and is still being developed and refined today.

One of the pivotal scientists in that field today is Professor Adrian Bejan, who was educated at MIT. But before that, he grew up in the harsh and unforgiving Romanian regime that was led by the communist dictator Nicolae Ceaușescu. So it is perhaps not surprising that the law he started formulating in 1995, while he was researching entropy, became an ode to freedom, flow and greater access—things that were very scarce in communist Romania.

This constructal theory is a fascinating and relatively new area of thermodynamics that deals with the natural tendency of flow systems to evolve and optimize their design over time. The theory is based on the principle that there is a natural tendency in nature for flow systems to evolve in a way that provides easier movement of matter and greater efficiency in flow.

In practical terms, this theory can be observed in the branching pattern of trees, lightning bolts, the shape and behavior of river basins, the architecture of the lungs, and even in human-made systems such as traffic flows and urban planning. In each case, the structure of the flow system develops to allow for easier and more efficient movement or transfer of some entity, whether it be air, blood, water or vehicles.

But here's where it gets really cool: you could actually use constructal law principles to build better technologies from the start. Like designing more efficient computing cooling systems by mimicking the branching patterns of tree leaves and nutrients. Or developing better distribution networks for goods and urban planning by modeling the pathways of river basins.

Constructal law also has broader implications beyond the sciences, touching on areas such as social dynamics, economics, and technology development. It provides a framework for understanding how systems evolve to handle stressors or flows more efficiently and offers insights into the design of more effective systems, whether they are ecological, biological, or engineered.

Flow is essential, and—even more crucially—it cannot be stopped. Because the constructal law works 'in reverse' as well, it does not just predict how a system will evolve, but also how a system will become toxic when it isolates itself and the natural flow and the access are willingly limited. This will eventually lead it to fossilize and die.

In other words, 'When movement stops, life ends.' Basically, we have to keep evolving, keep access open and keep the flow running. No matter our position, resting on our laurels sooner or later equals doom. Always continue to innovate and don't be afraid to redefine yourself. Those systems that increase flow, increase access and increase freedom are the ones that stay alive. The more dynamic you become, the more prosperous you'll be.

Simply put: when in doubt, go with the flow.

Looking At The Stars

So, fully understanding the eventuality of all things and fully aware of the Never Normal, I remain absolutely hopeful that all types of entities like companies, organizations, nations and individuals can harness the power of flow to maximize outcome and effect.

And that sense of hope is essential. It is vital to be able to seize the opportunity, and to re-invent ourselves and our systems to thrive in the Never Normal. As Oscar Wilde put it in his book *Lady Windermere's Fan*, 'We are all in the gutter, but some of us are looking at the stars.'

I fully understand how challenging it can be in a Never Normal world which, as Stephen Hawking puts it, seems to be 'the most dangerous time for our planet'. I'm sure it frightens many people to live in a world which seems more uncertain than ever before.

Richard Feynman is one of my greatest heroes. He'd certainly be on my Time Machine list, and I'm absolutely positive it would be a dinner-date to remember. Born in 1918, in Queens, New York, Feynman became a brilliant physicist whose contributions to the field of science are legendary. He single-handedly developed the theory of Quantum Electro Dynamics,[9] for which he received the Nobel Prize.

He had a gift for making the most complex scientific ideas accessible to any audience. His lectures became theatrical performances where he would captivate crowds with a charismatic blend of wit, charm, and an infectious passion for unraveling the mysteries of the universe.

Feynman was not a stuffy academic. At his core, he was driven by an unquenchable thirst for knowledge and understanding. He was relentless in his pursuit of pushing past the boundaries of the known, while inspiring others to join him in the endless quest to shed light on the great unknowns. His life was a testament to the importance of marrying scientific rigor with an imaginative, irreverent spirit—after all, it is those blessed with the courage to color outside the lines who so often end up redrawing them entirely.

That is why I absolutely love this wonderful phrasing by Feynman on progress, uncertainty and doubt:[10]

> We absolutely must leave room for doubt or there is no progress and there is no learning. There is no learning without having to pose a question. And a question requires doubt. People search for certainty. But there is no certainty. People are terrified—How can you live and not know?

It is not odd at all. You only think you know, as a matter of fact. And most of your actions are based on incomplete knowledge and you really don't know what it is all about, or what the purpose of the world is, or know a great deal of other things. It is possible to live and not know.

Positive In The Long Term

As the Irish playwright George Bernard Shaw said, 'The reasonable man adapts himself to the world; the unreasonable one persists in trying to adapt the world to himself. Therefore, all progress depends on the unreasonable man.'

That is why in the light of this seemingly menacing context of the Never Normal, and with the odds stacked against us in the bigger scheme of Cliodynamics, we have to relish and cherish the unreasonable heroes that guide us in our journey of progress.

One of the people that I admire greatly is Hans Rosling. Hans was a Swedish physician and statistician. I do not need to put Hans on my Time Machine list, because I had the absolute pleasure of working with him on a few occasions.[11] Sadly, he passed away in 2017.

An indefatigable optimist armed with statistics and showmanship, Hans had a magical ability to transform dense data into captivating narratives that spread hope about human progress. The professor's virtuoso talks, combining playful humor and mesmerizing animated data visuals, shattered myths about global development. His passionate belief in an upward trajectory for humanity reinvigorated optimism through the universal language of numbers.

Hans Rosling dedicated his life's work to challenging widespread pessimism and negative narratives about global development. He painted a powerful picture of human progress that offered a message of hope. Rather than dwelling on bleak statistics, Rosling celebrated the remarkable improvements in areas like health, education, and quality of life that have occurred across the world over recent decades.

Through the lens of data, Rosling revealed positive long-term trajectories that are often obscured by short-term crises. He showed that while challenges remain, the arc of human development has been decisively bent towards progress through achievements like rising life expectancies, falling child mortality, and increasing literacy rates.

His message was one of optimism tempered with pragmatism—acknowledging the world's very real problems, but demonstrating that sustained efforts by nations and people can and do create better living conditions for millions. Rosling's mission was to replace the cynicism often plaguing public discourse with a fact-based perspective rooted in possibility.

In the end, Hans Rosling's true gift was using the universal language of statistics to unite people across cultures in a shared narrative of hope for humanity's upward journey. His relentlessly positive worldview, backed by credible data, inspired optimism and encouraged continued efforts to create a brighter, more equitable future for all.[12]

When we look at our own evolution, the modern form of humans evolved only about 200,000 years ago. If the entire history of that human evolution was condensed into a day, it's interesting to look at what has happened in the last three minutes.

With the storming of the Bastille in Paris in 1789, history marked the beginning of **the social revolution**, which the French (being French) still call 'The French Revolution'. It was a landmark event that toppled the ancient monarchy and aristocratic privileges, paving the way for the ideals of liberty, equality, and fraternity to reshape society across the world. In the human day, that happened at 23:57.

Just 150 years ago, the Industrial Revolution **transformed economic and social systems** worldwide by introducing machine-based manufacturing, urbanization, and capitalist models that redefined labor, class structures, and quality of life. In many countries, the percentage of people working in agriculture went from 70% to less than 5% over time. In the human day, that happened at 23:58.

Today, the human clock stands at 23:59, and the **technological revolution** is rapidly reshaping nearly every aspect of human existence, driven by advances in robotics, computing power, artificial intelligence, biotechnology, and connectivity that are disrupting traditional systems and industries while opening up vast new frontiers of innovation, efficiency, and human potential.

Maybe we are heading for an apocalypse. But then I would prefer the real origin of the word.

Today, we use 'apocalypse' as a synonym for catastrophe, but the original Greek word apokálypsis, from which it is derived, actually means a **revelation**.

I, for one, cannot wait to unveil and reveal the enormous potential still ahead, and eagerly long for the moment our human clock strikes midnight.

tl
dr

Many people seem to believe that 'This is the most dangerous time for our planet' (according to an op-ed by the late physicist Stephen Hawking), but as a perennial optimist, I believe that we need a better narrative than that. Yes, history moves in S-curves and waves and cycles that seem to follow a 'What goes up must come down' pattern. And yes, we currently have many macro challenges to deal with. And true, companies need to understand this bigger picture in order to make intelligent decisions.

But we also need hope.

Uncertainty may be part of the fabric of (company) life, but we *are* moving forward. Data wizards like Hans Rosling have uncovered positive long-term trajectories that are unfortunately often obscured by short-term crises. In short: entropy and uncertainty are real, but I believe that acceptance of this should not mean resignation. We embrace them and then find out how we can help build a better future. Not just in spite of them, but because of them.

▶ **TLDR**, **TL;DR** or **tl;dr** is short for 'too long; didn't read', internet slang often used to introduce a summary of an online post or news article. Instead of putting it at the beginning of each chapter, I decided to put it at the end though, so as not to spoil the reading experience by offering everything up front. This way, it functions more like a little memory refresher for what you read in the chapter.

3

WTF? (What Is The Future?)

History teaches us nothing, except that something will happen. —HUGH TREVOR-ROPER

In today's Never Normal world, we tend to see that more and more of the traditional ways of observing the future are becoming less and less efficient and relevant. What would new mechanisms that allow us to turn insights into foresights entail? Before you say 'AI',[13] let me take you down a history of strategic foresight thinking. And what better place to start than in Middle Earth?

Palantíri And Mutually Assured Destruction

In the epic fantasy world of *The Lord of the Rings*, the writer J.R.R. Tolkien conceived the concept of the Palantíri (singular: Palantír): indestructible crystal balls that had been crafted by the Elves of Valinor in the First Age.

These Palantíri were ancient seeing-stones used for communication and viewing across vast distances. In Tolkien's world, the control of Palantíri offered foresight and huge strategic advantages amidst the epic struggle against Sauron. In the corporate world, having foresight about emerging risks and opportunities is invaluable amidst intense market competition.

The very idea of building contemporary Palantíri has been the Holy Grail in the world of forecasting for decades, both in military and business contexts.

I believe I'm running out of passes for my Time Machine trips here, but I'd certainly love to spend one on Herman Kahn, one of the most preeminent futurists of the twentieth century. He spent his entire life trying to conceive Palantíri, mostly to help the United States maintain their edge during the Cold War.

Herman Kahn was born in the US, to parents who were Jewish immigrants from Eastern Europe. He served in the US Army in the Burma campaign during World War II, and got a science degree in Caltech after the war. He was then recruited by the RAND corporation as a mathematician, to build scenarios of Cold War warfare.

His job at the RAND corporation was to contemplate 'the unthinkable', namely full blast nuclear combat between the US and Russia. He had to figure out if there were scenarios that would have a better post-nuclear outcome than others. In other words: how could the US go full-nuclear with the USSR, and still 'win'. That resulted in one of the most iconic books on strategic thinking: *On Thermonuclear War*. I have a copy of his book on the shelf of my office that I absolutely cherish.

Allow me to introduce a bit of context here.

THE Think Tank

Let us start with the RAND corporation itself.[14] Few organizations have a more mythical iconic and controversial status than this fabled think tank based out in Santa Monica, California.

The name RAND comes from 'Research And Development', and the non-profit was founded in 1948 as a joint venture between the US Air Force and the Douglas Aircraft Company, one of the crucial industrial players in the US during WWII. Douglas produced almost 30,000 aircraft for the US military between 1942 and 1945.

During the war, it was easy for the military to have access to the best and brightest minds of the nation, as I will describe later on when we deep dive into the relationship between war and innovation. Look at the role that MIT played in developing radar technology, where the smartest engineers in Boston worked for the military. Or the all-star crew of scientists that worked on the Manhattan Project.

But post-war, the US Air Force realized it would become much more difficult to tap into the brainpower of the best mathematicians, statisticians, physicists and engineers to lead the US into dominance during an unstable post-nuclear era, which we would later categorize as the 'Cold War' between US and Russia.

So they set up the RAND corporation, to bring the brains on board. RAND is not big, with less than 2,000 employees, but to give you an idea of the brainpower on board: 32 recipients of the Nobel Prize, primarily in the fields of economics and physics, have been associated with RAND at some point in their career. Pretty impressive. RAND was not the very first think tank, but it became so powerful and dominant that it became known as THE Think Tank.

The RAND corporation employees were pioneers. One of their first major focus areas was to build a nuclear military strategy for the US, which eventually led to the concept of the 'nuclear triad': a three-pronged nuclear deterrent capability that combined land-based missiles, submarine-launched missiles, and nuclear bomber aircraft.

This strategy aimed to ensure a credible retaliatory capability that could survive a Soviet first strike. RAND also advanced theories like deterrence through 'Mutually Assured Destruction' that shaped America's nuclear posture.

Herman Kahn was the scientist at the very heart of that mission, as the chief strategist at RAND. In *On Thermonuclear War*, he clearly stated the idea that a nuclear confrontation with the Soviets was 'winnable', based on the mathematics of game theory.

Needless to say, this was also highly controversial. During the Cold War, with the US entering into wars in Korea and Vietnam, many citizens became extremely anti-conflict and the topics of 'Mutually Assured Destruction' and 'Winnable Nuclear Confrontations' seemed insane.

It also resulted in Dr. Kahn being immortalized in arguably one of the best movies ever made. *Dr. Strangelove* by Stanley Kubrick is a brilliant 1964 political satire on the Cold War about that very idea—that the US and the Soviet Union battle out a nuclear confrontation. Peter Sellers plays one of the best roles of his entire career, as Dr. Strangelove, a wheelchair-based nuclear war expert, a character that was based on Herman Kahn. In the movie, Dr. Strangelove works for the BLAND corporation, a Kubrick play on RAND.

Kahn wanted to build Palantíri to help the US navigate nuclear strategies. He combined systems theory and game theory, used extensive number crunching and early computing capabilities, and applied it to military strategy, and later to economic strategies. In his later years, he published *The Next 200 Years*, in which he contemplated what the world would look like in 2176.

But Kahn also built the foundation of what came to be known as 'scenario thinking', scenario planning or scenario analysis. By cross-pollination of ideas across domains like economics and physics he laid the foundations for a now popular strategic planning method that involves creating multiple plausible scenarios of the future to help organizations anticipate and prepare for different outcomes.

Just as the Palantíri enabled their users to see far ahead, scenario planning equips organizations with a form of long-range strategic foresight. It allows them to peer into different potential futures before they unfold. Scenario thinking explores multiple diverging storylines and perspectives about the future rather than relying on ONE single prediction.

So in many ways, the Palantíri[15] represent the aspirational qualities of an effective scenario planning process—granting decision makers a deeper perception of potential futures to better prepare strategies amid an uncertain environment. Used wisely, such foresight is powerful; but abused, it can distort reality.

Shell And The 1973 Oil Crisis

The second father of scenario planning must be Pierre Wack, who would extract the concept of scenario thinking from the military realm, and introduce it to the world of business, at the Royal Dutch Shell corporation.

Pierre Wack was born in 1922 in the French Alsace region, a borderland between France and Germany. He studied in Heidelberg and Frankfurt, and combined economics with statistics. After the war, Wack had a chance to visit the East extensively, and became fascinated by Japan's economic reconstruction. He was particularly fascinated by the country's ability to drive and manage its growth with such efficiency. Following a brief stint at Michelin, he joined Shell in 1961.

Shell was, and still is, a major global energy player that was formed due to the merger of the Royal Dutch Petroleum Company and the British 'Shell' Transport and Trading Company in 1907. The combined entity rapidly became the leading competitor of the American Standard Oil corporation (Rockefeller). At the end of the 1920s, Shell was the largest producer of oil in the world.

In the early 1960s, Wack was working in the forecasting division at Shell, and was getting mightily frustrated with their very traditional 'straight line forecasting' approach based on regression models. There was very little attention to shorter and longer-term planning cycles, and virtually no input in terms of uncertainty, volatility and circularity.

When Wack was working in Algeria, a big part of the Shell operation by then, he realized that you needed to take the 'full' context into consideration if you wanted to understand the future.

During a sabbatical in Japan, he immersed himself in the work of Herman Kahn, becoming captivated by the mathematical foundations that underpinned Kahn's approach to scenario thinking. When he returned to

London, he bet his job on his conviction that, for a company like Shell, the only way to look ahead was to embrace the scenario-based approach to strategy.

Wack took the obscure methodology out of military and government circles and recognized its potential value for businesses operating in an increasingly volatile, global landscape. He spearheaded efforts at Shell to craft plausible scenarios about different future states of the world and their impact on the energy markets that were central to Shell's business.

They were just in time.

The Discontinuity Case

The 'Discontinuity Case' was a scenario developed by Pierre Wack and his Shell team in the early 1970s that presaged the 1973 OPEC oil embargo. This scenario highlighted the potential for a significant disruption in the global oil market due to geopolitical tensions in the Middle East and the growing power of oil-producing countries.

In the Discontinuity Case, Wack and his team explored a range of factors that could lead to a sudden and severe oil crisis, including political instability in the Middle East, tensions between oil-producing countries and Western nations, and the possibility of coordinated action by oil exporters to restrict supply.

The scenario challenged conventional wisdom at the time, which viewed the global oil market as relatively stable and predictable. By considering alternative futures and questioning existing assumptions, Wack and his team were able to identify potential risks that other oil companies had overlooked.

The significance of the Discontinuity Case became apparent when the 1973 OPEC oil embargo occurred. Following the outbreak of the Yom Kippur War between Israel and a coalition of Arab states, OPEC members announced an embargo on oil exports to countries perceived as supporting Israel, including the United States and several European nations. This led to a sharp increase in oil prices, long lines at gas stations, and widespread economic disruption in oil-importing countries.

Shell's scenario planning efforts, including the Discontinuity Case, positioned the company to respond more effectively to the oil crisis than all of its competitors. By anticipating the possibility of a major disruption in the global oil market, Shell had already begun taking steps to diversify its sources of supply, invest in alternative energy sources, and develop contingency plans to mitigate the impact of an oil shock.

The success of Shell's scenario planning approach during the 1973 oil crisis underscored the importance of anticipating and preparing for uncertainty in the business environment. It demonstrated the value of scenario planning as a strategic tool for navigating complex and rapidly changing markets, and highlighted the benefits of challenging conventional wisdom and exploring alternative futures.

Wack's innovative scenarios helped Shell avoid the worst effects that crippled many of its competitors. His approach moved scenario planning away from just extrapolating trends to exploring disruptions and discontinuities that could fundamentally reshape the business environment.

His approach to scenario planning was unique in that it emphasized a qualitative, narrative-driven approach over quantitative—data-driven and statistical—forecasting. He believed that traditional forecasting methods were inadequate for dealing with the uncertainty and complexity of the future, particularly in industries like energy where geopolitical factors and market dynamics could change rapidly.

Blinded By Beliefs

Wack's key contribution to scenario planning was his emphasis on 'mindsets' and 'mental models'. He argued that decision makers often operate within a set of implicit assumptions and beliefs about the world, which can blind them to emerging trends and disruptors. By challenging these mental models and exploring alternative perspectives through scenarios, organizations could develop a more robust and flexible approach to strategic planning.

Beyond the scenarios themselves, Wack was instrumental in institutionalizing scenario planning into Shell's corporate strategy and decision-making processes. He trained leadership to think more profoundly about uncertainty and to be prepared for multiple eventualities rather than just pursuing a single strategic path. Wack demonstrated that effective scenario planning required an egalitarian process of information sharing and intellectual humility—never just imposing a viewpoint, but allowing divergent stories of the future to be built collaboratively.

After pioneering successes at Shell, Wack shared his scenario planning methodology with other companies and aided its adoption as a widespread strategic tool still used by major firms today. His insights on fostering the institutional culture and imagination to truly 're-perceive reality' left a lasting legacy in the field of strategic foresight.

Though I do realize that Shell was, and still is, far from innocent, it must have been absolutely intellectually exhilarating to work there in the 1970s in London. Just like the concentration of brainpower at RAND, the scenario thinking group at Shell was at the very cutting edge of understanding how to build mechanisms to turn insights into foresights. At that moment, Shell had the best Palantíri in the business world.

Preparing For Uncertainty

At its very core, scenario planning is about understanding uncertainty and preparing for it. Rather than relying on single-point forecasts or predictions, it recognizes that the future is inherently unpredictable and complex. By developing a range of scenarios, organizations can explore different possible futures, identify key uncertainties, and devise strategies to thrive in various situations.

For a company like Shell, which operates in highly volatile and uncertain markets and regions, scenario planning was particularly valuable. It allowed them to consider a wide range of factors that could impact their business, including geopolitical events, technological advancements, regulatory changes, and shifts in consumer behavior. By examining how these factors could interact and evolve over time, Shell could better anticipate risks and opportunities and make more informed strategic decisions.

The process of scenario planning typically involves several steps. First, Shell's strategists gather information about current trends, uncertainties, and potential disruptors in their industry and the broader environment. They then identify the most critical uncertainties that could significantly impact Shell's future, such as oil prices, regulatory policies, or the adoption of renewable energy.

Next, Shell develops a set of scenarios—exploring a different set of assumptions and possibilities—that represent different combinations of these uncertainties. These scenarios are not predictions of the future but rather plausible narratives or stories that describe how the future might unfold under different conditions.

Once the scenarios are developed, Shell evaluates the implications of each scenario for their business strategy, operations, and investments. They identify key vulnerabilities and opportunities associated with each scenario and develop strategies to mitigate risks and capitalize on opportunities. This allows Shell to be more agile and resilient in the face of uncertainty, adjusting their plans and actions as the future unfolds.

Ultimately, scenario planning enables big companies like Shell to avoid institutionalized blind spots. It nurtures a learning organization comfortable with uncertainty and long-term thinking—key strengths for navigating their highly complex, future-oriented business environment.

Great! So, we found our Palantíri!

Well, not really.

Great, But Not Perfect

It certainly has its critics. One of them is Nassim Nicholas Taleb, who wrote the book *The Black Swan* about unpredictable events, and how society is ill-equipped to deal with these rare events. Taleb voiced his dislike for scenario thinking in the McKinsey Quarterly: 'I don't like scenario planning because people don't think out of the box. It may focus on four, five or six scenarios that you can envision, at the expense of others you can't.'

Let's consider some of the more challenging aspects of scenario planning…

While scenario planning can be an extremely valuable tool, there are indeed some potential downsides and situations where it may not work as effectively. One risk is that it can lead to overconfidence and complacency. If the team is not truly exploring all plausible alternatives, they may convince themselves they are fully prepared, even though blind spots still exist. Because, no matter how thorough, scenario planning has limits when truly unanticipated, black swan events occur.

Meanwhile, in environments that are extremely volatile or evolving at an unprecedented pace, the scenarios developed can quickly become outdated or disrupted by unforeseen variables.

On top of that, for scenario planning to be effective, it requires buy-in and commitment from key stakeholders and leadership and needs to be tied to tangible strategic decisions and resource allocations. If only portions of the organization embrace the scenarios, the exercise can become siloed and have limited impact. Also, with an overabundance of scenarios, organizations can get stuck in endless analysis rather than making decisions. There is a delicate balance between preparedness and overcaution or indecision.

So yes, scenario planning provides significant advantages, but in order to work best, users also need to understand its limitations. Like any methodology, it is a means to an end, not an end in itself.

In 2013, Roland Kupers, a professor at Arizona State University, together with Angela Wilkinson, wrote a brilliant HBR[16] paper on the learnings of scenario planning at Shell. As they state: 'Scenario planning has now been in use at Shell for more than 45 years, spanning times of great triumph and prominence—especially in the 1970s—but also long stretches during which company leaders struggled to see its value. It has come close to being shut down at least three times.'

The team at Shell, run by Pierre Wack, started to realize that in order for Shell to really leverage the potential of their ideas, concepts and tools, it would mean that the company would have to change as well.

The Living Company

Enter Arie De Geus. Arie was born in Rotterdam in 1930, and joined the Royal Dutch Shell corporation at the age of 21. He worked there for 38 years until his retirement, eventually running the Strategic Planning Group, responsible for the scenario planning activities.

He realized that it was not enough for companies like Shell to have *access* to the Palantíri. You still needed a company that was capable of *executing* on the intelligence and foresight that they brought. And that was a whole different kettle of fish.

He wrote a brilliant book on this, *The Living Company*, which came out in 1997. It is probably in my collection of the top 10 favorite business books of all times.[17]

At the heart of this book is a simple question with sweeping implications: 'what if we thought about a company as a living being?'

During his tenure at Royal Dutch Shell, Arie ran a massive study on corporate longevity. The research revealed that the average lifespan of

Fortune 500 companies, from inception to decline, was only 40 to 50 years. However, the study also identified a select group of companies that had thrived for over 200 years.

Arie was convinced that most corporations die prematurely—the vast majority before their 50th birthday. Most large corporations, he said, suffer from learning disabilities. They are somehow unable to adapt and evolve as the world around them changes.

Peter Senge—author of *The Fifth Discipline* and lecturer at MIT Sloan—wrote the foreword for Arie's *The Living Company*. In it, he writes:

> Like individuals who are unhealthy and can expect an early demise, most large, apparently successful corporations are profoundly unhealthy. The members of these organizations do not experience that their company is suffering from low life expectancy. They experience most corporate health as work stress, endless struggles for power and control, and the cynicism and resignation that result from a work environment that stifles rather than releases human imagination, energy and commitment. The day-to-day climate of most organizations is probably more toxic than we care to admit, whether or not these companies are in the midst of obvious decline.

Run Like Machines

De Geus's core question, *'What if we thought of companies as living beings?'*, leads directly to his belief that *'Only living beings can learn'*. Seeing a company as a living being implies that it creates its own processes, has its own purpose and evolves naturally.

The problem, as De Geus states, is that most companies are run like machines. It is a brilliant metaphor that helps companies achieve greatness. Briefly. But the machine metaphor can become so powerful in itself, that it shapes the character of most organizations. They become more like machines than living things because their members *think* of them that way.

The machine narrative conditions us to see everything in terms of parts and resources (hence the horrible use of the concept of 'human resources') and it forces us to overuse the concepts of output, throughput, efficiency and control.

But if we really want to unlock the potential of organizations, we have to re-think that.

In Swedish, the oldest term for 'business' is näringslivet. It literally means 'nourishment for life'.

As Peter Senge highlights, the ancient Chinese characters for 'business', which date back more than 3,000 years, are:

生 意

The first of these characters basically means 'life', or 'live', and can also be translated as 'survive' and 'birth'. The second translates as 'meaning'. Business is life and meaning combined.

At Shell, when De Geus was analyzing the longevity of organizations, and trying to find the Corporate Elixir of Life, he discovered a simple truth: companies that endured for very long periods in an ever-changing world had leaders that excelled at managing change.

He boiled down the essence of a living organization to four components:

1 Sensitivity to its environment

This is the very core capacity of a learning organization: understanding the world it operates in and being 'in tune' with the changing nature. Most companies die prematurely, however, because they suffer from learning disabilities. If companies want to understand how to navigate the Never Normal, the imperative is to master the Art of Learning. And learn how to leverage the Palantíri.

2 Cohesion

Cohesion is the talent to define a strong and lasting sense of identity. The path to that journey starts with a simple question, that of corporate purpose: what are corporations for?[18] What are you trying to achieve in the biggest scope of the Never Normal?

3 Tolerance

Tolerance is the symptom of a company's ecological awareness: its ability to build constructive relationships with other entities, within and outside itself. When companies grow according to machine philosophy, they focus on 'mono-culture' and destroy everything that doesn't look like the 'core crop'. But companies that last, living organizations, can 'tolerate' and have learned to leverage and harvest diversity. Which is quite interesting in the light of so many companies like Accenture, Amazon, Google, Meta, Walmart and McDonald's that have scaled back their DEI efforts these last few months.

4 Conservatism

For me, the most surprising of the four components is an element of conservatism when it comes to financing. De Geus's research revealed a clear link between long-term success and a company's ability to effectively govern its growth and evolution. This stands in sharp contrast to the hyper-aggressive venture capitalist approach in the world of Unicorns but it is indeed a defining trait of Phoenix companies—those that rise, adapt, and endure.

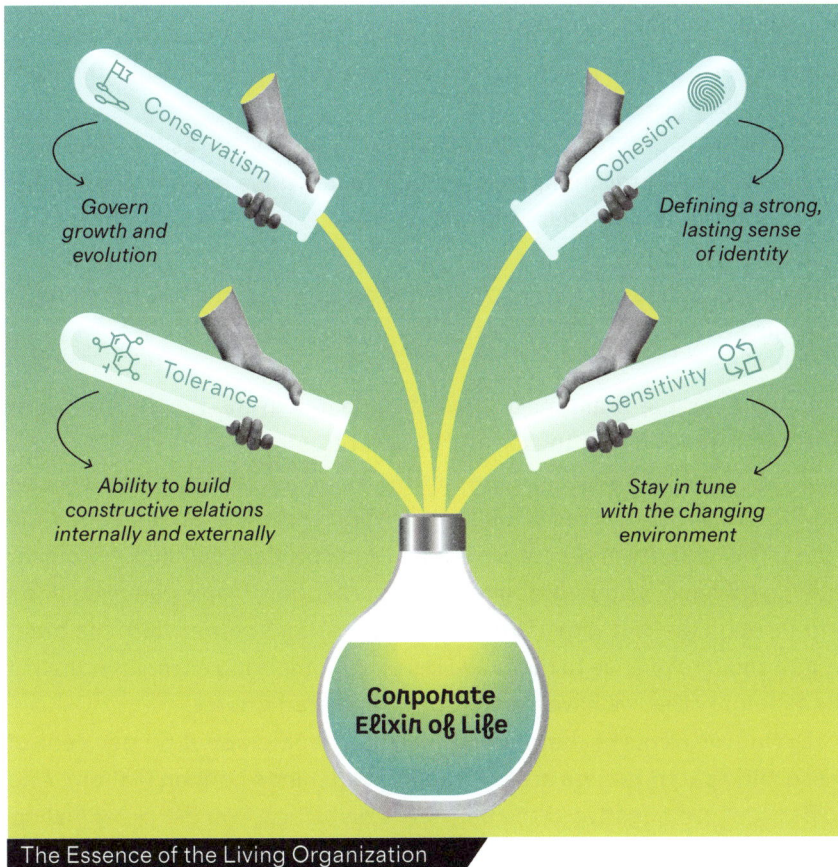

Conservatism
Govern growth and evolution

Cohesion
Defining a strong, lasting sense of identity

Tolerance
Ability to build constructive relations internally and externally

Sensitivity
Stay in tune with the changing environment

Corporate Elixir of Life

The Essence of the Living Organization

The Memory Of The Future

What Herman Kahn did at the RAND corporation was to think the 'unthinkable'. What Pierre Wack and Arie De Geus did at Shell was to build scenarios outside of the normal planning cycles and corporate comfort zones.

But, really, what they all did was build 'memories of the future'.

At Shell, the scenario planning group was heavily influenced by the work of Dr. David Henschen Ingvar, a Swede and one of the major 20th century figures in brain physiology. His research shows that the human brain is constantly attempting to make sense of the future. Every moment, we instinctively create action plans and programs for the future—anticipating the moment at hand, the next minutes, the emerging hours, the following days, the ongoing weeks and the years to come—in one part of our mind. This brain activity takes place throughout the daytime, independent of whatever else we are doing; it occurs in an even more concentrated form at night, during sleep.

These plans of the future are sequentially organized, as a series of potential actions: 'If this happens, I will do that.' These are not predictions. They do not pretend to tell what will happen. They are time paths into an anticipated future.

Each combines a future hypothetical condition of the environment ('if the train arrives late') with an option for action ('I'll take a cab').

Not only does the brain make those time paths in the pre-frontal lobes, it stores them. We visit these futures and remember our visits. We have, in other words, a 'memory of the future', as Ingvar calls it, continually being formed and optimized in our imagination and revisited time and time again. The memory of the future is an internal process within the brain, related to humans' language ability and to perception. It apparently helps us sort through the plethora of images and sensations coming into the brain, by assigning relevance to them. We perceive something as meaningful if it fits a memory that we have made of an anticipated future.

Dr. Ingvar remarks that among 'normal' people about 60 per cent of these anticipated futures are favorable: good things happen in them. And 40 per cent are negative. If the balance is disturbed, you get perennial optimists or incorrigible pessimists, depending on whether their prevailing memories of the future are positive or negative. In any case, the healthier the brain, the more alternative time paths it makes, striking a reasonable balance between favorable conditions and unfavorable ones. We make and store a great many options for the future, far more than we will ever fulfill.

For the group at Shell, the message of this research, applied to corporations, was crystal clear: *'We will not perceive a signal from the outside world unless it is relevant to an option for the future which we have already worked out in our imagination. The more memories of the future we develop, the more open and receptive we will be to signals from the outside world.'*

Our brains are hard-wired to perform this sort of active engagement to build 'memories of the future'. But companies are not. Corporations can develop the sensitivity they need, by finding ways to build up these organizational memories of the future.

And here comes the hard part. Identifying the opportunity or the threat is one matter; stimulating the change necessary to take advantage of the opportunity is another. There is a considerable difference between companies that stare blindly at threat and opportunity and those that react and change in time.

Lack Of Imagination

I was first introduced to the concept of 'lack of imagination' by the work of General Stanley McChrystal. In fact, I will dedicate a whole chapter on his influence on my thinking later in this book, when I talk about 'risk'. McChrystal served as the commander of the US and International Security Assistance Forces in Afghanistan. He also wrote *Team of Teams*, where he argues that traditional hierarchical structures and rigid thinking are ill-suited to the complexities of modern warfare and global security threats.

In the official report into the events leading up to the September 11, 2001 terrorist attacks—*The 9/11 Commission Report*—the term 'lack of imagination' was used to highlight a significant shortcoming in the US intelligence and security agencies' ability to foresee and prevent this disaster. This phrase captures the essence of their failure to anticipate the methods and scale of the terrorist threat posed by Al-Qaeda, despite various warning signs.

Prior to the attacks, US intelligence was actually well aware of threats from militant Islamic terrorists. They knew that Al-Qaeda harbored intentions to strike within the United States. However, there was a prevalent assumption that any attack would follow familiar patterns, such as bombings or hijackings aimed at making political demands. The possibility of terrorists using commercial airplanes as weapons to carry out a coordinated assault was not seriously considered. This oversight exemplifies the 'lack of imagination' the Commission referred to, highlighting the failure to think beyond conventional scenarios.

This failure was not just about predicting the exact nature of the attack but also involved underestimating the boldness and capabilities of terrorist groups. Intelligence agencies had intercepted communications and possessed information suggesting an impending significant event. Yet, the idea that terrorists could execute an attack as complex and coordinated as the one on September 11 seemed inconceivable to many officials at the time.

The report criticized how intelligence was managed and shared among various agencies, suggesting that a more imaginative and open-minded approach to threat analysis might have led to a different outcome. It argued that if agencies had considered and prepared for worst-case scenarios, even those that seemed improbable, the tragic events of 9/11 might have been averted.

In his book, McChrystal argues for operating more like a 'team of teams', and going beyond traditional hierarchical structures and rigid thinking. He advocates for a more flexible, collaborative, networked approach, where information flows freely, and individuals at all levels are empowered to make decisions. This paradigm shift is necessary to foster the kind of imaginative and anticipatory thinking that was found lacking in the lead-up to 9/11. Had they done so, they might have been more likely to consider and prepare for a wider array of potential terrorist scenarios.

McChrystal has a deep focus on shared consciousness which he believes ensures that all members of an organization have access to the same information and understand the broader context of their actions. This parallels the report's call for improved information sharing among intelligence agencies.

Very similarly, by breaking down silos in companies and creating a flatter, more integrated, networked and responsive organizational culture, the likelihood of missing critical signs due to a lack of imagination could be significantly reduced.

Tools For Foresight

A company needs an arsenal of 'Tools for Foresight', in order to brace against the Unknown Unknowns, and leverage the potential of the Never Normal. It's not that they will show you exactly what the future is. But they will help you make sense of the changing landscape, and understand how to move forward.

In the words of Pierre Wack, the most important is that these scenarios for the future are 'relevant'. As he puts it, *'In this sense, scenarios are neither a mystery nor a superior way of "planning". They are tools for foresight: discussions and documents whose purpose is not a prediction or a plan, but a change in the mindset of the people who use them. By telling stories about the future in the context of our own perceptions of the present, we open our eyes for developments which in the normal course of daily life are indeed "unthinkable".'*

Remarkable People

In many corporate settings the concepts of planning cycles, budget periods, and the entire governance of financial planning often gives a false sense of security and the illusion of certainty. But it is one of the most difficult habits to give up.[19,20]

Beyond tools, you also need 'Remarkable People' to make this happen.

The term was probably coined by Peter Schwartz, one of the leading scenario thinkers of the last century. During the mid-1980s, he worked for Royal Dutch Shell as head of scenario planning.[21] He was also the lead futurist behind the development of *Minority Report* and consulted on films like *Deep Impact*, *Sneakers*, and *War Games*. Today, he serves as the Chief Futurist at Salesforce. Schwartz deeply understands the necessity to 'look outside' and to talk to people with different points of view, people 'with whom you disagree deeply, but can talk amicably'.

His 'Remarkable People' are individuals who possess unique perspectives, deep expertise, and the ability to think creatively about complex problems. They often come from diverse backgrounds and bring unconventional insights that can challenge the status quo. Schwartz believed that involving such individuals in the scenario planning process was crucial because they provide fresh, often overlooked viewpoints that enrich the scenarios and make them more comprehensive and insightful. They shake up conventional thinking and push organizations to explore unexpected possibilities. By engaging with these trailblazers with diverse backgrounds and talents, companies can challenge hidden assumptions, spot emerging trends, and stay ahead of disruption.

As David Bowie said: 'Tomorrow belongs to those who can hear it coming.'

Bowie is one of my musical heroes. And an absolutely 'remarkable person' by Schwartz's definition. In fact, he was not only a musician but also an actor, a painter and cultural icon who constantly pushed boundaries and challenged conventional norms. His impact went beyond music; he influenced fashion, art, and social norms, often addressing themes that were ahead of their time. His ability to foresee and influence cultural trends, while continuously evolving his musical and personal style, demonstrated a profound understanding of the zeitgeist and a willingness to explore new frontiers.

He would have made one hell of a scenario thinker.

tl
dr

To leverage the full potential of the Never Normal, companies need tools of foresight. Where quantitative—data-driven and statistical—methods of forecasting are obviously useful, they tend to be less so in highly uncertain and volatile environments. That's where scenario planning comes in, a qualitative, narrative-driven approach that helps avoid blind spots and brings greater openness to the many possibilities that the future could bring.

But tools to help you foresee what might happen are not enough. You also need a living, learning, adaptive organization that is able to execute on the intelligence offered by the scenarios. One that functions like a 'team of teams' in a collaborative and networked approach and where information flows through the entire organization. Last, but not least, you need remarkable people from diverse backgrounds that shake up conventional thinking and challenge the status quo. Being able to 'see' the future is not enough, you need the structures and workforce necessary to act on it.

4

Game-changers: The Good, The Bad And The Ugly

*Fluctuat nec mergitur
(Rocked by the waves,
but never sunk.)* —PARIS MOTTO

The Silicon Valley Of The 14th Century

Murano is a small and currently very popular island in the Venetian Lagoon, which could be labelled the 'Silicon Valley of the 14th century' due to its booming glass industry, and incredible innovations back then.

The glass-making process involved the use of furnaces that reached very high temperatures, with an extremely high risk of fire. In those days Venice featured mostly wooden buildings and structures, and the glass foundries in the city had a nasty habit of repeatedly burning down large parts of the city. By relocating the glass factories on an island separate from the main city of Venice, the risk of fire spreading to the rest of the city was significantly reduced. On top of that, Murano's proximity to the saltwater lagoon gave it an ample supply of sand, an essential ingredient in glassmaking.

But the Republic of Venice had another motive to relocate the thriving glass industry to the island: containment. It wanted to keep absolute control over the glass industry and all of its intricate secrets. By relocating the 'glass entrepreneurs' to the island of Murano, and forbidding them to leave the island or disclose their techniques to others, they sealed their precious and unique knowledge from the rest of the world.

During this period, the glass industry on Murano was highly advanced and technologically sophisticated. Glassblowers on the island developed new techniques and methods for shaping and coloring glass, and they were known for producing high-quality, intricate glassware. The products from Murano were highly sought after luxury items and were exported throughout Europe and the Middle East. All these factors combined led to the island's reputation as the innovation epicenter of glass and mirrors.

In hindsight, the Venetian Senate probably created the first knowledge hub in the history of humankind. The concentration of talent, knowledge and creativity, combined with a surge of mercantile entrepreneurship, together with the financial firepower of the Republic of Venice created an innovation concentration that led to a veritable Cambrian explosion of inventions.

Like clear glass.

Angelo Barovier was born into a prominent family of glass artisans on the island of Murano. His most significant contribution came in the form of a type of exceptionally clear glass that revolutionized the industry around the mid-15th century. Before his time, Venetian glass was already of high quality, but it had a slightly tinted or cloudy appearance due to impurities in the materials. Through meticulous experimentation, Barovier managed to create a formula for glass, combining seaweed mixed with molten glass, that was nearly colorless and exceptionally transparent, mimicking the look of rock crystal. That's why he named it 'cristallo'.

His innovation immediately set Murano glass apart from other products across Europe. Cristallo allowed for the creation of finer, more delicate glass objects, which were in great demand among European elites. Angelo Barovier's work not only propelled Murano's fame but also transformed glass from a functional material into an object of beauty and status, cementing Venice's place at the heart of the luxury glass market.

It also brought us the mirror.

Through The Looking Glass

The process of creating highly reflective, clear glass mirrors was only perfected in Murano during the 16th century by the Dal Gallo brothers. Prior to their innovation, mirrors were typically made of polished metal, which could only offer a dim and distorted reflection. Although glass offered greater clarity, its low quality and the absence of effective coating techniques made it insufficiently reflective. The Dal Gallo brothers solved this issue by perfecting a method known as 'silvering', where they applied a reflective layer of mercury to the back of a thin, perfectly clear pane of glass. This process created a mirror that produced a sharp, clear, and accurate reflection, a leap forward from anything previously available. Evidently, the Dal Gallo brothers could not have developed their innovation without the ground-breaking work of Angelo Barovier.

But the mirror was a whole different level.

The significance of these mirrors cannot be overstated. In the 16th century, mirrors were not just practical household items; they were revolutionary in terms of self-perception and the concept of personal identity. The ability to see oneself clearly was an experience previously reserved for royalty or the wealthy. Venetian mirrors rapidly became a luxury status symbol, reflecting not just physical appearance but also the wealth and sophistication of the owner. Their production was so important that the Republic of Venice sought to monopolize mirror-making, strictly controlling the export of both the techniques and the craftsmen who knew the secrets of Murano glass and mirrors.

The Dal Gallo brothers' contribution to mirror-making coincided with the Renaissance period, a time when art, science, and innovation were flourishing. The rise of humanism and the emphasis on the individual made mirrors highly desirable for both practical and philosophical reasons. Artists used them to study perspective and light, while the nobility adorned their palaces with these stunning reflective surfaces to demonstrate their wealth and intellectual refinement. As mirrors became more common in aristocratic circles, they also transformed the interiors of palaces and homes, amplifying light and space in ways that were previously unimaginable.

As demand for mirrors skyrocketed, Murano's influence spread across Europe. Monarchs and wealthy patrons would commission custom mirrors, and the Murano craftsmen continued to refine their techniques, producing larger, more intricate mirrors that became central to the opulent décor of the period.

Mirror Envy

In the 17th century, the Republic of Venice tightly guarded its mirror-making secrets, refusing to allow the techniques to spread beyond Murano, a source of great frustration for many European monarchs. Their monopoly especially infuriated Louis XIV, who was going to need vast quantities of high-quality and exorbitantly expensive mirrors for his pet project Versailles. The latter was a reflection of his desire to project absolute power and divine right, while its Hall of Mirrors was intended as its extravagant centerpiece. To help you understand their value, each Venetian mirror then cost as much as a painting by Van Gogh today.

So Louis XIV became determined to break Venice's monopoly on glass-making to boost France's prestige and undermine Venetian economic power. His finance minister, Jean-Baptiste Colbert, orchestrated a covert operation to acquire the secrets of Murano's glassmakers by discreetly recruiting skilled artisans through the French ambassador in Venice, offering them financial incentives and a chance to escape strict local controls.

When recruitment alone proved insufficient, however, Colbert escalated his tactics by kidnapping top glassmakers to rapidly establish a French glass industry. In response, Venice resorted to desperate measures—such as poisoning key craftsmen—to thwart the French efforts, underscoring the intense competition and high stakes involved in this industrial espionage. But it was of little avail.

With this influx of Venetian expertise, Louis XIV was able to establish his own mirror-making industry and began producing mirrors that rivaled the quality of those from Murano. This breakthrough allowed him to fulfill his dream of the Hall of Mirrors, which became the crowning jewel of Versailles. Spanning more than 70 meters and lined with 357 mirrors, the room was an architectural marvel and a powerful symbol of Louis XIV's absolute rule. The mirrors reflected not only light but also the wealth, grandeur, and divine authority of the Sun King.

Death (Of The Mirror Monopoly) In Venice

Venice's reaction to this industrial espionage was one of outrage. The loss of its mirror-making monopoly was a significant blow to the Republic's economic power and prestige. Its authorities tried to maintain control by reinforcing laws against the emigration of glassmakers and imposing even stricter penalties, but the damage had been done. France had successfully broken Venice's hold on the luxury glass market, and the shift in mirror-making dominance marked the beginning of a decline in the exclusive status of Venice. The island was also hit hard by the Black Death and other plagues, and many skilled artisans perished. Additionally, the glass industry began to shift to other parts of Europe, where it was less expensive and more efficient to produce glass.

Louis XIV's efforts to steal Venice's glass-making secrets are a vivid example of how valuable technological knowledge was in the early modern period. It illustrates how industrial espionage played a role in shaping not only economies but also the cultural and political landscapes of Europe. By claiming the secrets of Venetian mirror-making, Louis XIV didn't just build the Hall of Mirrors—he also asserted France's rising dominance in the arts, industry, and international affairs.[22]

The Reinvention Of Saint-Gobain

I learned of this amazing story when I had the chance to work for Saint-Gobain, one of the largest glassmakers in the world. For me it is a true example of a Phoenix company, having transformed itself over and over again to become and remain a world leader in its industry. Interestingly, its origins go to the very heart of the industrial espionage performed by Louis XIV and Jean-Baptiste Colbert, and their successful attempt to steal away the Murano glass innovators and their secrets to France.

In 1665, following the successful recruitment of Venetian glassmakers, Colbert established the pioneering 'Manufacture Royale des Glaces de Miroirs' (translated as The Royal Mirror Glass Factory). The purpose of this hub, located in the Northern village of Saint-Gobain, was to lay the foundation for France's dominance in the glass industry. Over the years, the company expanded beyond mirrors into a wide variety of glass products, developing new techniques and improving the scale and efficiency of its operations. This growth marked the beginning of Saint-Gobain as a global leader in the glass industry.

As the company evolved, it expanded its reach beyond luxury goods like mirrors and began producing industrial and architectural glass, further solidifying its position in the global market. By the 19th century, Saint-Gobain had become a key supplier of glass for a range of uses. Today, it still is one of the largest glassmakers in the world, with operations in over 70 countries. It produces not only glass for construction and automotive industries but also high-tech materials for energy efficiency, sustainable buildings, and more. The Pyramid of the Louvre, for example, is covered in glass from Saint-Gobain.

It's pretty interesting to juxtapose Saint-Gobain with the Murano history. Though the latter had once been a powerful innovation hub, it was unable to reinvent itself in the face of industrial changes; instead, it held onto its secrets and its past. Saint-Gobain, on the other hand, transformed from a royal glassworks company into an industrial powerhouse. It rose from the limits of being a specialized luxury producer to become a global leader in glass manufacturing and materials science. It was able to reinvent itself time and again, like a phoenix.

The Phoenix Phenomenon

In my previous book, *The Phoenix & The Unicorn*, I juxtaposed two very different organizational forms. The 'phoenix' symbolized those near-mythical companies that are able to permanently evolve and renew themselves, while the 'unicorn' of course represented those rare, disruptive startups that achieve massive success seemingly overnight.

The search for longevity in organizations, much like the quest for eternal life, unfortunately remains elusive for most. While quite a few companies manage to extend their lifespans through incremental improvements, few are capable of the radical reinvention needed to become phoenixes. That's because it requires a lot more than just spotting trends or technological advancements and adapting to them; it demands deep cultural shifts, the ability to inspire new generations of leadership, and a vision that looks beyond the immediate horizon. In fact, the most resilient organizations don't merely react to disruptions but actively disrupt themselves before external forces dictate the need for change.

In Search Of Excellence

I have two personal heroes who have tried to figure out exactly the same problem: how can companies survive and thrive over longer periods of time? The first is Tom Peters, whose book *In Search of Excellence*, co-authored with Robert H. Waterman, identified the key characteristics that made certain companies capable of longevity, reinvention and thriving in a competitive and constantly evolving environment.

One of the major insights from *In Search of Excellence* was Peters' emphasis on the importance of staying close to the customer. This principle requires organizations to continuously evolve in response to the needs and desires of their customer base. Companies that are able to maintain this closeness avoid becoming complacent, and they are more likely to notice shifts in consumer behavior, allowing them to pivot before the market forces their hand. Peters argued that this customer-centricity was one of the critical ways in which companies could stay nimble and avoid the fate of stagnation.

He also recognized that companies needed to balance what he called 'hard' and 'soft' factors: structure, strategy, and systems on the one hand, and culture, values, and leadership style on the other. According to Peters, structure and culture had to work together to allow companies to sustain their excellence. Many companies failed because they became too bureaucratic and rigid over time, lacking the flexibility to respond to external pressures. Instead, Peters advocated for what he called 'loose-tight' properties: organizations needed to maintain tight controls and a strong sense of purpose while simultaneously allowing flexibility at the edges for innovation and adaptability.

Despite its initial impact, *In Search of Excellence* also faced criticism over the years, as many of the companies Peters identified as 'excellent' later faced significant difficulties or decline. True, it is rather strange to see companies that are struggling to stay relevant—like Boeing or Intel— on the long list. In fact, many of the 43 companies highlighted in the book, such as Xerox, eventually fell into obscurity. Others are not even around anymore. Kmart, for instance, was seen as a shining example of an 'excellent company' but it soon struggled to compete with Walmart's low prices and Target's trendier offerings. In early 2002, it filed for Chapter 11 bankruptcy protection. A few years later hedge fund executive Edward Lampert tried to combine Sears and Kmart, but eventually the last full-scale US store was closed in 2024.[23]

So yes, the book has its issues, especially since it dates from the early 1980s, but to me, it remains a critical reflection on the very issue of how companies keep themselves relevant in times of change.

Let me do a deeper dive in two companies in particular that were highlighted by Tom Peters: Intel and Xerox.

Xerox: Seeing But Not Building The Future

The story of Xerox, once an absolute titan of innovation, is one of the most striking examples of how a company can pioneer transformative innovations yet fail to capitalize on them. In 1959, the Xerox 914 revolutionized office work with the first commercially successful plain paper copier. It catapulted Xerox to enormous success and profitability, making the company a dominant player in the business technology world.

The people at Xerox did not give in to complacency, though. They realized their success would not last forever, and knew they had to study and conquer the 'Day After Tomorrow'. Luckily, with their newfound wealth, they had the resources to do so. So Xerox's leadership established a research lab in California in the '70s to explore cutting-edge technologies. The legendary Xerox PARC (Palo Alto Research Center) was born.

Xerox PARC became the exciting birthplace of some of the most important innovations that still shape the world today. Its researchers developed technologies that would become the foundation for modern computing. They invented the graphical user interface (GUI), the computer mouse, Ethernet networking, laser printing, and the concept of object-oriented programming. Perhaps the most significant development of all was the Alto, a personal computer with a graphical user interface that was far ahead of its time. The Alto was the precursor to the modern personal computer, complete with windows, icons, and a mouse to navigate the interface.

And yet, despite these groundbreaking innovations, Xerox failed to commercialize any of them effectively. Its leadership was far too addicted to the lucrative photocopying business to see the commercial potential in

PARC's inventions. They continued to invest heavily in their core copier business, unwilling to pivot their strategy toward the computing world that PARC was envisioning. It was as ironic as it was tragic. They saw the future. They invented the future. But they decided not to make the future. Their obsession with the past and incremental improvements became their downfall.

One of my favorite books on this missed potential is the 1998 gem *Fumbling the Future: How Xerox invented, then ignored the first personal computer*, by Douglas Smith and Robert Alexander. It is a grueling tale about how some of the most talented innovators in the computing business built amazing products, and then became absolutely frustrated because their senior leadership did not have the guts and capabilities to commercialize their inventions.

The most famous example of Xerox PARC's missed opportunity happened in 1979, when Steve Jobs was given a demonstration of the Alto. Jobs quickly realized the potential of its graphical user interface and mouse-driven navigation for the personal computer revolution and famously incorporated these ideas into Apple's Lisa and later the Macintosh, both of which became iconic products. Xerox had the opportunity to be at the forefront of the personal computing revolution, but they let it slip through their fingers. Apple, in contrast, copied (see what I did there?) what it saw at PARC and changed the world.

This failure to capitalize on innovation went beyond personal computing. The Ethernet, another PARC invention, became the standard networking protocol that powered the growth of the internet and corporate networks. Yet it was commercialized by others, including 3Com, a company founded by a former PARC researcher. Similarly, object-oriented programming, a powerful software development paradigm, became central to the software industry, but Xerox did not leverage it commercially. These innovations, if properly harnessed, could have made Xerox the dominant player in both hardware and software development for the burgeoning computer age.

Instead, Xerox's management missed the bigger picture, and the personal computing wave. While companies like Apple, Microsoft, and 3Com capitalized on the technologies born in PARC, Xerox itself stagnated. And by the time it attempted to enter the personal computing market, it was way too late.

With that tragic story of failed re-invention, Xerox PARC became a symbol of untapped potential and missed opportunities. The lab, which could have made Xerox the equivalent of Apple, Google, or Microsoft, became instead a shrine to impactless innovation.

The Moses Trap

One of the best books ever written on this subject is *Loonshots: How to Nurture the Crazy Ideas That Win Wars, Cure Diseases, and Transform Industries* by the American physicist and entrepreneur Safi Bahcall. It is centered on Bahcall's theory of 'phase transitions' as they apply to the development of new ideas and technologies. He argues that just as water undergoes a phase transition from liquid to gas when heated, organizations and systems can undergo similar phase transitions that allow 'loonshots'—unconventional ideas that at first seem crazy—to emerge and thrive.

According to him, you have to 'separate' the phases of core business and innovation. If you keep them too close together, the innovation won't be radical enough, as the 'mothership' is always looking over their shoulder, stifling innovation. Xerox did that right, at least: they separated the core copier business from the 'new' digital business and put the latter in Xerox PARC, on the other side of the country far removed from the corporate HQ.

But. Bahcall also argues that while you separate the phases, you need to nurture a 'dynamic equilibrium' where you constantly engage the 'old' business to understand the new potential, and where you 'invite' the new business to leverage the experience of the past. You need to separate them *and* keep them closely entangled. And that is where Xerox totally failed.

Safi Bahcall calls it the 'Moses Trap', a pitfall that many large companies fall into when they attempt to manage innovation. The 'Moses Trap' refers to the tendency of organizations to anoint a single visionary or leader (like Moses) to lead innovative projects separately from the core business, rather than embedding innovation as a more integrated, cross-functional part of the organization.

Bahcall argues that, in many organizations, the people who champion and nurture early-stage loonshots (the 'Moseses') often get pushed aside or sidelined once the latter start to gain traction and reach the 'Promised Land' of commercial success. This happens because the skillset and management style required to shepherd a loonshot through its early, uncertain stages is often quite different from what's needed to scale and commercialize it.

And that is exactly why Xerox's story is a cautionary tale about the importance of leadership in recognizing and acting on innovation. Its rise and fall, much like Intel's later story, shows that in the fast-moving world of technology, it is not enough to invent the future—you also have to seize it.

Intel, And Why Paranoia Still Rules

There is, unfortunately, a very similar story to tell about Intel, once *the* dominant player in the semiconductor industry.

Intel's meteoric rise to success is a legendary story of innovation, guts, leadership, and strategic foresight. Founded in 1968 by Gordon Moore and Robert Noyce, it quickly became synonymous with microprocessors, the essential chips that powered the burgeoning personal computer market. By the 1980s, under the leadership of Andy Grove, Intel solidified its position as the absolute king of microcomputers, especially with the release of its groundbreaking x86 processors. Intel's chips became the standard for PCs, and the company was riding high on its success, seemingly invincible in the rapidly growing tech industry.

Andy Grove, who became Intel's CEO in 1987, was instrumental in driving the company's relentless focus on innovation and market leadership. His management philosophy, encapsulated in his famous catchphrase 'only the paranoid survive', reflected his need to anticipate disruption and stay ahead of competitors. Grove's paranoia wasn't about fear, though. It was about vigilance and a refusal to grow complacent, even at the height of success. This mindset led to one of the most iconic marketing moves in tech history: the 'Intel Inside' campaign. Before that most people had no idea what a microprocessor was, but after that campaign, everyone wanted a PC with 'Intel inside'. By branding its microprocessors and making the Intel logo a household name, Grove transformed what had been a largely invisible component into a symbol of quality and innovation. Intel didn't just sell chips, it sold trust and performance.

And it worked.

During Grove's leadership, Intel soared. Its chips were powering virtually every PC made by companies like IBM, Compaq, and later, Dell and HP. In the 1990s, Intel experienced unprecedented growth and became one of the most valuable technology firms. At its peak, Intel was a symbol of American technological supremacy, driving innovation in computing and setting the standard for performance and reliability.

However, despite Andy Grove's 'healthy paranoia', Intel eventually began to stumble. The company failed to foresee the tectonic shifts in technology that were looming in the late 2000s and early 2010s, most notably the rise of mobile computing. As the world moved from desktop PCs to mobile devices like smartphones and tablets, Intel's dominance began to be eroded. While companies like ARM and Qualcomm embraced the mobile revolution, designing chips optimized for mobile performance and battery life, Intel clung to its PC-centric business model. It did try to enter the mobile market, but its chips were not competitive in terms of power efficiency, and it failed to gain significant traction.

The next major wave Intel failed to ride was the rise of the cloud and data centers. While Intel continued to dominate in traditional server markets, the cloud computing revolution, led by companies like Amazon Web Services and Microsoft Azure, required new kinds of chips optimized for massive, distributed workloads. Nvidia, a company once known primarily for its graphics processing units (GPUs), capitalized on this shift. Its GPUs became the gold standard for cloud-based AI workloads. Intel, meanwhile, missed out on the emerging growth areas of cloud and AI. Nvidia's monumental rise in the AI chip market—from data centers to autonomous vehicles—fueled by its GPUs' ability to handle parallel processing for AI algorithms, left Intel struggling to compete.

Intel's failure to catch these critical technology waves—mobile, cloud, and AI—was compounded by internal challenges. Leadership changes, a lack of strategic focus, and delays in its manufacturing process all contributed to Intel's fall from its once-dominant position. While competitors like AMD and Nvidia began to make significant gains in performance and innovation, Intel found itself scrambling to keep up in key areas like power efficiency and processing power. It became a cautionary tale of how even the most successful companies can falter when they fail to anticipate major shifts in their industry.

While Peters' *In Search of Excellence* was truly groundbreaking in its time, some of the companies hailed as models of success clearly did not stand the test of time. Unsurprisingly, this raised questions about the durability of 'excellence' as Peters and Waterman defined it. It uncovered how the success factors they identified were often based on short-term performance, making them vulnerable to shifts in market dynamics, technological changes, and leadership missteps. What seemed like a timeless formula for success turned out to be more situational.

On the other hand, some of the companies on their list have proven to be tried and tested Phoenixes. Companies like Walmart or Disney were not just shining examples of 'well run companies' in the '80s. Today, they are stronger than ever, and have truly been able to re-invent themselves.

This highlights the inherent challenge of re-invention and the complexity of sustaining excellence over the long term. While Peters provided a valuable framework for identifying what made companies successful at a given point in time, the realities of business are constantly changing. Even the most 'excellent' companies must continually evolve, and often fail to do so. Success is never static.

What Peters began with *In Search of Excellence* laid the groundwork for future discussions on organizational reinvention. The very challenges he identified—staying customer-focused, fostering innovation, and maintaining a balance between structure and adaptability—remain as relevant today as ever. The most important lesson, however, is that excellence, as Peters defined it, is not a permanent state but a fleeting one. Unless it is coupled with the ability to anticipate and respond to the future. And that is exactly what defines the Phoenix.

Built To Last

My second personal hero thinker in this field was Jim Collins. He wrote and published *Built to Last* with Jerry Porras in 1994, which sought to address why most companies failed to stand the test of time. While Tom Peters focused on what made some of them excellent in a specific period, Collins and Porras aimed to uncover the deeper, more enduring characteristics of companies that were built for long-term success. Their research compared 'visionary companies' with others that were strong but didn't exhibit the same lasting success. They wanted to identify the patterns and traits that allowed certain organizations to not only thrive for a moment but to continue thriving across decades or even centuries. Interestingly, unlike their counterparts in *In Search of Excellence*, many of the visionary companies identified in *Built to Last* were able to thrive over longer periods: 3M, Procter & Gamble, or Disney to name but a few.

Collins and Porras introduced the ideas of 'clock-building' and 'time-telling'. Companies that prioritize building a self-sustaining, innovative organization (like a clock that keeps ticking on its own) outperform those that depend solely on the vision of a single leader (time-telling). Visionary companies, they argued, were built to last because they created a structure, culture, and ethos that transcended individual leaders or trends. These Phoenixes endure because their foundations were designed for long-term growth.

Built to Last advocates preserving the core, and stimulating progress. Collins and Porras found that visionary companies were able to stay relevant because they had a clear set of core values or purpose that remained consistent over time, even as the strategies and products evolved. It's hard, though. Many businesses focus too much on either side: clinging rigidly to outdated practices in the name of preserving the core *or*, conversely, chasing trends without a clear guiding purpose. Balance between both is what separates Phoenix companies from the one-hit-wonders.

Ultimately, *Built to Last* shifted the conversation from short-term excellence to long-term resilience. Collins and Porras challenged the idea that success is about finding the right strategy at a given time; instead, they argued that it is about creating an organizational system that is capable of continuous renewal, and evolution.

The Zoo

My book, *The Phoenix and the Unicorn*, offered a rather binary visualization of the world at large. You were either a young and hungry newcomer, eager to eat the lunch of older players. Or you were an established entity with much to lose, and the necessity to re-invent yourself. Since then, I have come to believe that there's more between heaven and earth than merely Phoenixes and Unicorns.

So I broadened the scope of my classification to six:

→ Ponies   → Dinosaurs
→ Unicorns   → King Kongs
→ Godzillas   → Phoenixes

Let me guide you.

Ponies

In the context of startups and venture capital, 'ponies' refer to small, early-stage companies that are aspiring to perhaps one day become the elusive 'unicorns'. Ponies are still fragile, unproven entities, with a lot to potentially lose if they don't manage to scale and succeed. They are still in the very early, uncertain stages of development, but the idea is that a small, scrappy company can rapidly transform into a massive success. There's an allure and romanticism to being part of this high-risk, high-reward start-up journey.

Over the years, the 'pony' appeal has only grown stronger. When I graduated as a young engineer, a long time ago, the vast majority of the students would choose a corporate career. Today, however, many young people are willing to take the risk of being part of a 'pony' experience, knowing full well the danger and potential demise, but also realizing that the learning journey of that 'pony' experience could be thrilling and exponential.

Unicorns

The 'unicorn' phenomenon—a private startup company valued at $1 billion or more—was fueled by the abundant and cheap venture capital funding that became available in the wake of the 2008 financial crisis, as central banks around the world maintained extremely low interest rates. Investors, eager to back the 'next big thing', poured money into high-risk, high-growth startups, allowing these unicorns to prioritize rapid expansion over profitability. Easy access to capital enabled these companies to disrupt established industries, as they were able to grow at an unprecedented pace without the same pressure to become profitable as previous generations of disruptors.

However, this unicorn boom was intrinsically tied to the low-interest rate environment. The shift towards higher interest rates since 2022 has led to a slowdown in venture capital funding and a greater emphasis on profitability over growth at all costs. The unicorn phenomenon, fueled by cheap and abundant capital, has given way to a more cautious startup ecosystem, where the viability of these high-flying, money-losing enterprises is being called into question. The current pressure on unicorns is no longer to grow at any cost, but to grow towards sustainable and profitable business ventures. And that is a lot more difficult than just throwing vast amounts of money at the problem.

The result is that in many sectors there is less anxiety about the disruptive potential of unicorns. The relationship between traditional companies and startups has thus evolved from one of confrontation to potential collaboration. Incumbents can now selectively acquire or partner with startups to enhance their digital capabilities, while maintaining their core competitive advantages.

Godzillas

Now, what the incumbents fear more is the phenomenal rise of the Godzillas, the nickname for Big Tech platforms like Google, Amazon, Meta, and Apple. They represent one of the most significant shifts in corporate power in modern history. These companies have grown to unprecedented size and influence, partly during the COVID-19 pandemic when digital services became essential to daily life. But also now that Trump is clearly set to stimulate the tech industry—especially AI—to boost the economy and keep geopolitical power at an all-time high. Like their namesake, these tech giants have become seemingly unstoppable forces, reshaping entire industries and economies through their sheer scale and reach.

What makes these Godzillas particularly formidable is their ability to leverage network effects and vast amounts of user data to create nearly impenetrable competitive advantages. Their platforms have become so integral to modern life that they essentially function as private infrastructure—digital utilities that billions of people and businesses depend on daily. This reach gives them unprecedented power over markets, user behavior, and even public discourse. Traditional antitrust measures and regulatory frameworks have struggled to effectively address their dominance, much like conventional weapons proving ineffective against the fictional Godzilla.

But they will be tested. The Justice Department's 2024 victory against Google—proving it leveraged its vast financial power and exclusive deals to dominate search and act as a monopoly in its search business—marks the first major legal triumph against a tech giant in a generation.

The ruling is particularly significant because it challenges one of the core mechanisms these Godzillas use to maintain their power: their ability to leverage their dominance in one area to control access points and effectively lock out competition. In Google's case, paying billions to Apple and other companies to be the default search engine on browsers and devices helped ensure its continued dominance, creating a self-reinforcing cycle where more users led to better search results, which led to more users, and so on.

Traditional antitrust frameworks were developed in an era of industrial monopolies, where power was often measured in physical assets and market share. But these Godzillas operate differently—their power comes from control of digital infrastructure, network effects, and data advantages that can make their dominance self-perpetuating even without traditional monopolistic practices.

Unlike the unicorns, whose fortunes have waned with rising interest rates, these Godzillas have only grown stronger, benefiting from their established market positions and seemingly unlimited resources. Their ability to weather economic uncertainties, combined with their essential role in the digital economy, has made them more powerful than traditional nation-states in some respects. This raises important questions about competition, innovation, privacy, and the concentration of power in the digital age, as society grapples with how to ensure these digital giants serve the public good while maintaining their innovative capacity.

King Kongs

Most companies I meet today are what I call King Kongs. They resemble the giant at the top of the Empire State Building: they're massive, loud, and seemingly powerful, but they're also in a very precarious position, clinging to the structures that brought them success without fully understanding how they got there or what to do next. Just as King Kong scaled the tower with little understanding of the modern city's layout or the mechanics of the building he clings to, large organizations often reach the peak of their industry by leveraging past strategies and familiar tools.

Like King Kong's brute strength, many companies rely on their substantial resources and sheer size to maintain dominance. They throw their weight around through aggressive market positioning, high-budget marketing, and extensive acquisitions. This strength might keep them at the top temporarily, but it doesn't address the shifts in customer expectations, technological advancements, or agile competition rising from below. They know how to fight and protect their territory, but they often lack the agility and innovation required to truly evolve. The bigger and more complex they become, the harder it is to experiment with new ideas without disrupting the structures they're built on.

These companies often end up isolated, separated from the cultural and technological currents reshaping the world around them. Like King Kong, who stands above a city he doesn't understand, large corporations can find themselves out of touch with emerging trends, unable to connect with newer markets or younger consumers. Their decisions become increasingly reactionary, fending off changes rather than driving them.

In this state, these companies risk becoming symbols of a bygone era, trapped at the peak of their legacy but unsure how to descend safely or move forward.

Dinosaurs

And if they're not careful, they're heading into Dinosaur territory.

In the corporate ecosystem, 'Dinosaurs' represent once-mighty companies that failed to adapt to changing times, ultimately facing extinction much like their prehistoric namesakes. These are organizations that dominated their industries during certain eras but proved unable or unwilling to evolve when faced with technological disruption or shifting consumer behaviors.

BlackBerry (formerly Research In Motion) exemplifies a dinosaur that saw the meteor coming but couldn't evolve quickly enough. Despite dominating the corporate mobile phone market in the early 2000s, BlackBerry failed to recognize how the iPhone's consumer-friendly approach would revolutionize mobile computing. Their attachment to physical keyboards and enterprise-focused features made them increasingly irrelevant as smartphones became more sophisticated and consumer-oriented. Like a species that couldn't adapt fast enough to a changing climate, BlackBerry's market share plummeted as more agile competitors took over.

These corporate dinosaurs share common characteristics: a deep-seated resistance to change, an overconfidence in their market position, and a failure to recognize how fundamentally their business environment was shifting. Their fate serves as a warning to today's market leaders, particularly in an era where technological change occurs at an ever-accelerating pace.

Even today's mighty Godzillas of Big Tech must remain vigilant, as the next extinction-level event—whether it's blockchain, artificial intelligence, or some yet-unknown innovation—could be on the horizon.

The Godzilla Phoenix

The monopoly ruling against Google I mentioned earlier is a testimony to the need of everyone in this Organizational Zoo to focus on re-invention, certainly in this Never Normal era.

Google's rise was a defining story of the internet age. Founded in 1998 by Larry Page and Sergey Brin during the aftermath of the first dot-com bubble, it distinguished itself with a revolutionary approach to search. Its

PageRank algorithm made it possible to sift through the growing chaos of the web, delivering highly relevant search results. By the mid-2000s, Google had not only become synonymous with search but had also evolved into a tech behemoth, expanding its footprint into advertising, video (through YouTube), email, and mobile (via Android). For nearly 23 years, its growth seemed unstoppable, and its parent company, Alphabet, became one of the world's most valuable corporations.

However, the explosive growth of AI in recent years has cast uncertainty over Google's future and its ability to maintain dominance.

The irony is that much of the AI technology driving the current revolution was pioneered by Google itself. Through its subsidiary DeepMind, Google made immense breakthroughs in machine learning, such as AlphaGo and AlphaFold (which got the Nobel Prize for Chemistry in 2024). Google Brain, then, pushed boundaries in neural networks and deep learning. Yet, despite its early leadership, Google now finds itself in a reactive position, scrambling to catch up with new AI-driven business models and applications. Companies like OpenAI, with its generative AI models like ChatGPT, have captured the public imagination, raising fundamental questions about the future of search, an area where Google once had no real competition. AI, with its ability to generate natural language responses, seems poised to challenge Google's dominance in how we access and interact with information.

While Google still remains a leader in AI development, it has struggled to translate that expertise into products that can capture the momentum generated by these newer entrants. In essence, Google must now fight to keep its crown in the very domain it once dominated: information retrieval.

Google's predicament mirrors the fate of other tech giants like Xerox and Intel, who also were once pioneers but later missed crucial shifts in their industries. The challenge for Google now is to avoid becoming a cautionary tale of a tech leader that failed to anticipate or respond quickly enough to a changing environment. While Google has been a Unicorn—and eventually a Godzilla for much of its existence, it now faces the necessity of becoming a Phoenix, capable of reinvention to thrive in an AI-driven future. The days when Google could rely solely on its dominance in search and online advertising are coming to an end. It must now rethink its business model, its core technology offerings, and how it engages with consumers and developers in the AI era.

Reimagining Search

One of the key challenges for Google will be reimagining the concept of search itself in an AI-dominated world. Instead of users typing in queries and receiving a list of websites, they now interact with AI systems that understand context, generate personalized responses, and even anticipate user needs. To stay relevant, Google must either develop a better AI-powered version of its search engine or create entirely new products that can leverage its vast data and AI capabilities to deliver better user experiences.

This transformation will not be easy, given Google's size and the weight of its legacy business model. The company's dominance in search has long been its strength, but it also represents a potential obstacle to radical innovation. Reinventing the core of a business that generates tens of billions of dollars in annual revenue comes with significant risks. However, just as Microsoft successfully reinvented itself by shifting its focus from traditional licensing to the cloud and AI under the leadership of Satya Nadella, Google must now find a way to pivot before it is overtaken by more agile competitors.

Moreover, Google's ability to become a Phoenix will also depend on its internal culture. The company's 'moonshot' mentality, embodied by Google X, was once celebrated for its bold experiments. Yet the execution and commercialization of these innovations have been slow, leaving the company vulnerable. In some ways, Google fell into the 'Moses Trap', just like Xerox did all those years ago.

After nearly 25 years of meteoric growth, Google faces a critical juncture. While it has the talent, resources, and early leadership in AI, the challenge now is to translate these assets into products and business models that align with the future of AI-driven information access. Google must become a Phoenix, shedding its reliance on traditional search and reimagining itself for an AI-first world. How Google handles this moment will determine whether it remains a dominant force in the tech industry or fades like some of its once-great predecessors.

Google is facing its Phoenix moment. But these near-mythical companies are not just present in the high-tech sector. They are everywhere. Sometimes in very traditional industries. And often with a very long history of re-invention.

One of my favorite examples is the French luxury group Hermès, which achieved enduring success across generations. Founded in 1837 by Thierry Hermès as a maker of fine harnesses and saddles for the French nobility, Hermès distinguished itself early on through its dedication to craftsmanship, elegance and quality.[24]

The second generation of a family business often has the potential to scale the business, and that is exactly what Thierry's son, Charles-Émile Hermès, did. He took the company's foundations and scaled them beyond their initial niche. Charles-Émile moved the Paris workshop to a more prominent location on Rue du Faubourg Saint-Honoré thus setting up Hermès for greater visibility and access to an affluent customer base. Under his leadership, Hermès would become the preferred saddle maker to the entire European nobility.

Then the third generation took the reins—a notoriously delicate and defining moment in the history of a family business. So when Émile-Maurice took over, he first wanted to sense their 'Day After Tomorrow'. He travelled to the 'New World' and observed two things in New York that would change his view, and the course of Hermès. The first was the automobile, quite a shock for the young Émile-Maurice who suddenly realized that perhaps making saddles for horses was not the most solid future foundation. His second epiphany came in the form of the humble yet underestimated zipper. So Émile-Maurice procured the exclusive rights to the zipper in continental Europe.

Imagine the scene where the grandson of the founder comes back from America, tries to convince his saddle-crafting artisans that the future is not in the horse business, and consequently tries to sell them on the concept of the zipper.

But he succeeded. It was during the third generation that Hermès began a series of reinventions that would set it apart as a modern luxury brand. He not only introduced zippers to Europe, which became a hallmark of Hermès bags and apparel, he also expanded the brand's product lines to include leather handbags, clothing, watches, and, eventually, silk scarves. Hermès was no longer a saddlery—it had redefined itself as a maker of high-end lifestyle products, anticipating changes in luxury consumption.

The company's evolution continued across successive generations. Throughout the 20th century, Hermès mastered the art of blending its heritage with innovation. It expanded internationally, while still insisting on limited production runs and superior craftsmanship, creating a sense of scarcity and exclusivity. Hermès resisted trends that might dilute its identity, choosing instead to stick to its artisanal roots even as the luxury market became increasingly industrialized. By keeping the family closely involved in its operations, Hermès preserved its values and quality, maintaining a reputation as a 'true' luxury brand, a standard increasingly rare in the global luxury market.

In the 1990s, under the guidance of Jean-Louis Dumas, the company made another leap by refining its image as a cultural and lifestyle icon. The Birkin and Kelly bags, for instance, became more than just handbags—they were symbols of luxury with years-long waitlists, driving Hermès' brand loyalty and prestige to new heights. Dumas also championed modern marketing techniques, balancing heritage with a contemporary image that would attract younger, international clients. The brand became synonymous with timeless elegance, making it resilient even in fluctuating markets.

Today, Hermès is one of the world's most valuable luxury companies, largely due to its ability to transform yet remain authentic. Under the leadership of the sixth and seventh generations, Hermès has embraced digital transformation cautiously and responsibly, ensuring that its craftsmanship remains the focus. The company continues to defy industry norms, choosing quality over quantity and longevity over short-term profits. Today, the company is one of the most active in looking at leather alternatives, to keep re-inventing the world of luxury towards a sustainable future beyond leather.

Hermès embodies the 'Phoenix' model by continuously reinventing its products without compromising its identity. Tom Peters and Jim Collins would have loved Hermès.

Unleashing The Tiger

The most amazing Phoenixes, however, are those companies that can claw their way back from a comatose-like state. Like Volvo.

I've had the chance to work for Volvo on many occasions, and one of the nicest gifts I received from them was a wonderful book called *Volvo's Comeback: How The Tiger Was Unleashed*, written by Swedish journalists Håkan Matson and Anders Nilsson. Its title comes from the very first speech that the brand new owner of Volvo, the Chinese entrepreneur Li Shufu, gave to the Volvo crowd in 2010 after he acquired the company. He told them 'I will unleash the Tiger'. No one in the audience had any idea what he was talking about.

Håkan Matson and Anders Nilsson were in the audience that day, and they started observing and documenting the miraculous and completely unexpected recovery of Volvo under Geely's ownership. When the latter acquired Volvo in 2010 for $1.8 billion, it was struggling. Ford, its previous owner, had focused more on extracting value than on nurturing Volvo's brand identity. So its product lineup was outdated, and its financial performance lagged.

The story of Geely's chairman, Li Shufu, is a remarkable tale of entrepreneurial vision and transformation. Born into a very poor farming family in Zhejiang province, China, Li started his business journey far from the automotive world. His entrepreneurial path led him to founding Geely in 1986, which initially produced refrigerators before moving into motorcycles and finally automobiles in the late 1990s.

Geely's acquisition of Volvo Cars is quite wonderful. Li traveled to the Detroit Auto show for years, going to the Ford Motor Company, and wanting to discuss the possible acquisition of Volvo. The Ford executives dismissed Li Shufu, until they essentially ran out of money in 2010, and then finally took him seriously.

Back then, this marriage was met with considerable skepticism from the automotive industry. Many doubted that a relatively young Chinese car company could successfully manage a prestigious Swedish brand with a long history and reputation for safety and quality. The acquisition price was remarkably low, as Ford had paid $6.45 billion for Volvo in 1999, but was forced to sell during the aftermath of the global financial crisis.

Li had struck a bargain, but he was not just a shrewd financial manager. He understood the inherent Phoenix potential of Volvo. That is why he stated in his first speech to the Volvo audience that he would unleash the Tiger. His vision was not to dismantle Volvo or turn it into a producer of budget cars, but rather to revive its reputation for quality, safety, and design on a global scale. And it worked.

Initially, many skeptics feared that Geely would shift production to China, undermining Volvo's Swedish roots and quality standards. Yet Shufu and Geely did the opposite: they invested in Volvo's infrastructure, research, and development in Sweden, allowing the brand to retain its core iconic Scandinavian character, heritage and engineering prowess. And they fueled Volvo's rebirth as an innovator in the luxury car market. One of the key strategic moves was Geely's decision to prioritize product development, especially in areas like safety and sustainability—values deeply embedded in Volvo's brand DNA. For instance, it invested heavily in Volvo's research into electric and hybrid vehicles, and clean technologies.

Geely's approach to reviving Volvo was pretty unique. Rather than imposing a top-down strategy, Li Shufu gave Volvo the freedom to chart its own course. Its leadership retained its headquarters in Sweden and continued to operate with a high degree of independence.

Under Geely's ownership, Volvo has experienced a remarkable renaissance. The company successfully modernized its product line, embraced electrification, and expanded its market presence, particularly in China. Li's strategy of allowing Volvo to maintain its distinctive identity while benefiting from Chinese investment and market access has turned what many viewed as a risky gamble into a textbook example of successful cross-cultural acquisition and revival.

Today, Volvo stands stronger than ever. Its 'Phoenix' transformation under Geely underlines how thoughtful ownership—balancing respect for heritage with bold investment in innovation—can breathe new life into a legacy brand.

Thrive, Not Survive

Warren Buffett's 'castle and moat' investment philosophy has long been a cornerstone of his success. In this approach, the 'castle' represents a company's strong market position and ability to generate consistent profits, while the 'moat' symbolizes the protective barriers that shield it from competitors. The most formidable moats are reinforced with powerful defenses; they are filled with 'sharks', like proprietary technology, strong brand loyalty, regulatory advantages, or economies of scale. These elements create a business fortress, which protects the core business from competitors. This strategy has served him well in stable, predictable environments, yielding impressive, long-term results. The moat approach prioritizes security and endurance, providing companies with a solid foundation to protect their position and withstand fluctuations.

The Limits Of The Moat

Yet in today's 'Never Normal' era, where technology, consumer preferences, and competitive landscapes are shifting at an unprecedented pace, the moat mentality can sometimes limit potential. Companies with traditional moats might still survive, but they also risk stagnating if they focus solely on protecting their territory rather than on evolving. Venture capitalist Jerry Chen from Greylock believes that having moats to survive no longer suffices. Those were built for defense, but thriving in the 'Never Normal' demands resilience, adaptability, and the willingness to explore beyond the walls of a secure business model.

'King Kong' companies, for instance, with their established positions and resources are primarily focused on survival and defending their existing models rather than innovating. They hope to maintain dominance by relying on their size and past successes. Yet, in rapidly evolving markets, these attributes can become liabilities. Their slow, risk-averse nature may keep them afloat for some time, but it rarely leads to meaningful growth. As the environment around them changes, King Kongs might find themselves clinging to outdated practices while more nimble, innovative companies take advantage of emerging opportunities.

By contrast, 'Phoenixes' aren't complacently content with a strong moat. They understand the importance of continuously reassessing their core strategies, embracing disruption, taking calculated risks and evolving with market changes. This is how they actively turn obstacles into opportunities and position themselves to lead rather than follow.

In the end, success in the Never Normal means shifting from a moat-centered approach to one that balances defense with reinvention. A strong castle and moat can provide stability, but it's the ability to adapt and reinvent that drives growth. That is how Phoenixes don't just *survive*, but actively *thrive*.

Veuve Clicquot

Barbe-Nicole Ponsardin, better known as Madame Clicquot, was a true pioneer in the early 19th century. When her husband François Clicquot died unexpectedly in 1805, she inherited his small champagne business that had been struggling due to the Napoleonic Wars and continental blockades. Her financial advisors urged her to shut down the business, but she was determined to lead the company *and* transform the business. In an era when women were largely excluded from the business world, this was completely unheard of, especially for one so young. Widows of 27 were usually expected to remarry and sell their late husband's business. The fact that the French wine industry was in turmoil—affected by political unrest, wars, and trade disruptions—made her decision to revolutionize the champagne industry all the bolder. But she did end up convincing her father-in-law to let her manage the company, displaying a powerful determination that would characterize her entire career.

She had a vision for what the business could become, and she believed in the quality of her champagne. With courage and keen business acumen, she worked tirelessly to stabilize operations and quickly grasped the importance of improving and differentiating her product.

One of her most famous innovations was the development of the riddling process, which allowed Veuve Clicquot champagne to be produced at a much higher quality. At the time, champagne tended to be cloudy due to the residual yeast left from fermentation, which affected its appearance and taste. Madame Clicquot devised a method where bottles were stored at an angle and rotated regularly to collect the yeast sediment in the neck. This process, called 'remuage', enabled her to produce a clear, refined champagne, with a taste and clarity that were previously unattainable. Like many Phoenix-like innovations, it didn't just improve her own company's products, it revolutionized the entire champagne industry. The technique was so effective that it became the standard method used by all champagne producers, a position it held for over 150 years until the invention of modern mechanical riddling.

This innovation set Veuve Clicquot apart and marked the start of its transformation from a regional product to an internationally renowned luxury good.

After product improvement followed scaling. Not an easy feat during the Napoleonic Wars, which blocked many trade routes. The relentless Madame Clicquot managed to bypass embargoes and sent her champagne to Russia. When the continental blockade ended in 1814, she took a bold gamble by secretly shipping 10,500 bottles of her 1811 vintage to Russia. This risky move paid off spectacularly—her champagne reached the Russian market before her competitors, establishing Veuve Clicquot as *the* luxury drink of choice for the Russian nobility and it created a lasting market presence. This success gave Veuve Clicquot international credibility, establishing the brand's name across Europe.

Madame Clicquot continually sought to improve her product and innovate in her field, earning her the nickname 'La Grande Dame de la Champagne'. She introduced the first vintage champagne in 1810, a concept that highlighted the uniqueness of a particular year's harvest. This innovation allowed her to position Veuve Clicquot as a champagne house that valued quality and refinement, setting a standard that other champagne makers would later follow. Her approach to branding through quality was groundbreaking and built a sense of exclusivity around her product.

Beyond production innovations, Madame Clicquot was also a strategic marketer ahead of her time. Like today's successful digital platforms, she understood the power of network effects and brand building. She cultivated relationships with royal courts across Europe, making her champagne synonymous with luxury and celebration. She used distinctive yellow labels to make her bottles' brand identity recognizable. She also had a unique flair for cultivating relationships with her clients and partners, creating a network of ambassadors who promoted Veuve Clicquot's reputation worldwide. This personal connection with her customers became part of the brand's allure, creating loyalty that lasted for generations.

As her success grew, Madame Clicquot maintained a commitment to excellence that became central to Veuve Clicquot's identity. She once famously said, 'Our wines must be flattering both to the palate and to the eye.' This insistence on quality over profit laid the foundation for the brand's longevity and reputation. She knew that her customers associated Veuve Clicquot with sophistication and trust, so she upheld these values, making the brand synonymous with celebration and refinement.

Madame Clicquot's leadership style was also revolutionary. She was deeply involved in all aspects of her business—from production to distribution—making decisions that demonstrated both courage and foresight. This holistic approach allowed her to understand the full scope of her business and adapt swiftly to changes, reinforcing her status as an entrepreneur ahead of her time. Under her leadership, Veuve Clicquot became more than just a business—it became an enduring symbol of elegance and resilience. Her legacy is seen in how Veuve Clicquot remains a major Phoenix player in the champagne industry, committed to balancing tradition with innovation.

The Diode Dilemma

I have drawn countless 2x2 models in my life. And I've seen even more of them in books, reports, articles and keynotes from others. And yet, people love to make fun of them. That's because the model is often seen as the quintessential 'magic trick' of consulting. But I personally love them. They allow us to simply yet powerfully visualize some of the most complex issues and concepts out there.

The 2x2 model that I'm about to describe is a particular favorite of mine. It is not just about understanding the 4 squares per se, and what they stand for, but more about how the dynamics of movement across the field play out. And it has a really cool name: The Diode Dilemma.*

Diodes

If you are not an electronics expert, you might not know what a diode does. Or, does *not* do, actually. A diode is a rather funny electronics component that allows current to flow in one direction, but not in another. It's basically the 'one-way street' on the electronic circuit boards. Diodes were originally named 'rectifiers', because the unique property of the diode allows it to convert alternating current (AC) to direct current (DC), by 'rectifying' the signal.

German engineer Karl Ferdinand Braun—who shared the 1909 Nobel Prize in Physics with Guglielmo Marconi, the inventor of wireless telegraphy—was crucial in the development of the diode. Braun was an amazing scientist who developed the first cathode-ray tube (CRT), which was the precursor to the television. Today, the latest generation of TVs works on the principle of OLED, which are Organic Light Emitting Diodes. Hah. Full circle back to the diode.[25]

So, a diode is a 'one-way street' for electrical current. You might ask yourself why in heaven's name that would be an interesting concept, and how it relates to business and Phoenix companies.

Well...

*This sounds as if it would have been a great episode of *The Big Bang Theory*. ◄

Relevance And Proficiency

The 2x2 model that I'd like to use here is the 'Relevance / Proficiency model'. I find it incredibly simple, yet it describes so many of the challenges that companies and organizations face in the Never Normal maelstrom of constant change.

Let's start with 'Relevance', which is embodied in the question 'Are you doing the right things?'.

Being Relevant is very, very different from being Essential. In any industry, in any market, you can only hope that what you offer, what you produce, or what you sell will be crucial in the lives of your customers. When you are a car manufacturer, you're playing on the role of being an essential partner of mobility for your clients. As a bank you hope to provide essential financial services to allow your clients to function. As a telecom provider, you help to provide essential communication services.

But this is the harsh truth: in many markets, being essential does not automatically mean that you are relevant. Relevance happens when you are acknowledged by your customers as being unique, as providing a set of services, offering a set of products that really 'hit the spot'. If that turns out not to be true, you risk falling into the 'Dumb Pipe Syndrome', a concept which makes the Telecom industry incredibly unhappy (seeing that it was named after them).

The term 'Dumb Pipe Syndrome' describes a scenario in which telecom service providers—such as broadband and mobile network operators—serve solely as conduits for data, without offering any additional value beyond basic connectivity. In this model, they function as passive carriers of commodity services, merely transmitting data without leveraging opportunities to enhance user experience in any way. To combat this challenge, traditional telecom service providers need to innovate not just in technology but also in their service offerings and business models. The future of telecom isn't just about providing pipes but about how creatively these pipes are used to deliver value-added services and improved customer experiences.

But the phenomenon is not just restricted to 'telecom'. You see banks struggling too. Many mobile apps of different financial players are starting to look very much similar, and therefore you get a commoditization effect: the dumb pipe in banking. Or insurance. Or retail.

So Relevance is one element. The other axis is about 'Proficiency'. If you want to understand how proficient your organization is, simply ask yourself if you have the right skills, competencies, resources, technology and governance to achieve greatness. In other words: *'Are you doing things Right?'*

So this 2x2 model is about answering two simple but powerful questions: *'Are you doing the Right Things?'*, and *'Are you doing things Right?'*

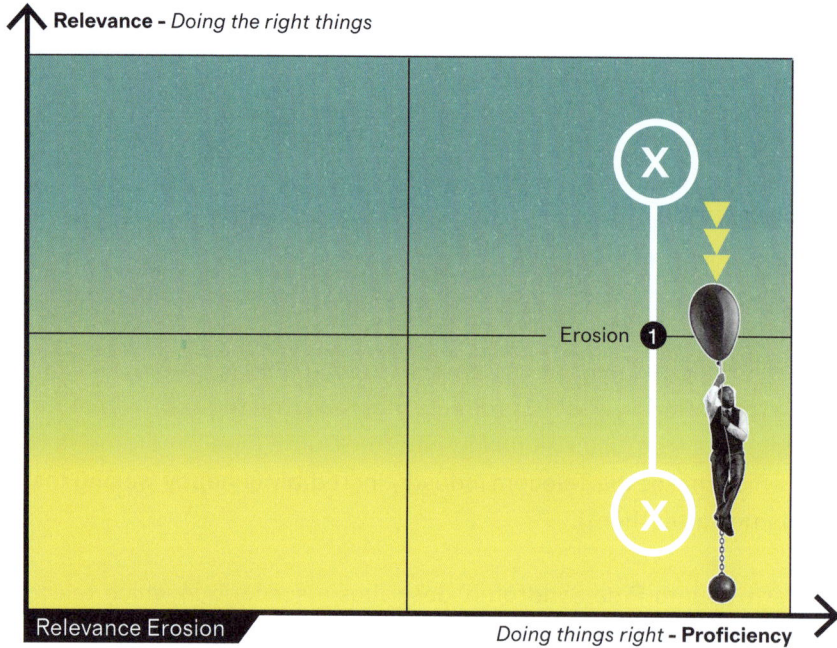

Relevance Erodes

Easy, right? We all want to do the right things, and therefore we need to do things right. It's pretty basic. But there is ONE fundamental law that you have to understand in this setup: *Relevance Erodes.*

I think of it as a force of nature, the equivalent of the laws of physics in an economic context. Just like entropy gets worse over time and breaks down order into chaos. Relevance Erodes. Beauty Fades. Entropy Increases.[26]

It's just a matter of time.

Whatever brilliant business model you have. Whatever amazing product you sell. Whatever insanely awesome proposition you have for your customers. Over time, it will get less brilliant, less amazing, less insanely awesome. Gradually, and then suddenly, Relevance Erosion will always set in.

That's what the Telecom industry went through. They were the absolute heroes of the end of the last century. They unlocked the potential of communication, gave us the mobile phone, and then the internet. They were awesome. And then they became a commodity, a 'dumb pipe'. They were boring. And only a source of frustration when they did not operate 100%.

The problem with the erosion process of relevance is that you can't just reverse it. It is a one-way street. And that's the Diode Dilemma.

It's like ageing. Most of us will try everything we can to look great, stay healthy, eat well, exercise when we can, sleep as much as possible. But we will still age. That is a natural process. And it is 'irreversible'. You can't just take a pill and become young again.[27]

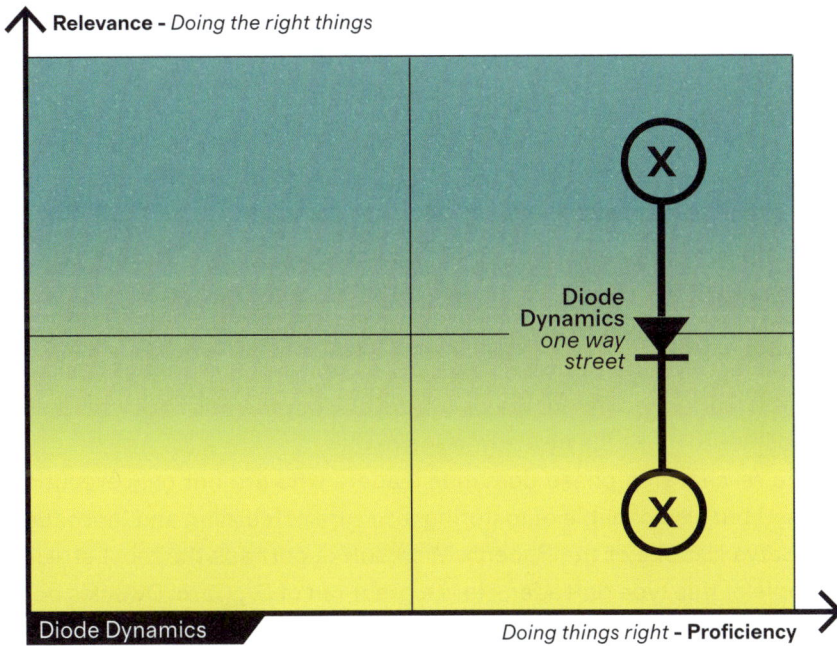

Actually, you *can* reverse the Erosion route. But not in the same way you got there… you have to use a detour and it involves a two-step approach. When a business finds itself losing relevance in the marketplace, it needs to undertake a strategic revitalization to regain its standing and ensure future success. This process can be thoughtfully described in two key phases: re-targeting and re-charging.

Re-target

The first step consists of re-targeting. That means getting back to understanding how to regain relevance. This involves taking a deep and introspective look at the marketplace to identify new or shifted customer needs, emerging trends, and potential opportunities. This phase is about understanding where the current offerings of the business fall short and pinpointing what customers now expect or desire that they are not getting.

It means you have to understand customers and markets, and do deep dives on pain points, trends, preferences, and expectations. It means redefining your value proposition. This could mean modifying existing products or services, introducing new ones, or even pivoting to a completely different set of offerings. And it means rethinking the brand messaging to align with the new focus.

Re-charge

Re-targeting is not enough, though. Companies also need to re-charge if they want to get out of a 'dumb pipe' situation. This is where they build or acquire the necessary skills, people, competencies, and capabilities to deliver on the new promise to customers.

In short, by first re-targeting, the business scans its environment and identifies what it needs to change to be relevant again to its customers. This is a strategic vision phase, where understanding and insight set the direction for the future. Following this, by re-charging, the business equips itself to execute on this vision, developing the necessary skills and capabilities to make the new strategy a reality.

The re-charging phase demands leaders who are not only execution-focused but also capable of fostering a culture of learning and innovation. And Satya Nadella of the Phoenix Microsoft is perhaps the most striking example of this type of leader. He is a great fan of Dr. Carol Dweck's book *Mindset: The New Psychology of Success*. She's the one who divided the world into 'learners' and 'non-learners', demonstrating that a 'fixed mindset' will limit you, while a 'growth mindset' will enable you to move forward. People with a 'fixed mindset' are more likely to stick to activities that utilize the skills that they've already mastered, rather than to risk embarrassment by failing at something new. People with a 'growth mindset' make it their mission to learn new things, understanding full well that they might not succeed (at all of them) at first.

When Satya Nadella transformed the then lagging Microsoft, he used the concept of the 'growth mindset' intensely while transforming its culture of 'Know-It-Alls' into a company of 'Learn-It-Alls', stimulating a mindset of curiosity and learning in employees throughout the organization.

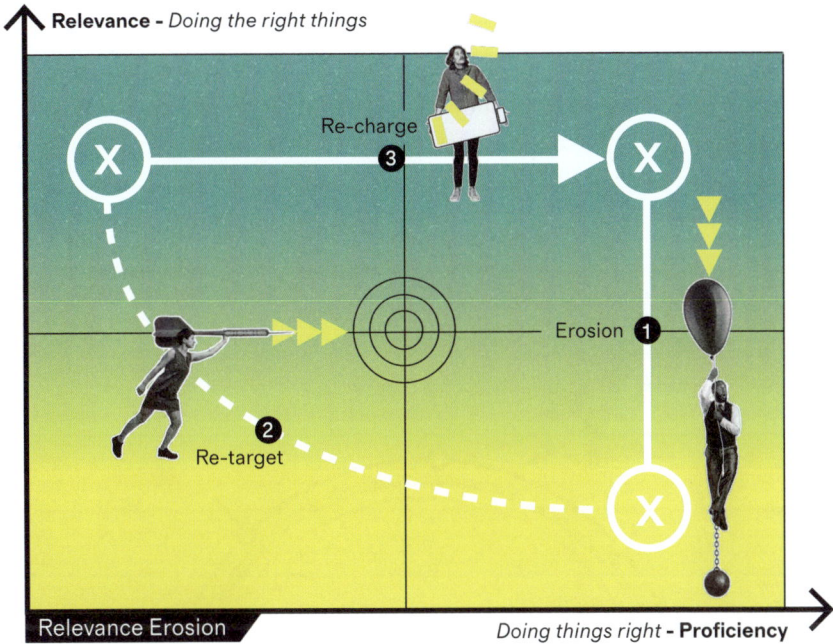

Companies that want to stay relevant in the Never Normal will repeat this loop continuously: relevance erodes, then they re-target to continue doing things that 'matter' to their customers and their market. Then they re-charge to make sure their capabilities allow them to do things right.

It's the same cycle, over and over again, which has only been speeding up in our Never Normal era.

Innovate When You Can

Mark Leslie is a name that resonates deeply in the world of Silicon Valley entrepreneurship and academia. A successful entrepreneur, investor, and lecturer, Leslie has had a significant impact on the way businesses think about growth, innovation, and reinvention. He is best known as the founder of Veritas Software, a company that became a major player in the data storage industry. Under his leadership, Veritas grew from a small startup into a multi-billion-dollar company, demonstrating his deep understanding of business strategy and scalability.

Beyond his success in the corporate world, Leslie has also been a vital part of Stanford University's entrepreneurial ecosystem. As a lecturer at Stanford Graduate School of Business, he has influenced a generation of business leaders, sharing insights on leadership, strategy, and innovation. One of his most impactful contributions has been his articulation of the *Theory of Optionality*, a concept that provides a framework for understanding how businesses (and individuals) should think about growth, peak performance, and reinvention. I love the way this simple concept makes what you need to do to become a Phoenix in the Never Normal super clear.

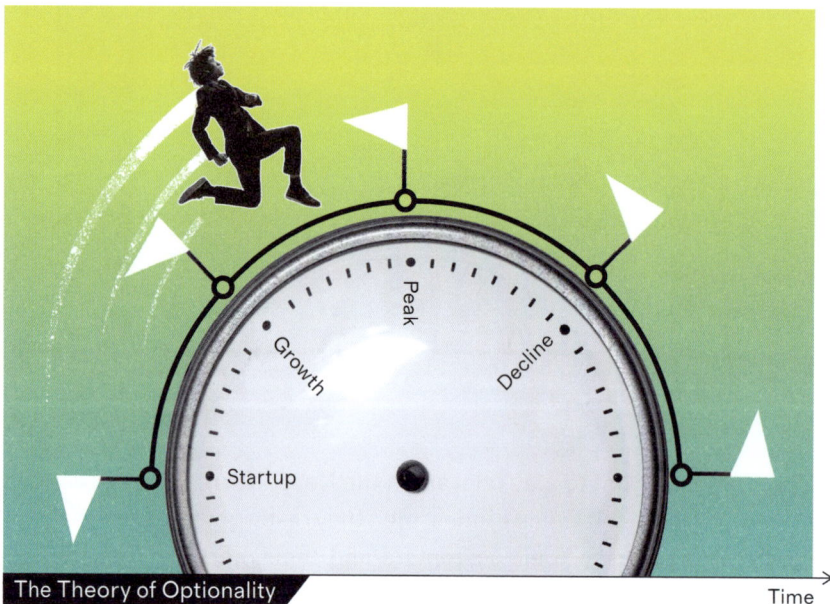

The Theory of Optionality

Time

The Theory of Optionality posits that everything in life—whether a company, a product, a strategy, or even an individual career—follows a predictable pattern. There is a beginning phase where things are nascent and full of potential, followed by a period of rapid growth. Then, at some point, a peak is reached, and what follows is a decline.

You can apply this arc to a product, a brand, a market, but even to companies, organizations, historical eras and life itself. In fact, it's the 'what goes up, must come down' dynamic that I referred to in chapter 2. You start, you grow, you peak and eventually you decline. It's the cycle of life stripped to its purest form.

In traditional business thinking, companies often wait until they have peaked before they begin to innovate. And historically, this approach tended to work because market conditions moved slower, and businesses had the luxury of time to pivot and transform.

The Theory of Optionality

However, the world today has changed; in the 'Never Normal', waiting until a company or strategy has peaked before innovating again is a very dangerous game. Once a business begins to decline, it often becomes too late to make any meaningful changes. This is because momentum works both ways—just as company growth creates its own form of inertia, decline does too. When a company is already on the downward trajectory, efforts to reinvent it are met with resistance, not just from external forces like the market and competitors, but also internally, where employees, investors, and leadership teams struggle to break away from entrenched mindsets and processes.

This is why Leslie's Theory of Optionality is so crucial: it teaches us that the best time to innovate is not when we need to but when we can.

The Theory of Optionality

Transformation

Peak

Growth

Decline

Startup

SWEET SPOT OF OPTION-ALITY

Time

This brings us to the idea of the 'sweet spot of optionality'. The sweet spot is that precise moment when a company still has momentum, resources, skills, and market goodwill but is close enough to its peak that it can see the potential risks of stagnation. At this stage, a company has maximum flexibility—it can experiment, take risks, and explore new directions without the existential threat of decline looming over it.

Unfortunately, this is also the moment where change feels the least necessary. Companies often continue doing what has worked in the past, relying on their existing business models, customer bases, and processes. The idea of disrupting themselves while they are still succeeding feels counterintuitive, if not outright foolish.

But history has shown us that companies that master the discipline of reinvention at the right time are the ones that survive and thrive. Take a Phoenix like Apple, for example. In the early 2000s, it could have continued to focus solely on computers, which was its original core business. Instead, it ventured into music with the iPod, then mobile phones with the iPhone, and later into wearables and services. Each time, it made these moves not because it was struggling, but because it recognized its sweet spot of optionality and acted before it was forced to do so.

Contrast this with companies that waited too long. Blockbuster had multiple opportunities to pivot when it was still dominant in the video rental market. It had a massive customer base, a strong brand, and extensive distribution channels. Yet, it dismissed streaming and digital distribution as minor trends. By the time it recognized its mistake, it was already in decline, and the inertia of failure was too strong to reverse. Similarly, Kodak invented the digital camera but refused to shift its focus from film photography until it was too late. The company's reluctance to innovate when it still had strength led to its downfall.

The key challenge is that acting on the sweet spot of optionality requires both guts and vision. Leaders must be willing to challenge their own successes, question their own assumptions, and embrace disruption even when everything appears to be going well.

Optimal Action Phase

So, to sum it all up: the Diode Dilemma describes a fundamental challenge for organizations trying to stay relevant in an ever-changing world. Relevance naturally erodes over time. Companies that were once at the top of their game slowly slip into commoditization, irrelevance, or outright obsolescence. And they can't just simply reverse the process. The Theory of Optionality, then, proves that you have to get your timing exactly right.

But how could you possibly know when that is? That's where the 'Optimal Action Phase' comes in.

Organizations don't operate in a vacuum. They constantly receive signals from the market, customers, competitors, and emerging trends. These signals tend to follow an S-curve[28]—weak at first, then gradually strengthening over time. The longer you wait, the clearer the signal becomes, and the easier it is to spot major shifts.

But here's the brutal catch: while the strength of the signal increases over time, the number of strategic options decreases. Wait too long, and your choices narrow significantly—sometimes to the point where you're just reacting rather than leading. By the time an industry shift is undeniable, companies often find themselves in damage control mode, struggling to adapt to a landscape that has already left them behind.

This is why there's an 'Optimal Action Phase'—an ideal window where the signal is strong enough to justify action, but where meaningful strategic options still exist. Move too early, and you might be betting on a trend that never materializes. Move too late, and you're forced into survival mode, with little room to maneuver.

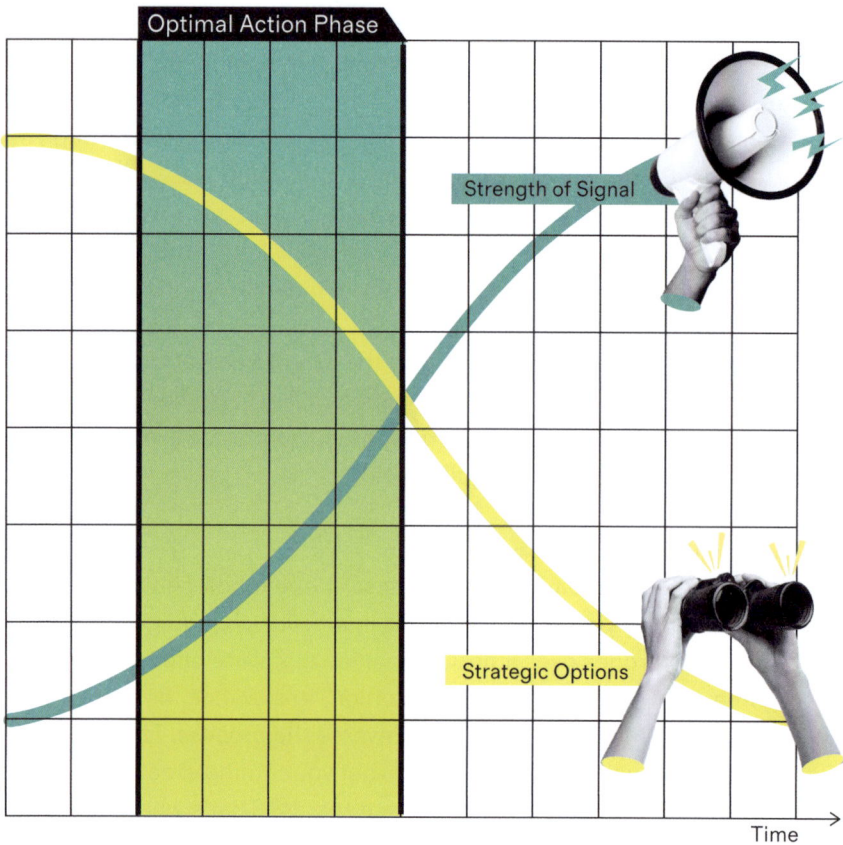

Optimal Action Phase

Strength of Signal

Strategic Options

Time

Waiting for clarity and (the illusion of) certainty, rather than accepting the quantum state of the future—where many scenarios and options are still possible—and acting on that, is where the true danger lies. It is this tension that has shaped the rise and fall of entire industries. Ironically, our obsession with certainty can be just as dangerous as uncertainty.

The conclusion here is as simple as the reality behind it is complex: bet on the future while you still have options. The future doesn't wait for perfect conditions. It arrives whether you're ready or not.

tl dr

Being a Phoenix company is really hard. It's just as difficult, if not more, for an organization to keep its success as it is to acquire it. But long-lived and long-term thinking companies like Saint-Gobain, Veuve Clicquot, Hermès and Volvo have proven that companies *can* keep their excellence and reinvent themselves time and time again.

These Phoenixes understand that long-lived success is all about maintaining a delicate balance between innovation and the core, between culture and structure, between the ability to see the future and the one to build it, between visionary leaders and self-sustaining organizations or between a defensive strategy and one that focuses on offense. There is no fail-safe ingredient for becoming a Phoenix, but there is one absolute pattern, and that is pointing towards equilibrium.

Another key ingredient of Phoenix companies is timing. They understand that they have to innovate when they *can*, not when they *need* to, if they want to stay relevant (and not just essential). Because it is just as important to know *when* to step into the future as it is to try to understand *what* it might become.

Only those who will
          risk going too far

can possibly find out
how far one can go. —*T.S. ELIOT*

5

Risk, The Root Of All Progress

I never fail,
I either win,
or I learn. —*NELSON MANDELA*

The Battle of Spotsylvania was one of the most brutal and blood-soaked clashes of the American Civil War. In this bucolic part of Virginia, the army lost 32,000 men (killed, wounded or missing) during the combat, which lasted for 12 days in the month of May, 1864. Its single casualty who will be remembered most was Major General John Sedgwick, a seasoned Union Army commander. When the Battle of Spotsylvania Court House took off, he was incredibly annoyed at his soldiers ducking for cover when the enemy started shooting. Angrily, he shouted out, 'Why are you dodging like this? They couldn't hit an elephant at this distance.' Those were his famous last words, as he was subsequently shot by a confederate sniper.

It is a telling story I picked up from General Stanley McChrystal, whom we met earlier, when I wrote about 'lack of imagination'. McChrystal is also the one who helped me better understand the nature of risk, which I have come to believe is the fundamental essence of progress, especially in the ever-changing landscape of the Never Normal. It is, in fact, the defining element that underpins our lives, innovation, and economies.

Mistrust makes life difficult, trust makes it risky.

—MASON COOLEY

The Ubiquity Of Risk

We make choices every single day, in our personal lives, our social circles, and in our professional activities. And every single choice we make is a judgment call, a statistical analysis, if you will, that starts with a risk assessment. The combination of these choices is life itself. And they have huge consequences.

The choice of your life partner is an example. In the US, the overall divorce rate amounts to over 44%, and the current estimate is that 60% of spouses married at 20–25 years old will eventually divorce. Similarly, the choice of schooling, your university, and your major will have huge consequences for your eventual life journey. The choice of your first employer will have a massive impact on your professional career. Even the friends you pick as a child could have a colossal impact on your personal development. Choices are risk assessments, and risk is what makes life exciting.

I had a Catholic upbringing, and one of the stories that shaped me was the 'Parable of the Talents'—also known as 'The Parable of the Bags of Gold'—as told in Matthew 25:14–30. A talent was a significant unit of weight in the ancient world, primarily used for measuring gold and silver. And it was immensely valuable. A single talent was worth more than 15 years' wages for a daily laborer.

The parable goes like this. A master leaves his house for a very long journey, but, before he does so, he entrusts his belongings to his servants. According to the abilities of each man, one servant received five talents, the second received two, and the third received only one. So, the total number of talents he left behind was eight, which was quite a significant amount of money in those days.

When the master returns home, after a long absence, he asks his three servants for an account of the talents he entrusted to them. The first and the second servants explain that they each put their talents to work, and have doubled the value of the property. They are promptly rewarded by the master. The third servant, however, had merely hidden his talent, burying it in the ground under a tree. He was afraid to risk the one talent he received, and did not want to lose it. This behavior infuriated the master, and he subsequently punishes the servant.

The point of this parable is to show how God expects his people to use the 'talents'—skills, money, assets, resources, abilities—that he has given them. Regardless of how much we've been given, we're expected to faithfully use those blessings in godly ways. We are not meant to bury them and do nothing.

As a kid, this story had a huge impact on me. Of course, the two servants who had put their talents to work had done very well. They had doubled the value of their assets by the time the master returned. But this story would also have been completely different had the two entrepreneurial servants seen their initial investment go up in smoke because they invested in really bad ideas. If the master returned in that scenario, the only one who would have had any resources left was the risk-averse servant who had buried it under a tree.

I did not grow up to become a religious man, but I've always cherished the message from this parable: 'Take the risk. Better to have tried, than to have done nothing.' Unfortunately, most people are not great at risk taking.

I grew up with a fascination for risk takers, heavily influenced by an overload of action movies and sci-fi flicks. I loved James Bond, facing danger with an absolutely cold stare, taking huge risks while never losing his cool. Indiana Jones was my childhood hero, consistently placing himself in dangerous and unpredictable situations in pursuit of ancient artefacts and knowledge. He epitomized the archetype of a risk-taking adventurer, willing to face peril and uncertainty in the pursuit of the greater good. It was extremely confusing to me that Han Solo was played by the same actor. But Han, too, is brash and confident, thriving on the thrill of the unknown and willing to undertake dangerous missions for the right price.

A Tale Of 3 Startups

With these heroes and parables in my background, I had the chance to run three technology startups. Startups are notoriously risky, often with a close to 90% chance of failure. But in 1995, at the age of 25, I started an internet-based technology company. I often think back to that period, and feel blessed that I had the chance to do a startup at such an early age. I had *no* idea how risky it was, though, what the consequences could have been, and what a massive gamble I was taking on. Thank God, or I would have never done it.

But let's rewind a little. After graduating as a young engineer, I joined Alcatel, one of the systemic players in the world of telecoms infrastructure at the time. This 'telephone' pioneer had its roots in the early 1900s and would grow to be a global giant supplying equipment to telecom operators. When I joined the company, it had more than 300,000 employees worldwide.

I admired Alcatel and was surrounded by absolutely brilliant engineers who had helped build the telecoms industry. This was the pre-world-wide-web era, in 1993. When I saw my first website two years later, I was mesmerized and wanted to understand how the technology worked. I spent all my off-duty hours building and debugging websites. But my enthusiasm was clearly not shared at work. On the contrary, most of the senior executives running the research department where I worked did not believe that this 'web technology' would ever amount to anything.

But I did. So I quit my job in 1995. Most of my colleagues believed I was nuts. Yet I started an internet company that developed a web-based platform for information management. Actually, we built a 'Sharepoint', long before there was Sharepoint, and grew the company steadily with customers all over the world. Ironically, four years after I left, Alcatel asked if it could acquire my company. The 'world-wide-web thing' had turned out to be something substantial after all...

If I had not been so passionate about the web, and not so disappointed with the lukewarm and often hostile attitude at Alcatel, I probably would never have left the company. And would never have taken the entrepreneurial risk associated with startups. I sometimes meet the people I went to university with at reunions. They often tell me things like 'I wish I had done something like you. But I joined the steel plant (or bank, or chemical company, or whatever), and then before you know it, it's 20 years later and you don't want to take the risk anymore.'

I took the risk of building a company, not because I wanted to be Han Solo, of course. I took the risk because I truly believed in my passion. And probably because I did not fully comprehend all the risks it involved.

Those became clear in my second startup, though. Giddy after the first success, probably a little too arrogant, and convinced that I had the 'Midas Touch', I started a second venture. This time in streaming video. I believed that the internet was not just going to be about websites. Video would come to play a huge role in it. I was absolutely right, ... but the timing was all wrong. We started this venture four years before YouTube entered the market. At a time when there was no bandwidth to support video, no video compression technology, and therefore no customers.

Still, I took the risk. We grew the company, burned a lot of money, and a few years down the line we were forced to sell the company for one symbolic euro (about the same as a symbolic dollar, really) in order to save it from bankruptcy. I had learned the hard way, and the final moments of that venture were nerve-racking. I could have lost all my financial stability, and it was eating me up.

Still, I had the courage to launch a third one. This time, we raised venture capital, and developed one of the first European cloud players of its day. We grew the company, and were able to list it in 2006. The IPO was one of the most interesting things I have ever done professionally. The combination of starting and running a company, and then going on to sell that narrative to investors, with all the legal and financial engineering involved, was intellectually probably one of the most rewarding things I've ever experienced. We ran the company as a listed company for almost four years, and were subsequently acquired by a Canadian company that was listed on the Toronto stock exchange and on the Nasdaq.

Three intense startups, back-to-back, in a period of 15 years. Exhilarating. And absolutely draining. Emotionally, physically and mentally, I was totally exhausted. Today, people would call it burnout, but back then, nobody talked about that.

On the other hand, my sense of appreciating risk had grown spectacularly. When you look at the normal odds of failing in a startup, I had achieved a massive victory. With two wins and just one defeat, I had a success ratio of 66% instead of a normal failure rate of 90%.

Instead of doubling down, and putting everything on 'red' again, I decided to completely change my life. Although I would still invest in startups, I wanted to work and live on a different part of the risk spectrum. I started teaching at London Business School, became a fellow at MIT Sloan, wrote a string of books and toured the world with keynotes. Startups will give you the 90% failure rate thrill, but academia and writing books is the complete opposite. You cannot get a more risk-averse comfort zone than the realm of a Business School, where tradition runs deep.

Uncertainty Balancers

Nathan Furr is professor of Strategy at INSEAD, the author of *The Upside of Uncertainty* and one of my esteemed colleagues. He actually co-wrote the book with his wife Susannah Furr, who is an entrepreneur. An interesting marriage on two sides of the risk spectrum.

One of the concepts that Nathan describes in his book is the idea behind 'uncertainty balancers'. People who take great risks professionally are sometimes very conservative in their personal lives. And vice versa. Look at Steve Jobs, arguably one of the most disruptive and innovative thinkers in the world of technology, who wore the exact same outfit every day, a combination of an Issey Miyake black mock turtleneck with a pair of Levi's 501 jeans. Or, the other way round, you also have government bureaucrats or accountants who perform the very same tedious routine tasks every single day at work, yet do bungee jumping and skydiving at the weekend, or tear through the countryside like unshaven bandanna-wearing road pirates on Harley-Davidsons.

This balancing act between professional and personal risk taking is a way for individuals to manage their overall exposure to uncertainty. By compartmentalizing their risk tolerance, they create a dynamic equilibrium that allows them to maintain a sense of control and fulfillment. This duality allows them to harness the benefits of taking calculated risks while ensuring they have a sanctuary of predictability to fall back on. This nuanced approach to managing uncertainty not only highlights the complexity of human behavior but also underscores the diverse ways in which people strive to achieve equilibrium in their lives.

It probably explains why I, on the one hand, loved starting up three companies, experiencing the risk more like excitement than anything else, while on the other hand being described by my family as the most steadfast, stable and stodgy person you can imagine. I could actually eat the same meal every day: Miracoli spaghetti, made by the Mars company. That's an extremely bare-bones Italian pasta dish with a simple tomato sauce and 'secret spice mix' that comes in a box.

When I moved from Europe to the US with my parents as a kid, that particular brand of boxed spaghetti was no longer available to us. So my parents begged family and friends who visited us in California to smuggle packets of Miracoli spaghetti sauce in their suitcases, to keep me satisfied. Even today, when I'm overwhelmed, I reach for the cupboard where there is always an ample supply of Miracoli boxes.

Food is quite literally an excellent indicator of risk appetite. I have to admit, I'm personally not on the adventurous side at all in that area. When we travel abroad, my family tries anything novel and exotic, while I look for the tried and tested, and prefer to avoid anything new. But when it comes to making a household purchase, I can easily and quickly choose and buy in record time, while my wife mulls over the options ad aeternum.

Everyone of us has a risk journey. Everyone of us has risk appetite, larger or smaller, and most of us have figured out a way to 'balance' the uncertainty in our lives by spreading the risk profile. As fascinating as this is for individuals, I have become ever more intrigued by the potential to apply this to organizations, their leadership and their cultures.

Be Prepared

When I was growing up in the US, I joined the Boy Scouts of America. It has been one of the most rewarding and enjoyable experiences of my childhood, and I still have very fond memories of what I learned there. Not just in practical skills, but also in terms of social interactions and understanding organizational dynamics. The Boy Scouts of America was a pretty formal organization, strict on hierarchy and structure. Their motto was drilled into young Scouts such as myself: 'Be Prepared'.

Our troop went for camping trips around Southern California on almost a monthly basis, and 'Be Prepared' was not to be taken lightly. It was a rigorous method of planning and preparation, and as young boys we learned the importance of looking ahead, and evaluating risk. We were told repeatedly that if we were to become stranded somewhere in the middle of nowhere, where rattlesnakes and black widow spiders were not uncommon, then being prepared could make the difference between life or death.

In 2020, however, The Boy Scouts of America filed for bankruptcy, 110 years after it was founded. They had to spend more than $150 million to settle hundreds of sexual abuse lawsuits. In a massive bankruptcy restructuring exercise, it changed its name to Scouting America, and committed to paying out more than $2 billion to men who say they were sexually abused as Scouts. So much for 'Being Prepared'.

It has been absolutely fascinating for me to see how organizations evolve and how, so often, the very seeds of their destruction were present from the very beginning.

My father was an engineer who worked in the Oil & Gas sector for his entire career. I had great admiration for my dad as a young boy and all I wanted was to follow in his footsteps and become an engineer myself. Interestingly, the core knowledge of my father was risk management. The year he joined Exxon, in 1976, one of the worst man-made environmental disasters took place in Seveso, in a small chemical manufacturing plant approximately 20 kilometers north of Milan in the Lombardy region of Italy.

The plant was producing 2,4,5-trichlorophenol, a chemical used in herbicides and pharmaceuticals. Due to a runaway reaction, a dense vapor cloud containing highly toxic dioxins was released into the atmosphere, contaminating an area of approximately 6 square kilometers. The effects were immediately visible on local fauna and flora; within days, animals began dying and plants started withering. The human impact was slower to manifest. Initially, residents reported skin lesions and inflammation, but the long-term effects were way more severe. Studies in the following years linked exposure to increased rates of certain cancers, reproductive issues, and developmental problems in children born after the accident. Over 80,000 animals, mostly pets and livestock, had to be slaughtered to prevent dioxins from entering the food chain.

The Seveso disaster had far-reaching consequences for industrial safety regulations, particularly in Europe. It led to the creation of the European Union's 'Seveso Directive' in 1982, which mandated strict controls on industrial activities involving dangerous substances, including risk assessments, emergency planning, and public information policies. It introduced the concept of a 'safety report' that companies must produce, detailing how they manage risk. That was my father's job. He was stationed in chemical plants around the world, in order to build safety systems, procedures and mechanisms to ensure that a disaster like 'Seveso' would never happen again.

Three Brain Safety

It's sometimes strange what you can remember from your childhood. One memory that is strongly implanted in my brain was the absolute excitement of my dad about a technology called 'Triconex', which he pioneered at Exxon. Essentially it was a solution called a TMR (Triple Modular Redundant) system, a brilliant technique of three intelligent 'brains' constantly monitoring the safety situation in an operational situation like a chemical plant: two 'brains' worked side-by-side, independently. Normally they would both come to the same conclusion about the safety of the situation. In the very unlikely case that the two side-by-side brains were *not* in sync, there was an 'uber-brain', the third brain, that would make the final decision on whether to shut down the plant or not.

As with many technologies, this technique had its origins in space. The first Triconex system had been used on the NASA space shuttles, and then the technology made its way into mainstream business like the petrochemical industry. My father's entire career entailed using the Triconex technology to make chemical plants around the world safe.

Then, in the summer of 2017, an incredible tech-spy-thriller story unfolded when malicious software (malware) was discovered in a petrochemical plant in Saudi Arabia. Hackers had deployed malware—which has since been dubbed 'Triton'—that let them take over the plant's safety instrument systems. It took over the Triconex systems remotely, and would have allowed the hacker to remotely detonate entire chemical plants, essentially causing several Seveso-scenarios around the world. The consequences could have been catastrophic, but fortunately, a flaw in the code gave the hackers away before they could do any damage. But it was a stern signal: this was the first time the cybersecurity world had seen code deliberately designed to put lives at risk. It was especially concerning if you realized that Triconex systems were also the last line of defense in everything from transportation systems to water treatment facilities to nuclear power stations.

For me, it was a closing of the loop to remember my father's excitement about how this new technology could make the world of chemical production so much safer, only to realize that this very same solution had become the attack vector to unleash potentially horrible terrorism on the world.

As I said, the seeds of an organization's destruction are often present from the very beginning.

Risk Is A Spectrum

My professional view on risk expanded significantly when I joined the board of a bank, back in Belgium where I live, back in 2021. I completely underestimated the enormous intellectual challenge of participating in the extremely heavily regulated and risk-averse world of finance. It meant that, at the age of 52, I had to go back and study, big time. I had to not only learn how the mechanics of banking worked, but also hit the books to understand the complex set of rules and regulations that govern the financial system.

The bank I joined was Belfius, a casualty of the financial crash of 2008, and 100% owned by the Belgian government. Back then, there was a larger financial player called Dexia, operating in multiple countries, but in the aftermath of 2008, when the bank collapsed, it was rescued in parts. The French government carved out their bank, and the Belgian government carved out what would become Belfius. Today, the bank is doing extremely well. It is a broad-spectrum bank, doing everything from retail banking serving households and individuals, to corporate banking and also private and wealth. It has become a true Phoenix, leveraging the power of technology to become stronger, with a mobile app that is ranked in the top three worldwide. In 2023, it recorded a healthy profit of 1 billion euros.

In essence, banking is not very difficult: you collect money from depositors and in return you pay them interest for using their money. The bank then lends that money to business and families who need it in the form of loans, and the borrowers pay back the loans with interest, which is higher than what the bank pays depositors. The bank makes money from the difference between the interest it receives from loans and the interest it pays to depositors. Easy, right? Well yes, but there is also plenty of risk involved.

Understanding risk is the very core of banking. Not all loans will be repaid: companies might go out of business, people could lose their jobs. You have to calculate the chances of a default on a loan, and understand the credit risk. Then there is liquidity risk: if too many people want their money back all at once (like during a panic), the bank might not have enough cash

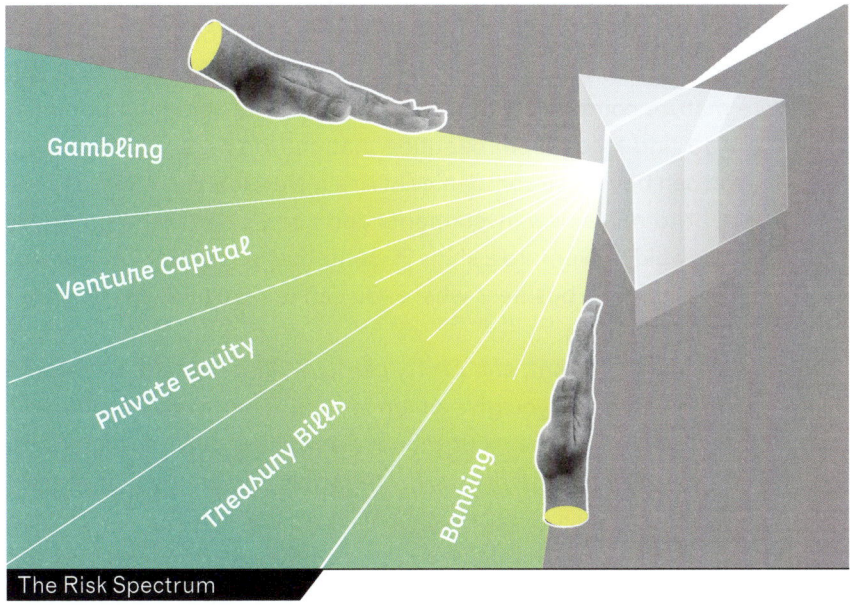

The Risk Spectrum

on hand because most of it is out as loans. Interest rates are unstable, and this creates interest risk. There is also market risk because market fluctuation can cause the value of the bank's investments (like stocks or bonds) to change. But banks have frameworks to deal with this, like the Risk Appetite Framework (RAF), which is a structured approach that defines the amount and type of risk a bank is willing to take on in pursuit of its business objectives. It's like a bank setting its own speed limit for risk taking.

Beginning my career in the startup world, dealing with venture capitalists, and ending up on the board of a bank has given me a great appreciation for the incredibly wide spectrum of risk that exists in the business world.

In the world of venture capital, it is quite normal that out of the 10 investments you make, seven turn out to be a complete failure. That is the risk you are willing to take. In fact, you actually want these startups to fail as quickly as possible, so they stop bleeding resources, and so that you can concentrate on the ones that will make it. Out of the three remaining investments, two might be mediocre performers, but you'll also have one 'home run' investment. One that will give you a 50x return (you get 50 times the money you put in), and that will make your entire fund extremely profitable even if 70% of your investments have died. It's all about that one home run.

I joined the advisory board of a private equity firm about 10 years ago, wanting to understand how that world worked. I learned that it is an absolutely beautiful mechanism, based on the concept of leveraged debt. Instead of finding raw young startups that still have to make their way, you find more mature companies, with much less risk yet very high potential. The trick is to find 'neglected' beauties that can be reinvigorated like a Phoenix. You can buy these companies at a relatively low valuation, use the power of debt to make new investments and acquisitions, and gradually turn your dusty old tanker into a shiny Phoenix that you can sell at a premium. It is a very lucrative business where you can double or even triple your money within a few years.

Banking is very different, and pretty complex. You give a mortgage to a family to buy a home, or you give a loan to a company to buy equipment, and you basically hope to get your money back years down the line, with interest of a few percentage points. In the world of insurance, it's about even more long-term risk calculation. Look at life insurance: you sign up a customer when they're in their 30s, and try to calculate how long they will live, and your risk of having to pay a premium.

These diverse financial solutions create a full spectrum, balancing time, risk, and reward. The key is to define your limits while continuously monitoring and strategically leveraging risk to maximize returns.

But it can also go completely pear-shaped.

The collapse of Silicon Valley Bank in March 2023 sent shock waves through the global financial system, when it found itself at the center of a perfect storm of risk management failures.

Silicon Valley Bank was originally founded in 1983 to focus on the needs of startup companies and venture capital companies. It was created by two former Bank of America managers and tennis buddies, who came up with the idea over a game of poker. At that time, the banking industry did not have a good understanding of startup companies, particularly those that lacked revenue. Many startups will go years in developing their ideas before they can start generating revenue, let alone profit. That did not work well in building a relationship with traditional banks, where all sorts of bells and warning lights go off if you can't provide stable cash flows.

So, Silicon Valley Bank worked differently. Initially, startup founders seeking loans from the bank had to pledge about half of their shares as collateral, but the rate later fell to about 7%. The bank covered losses by selling the shares to interested investors. The intimate relationship between the bank, the startups, investors and venture capitalists proved to be a brilliant combination, driving spectacular growth throughout the internet boom. Many entrepreneurs gained significant wealth through their ventures, and Silicon Valley Bank developed a very lucrative private banking business to cater to these new wealthy clients. By 2015, the bank stated that it served 65% of all US startups.

Venture capital had a golden era when the interest rates fell to almost zero, and the world became fascinated by the digital platform craze that seemed to create new economic giants that were fueled by 'network effects' instead of the old-school traditional expensive capital expenditures.

It was a gold rush for venture capital, and an absolute boom for Silicon Valley Bank. These hot new startups raised bigger and bigger fundraising rounds, and the bank just didn't know what to do with all the money that was pouring in. Instead of just lending this money out, SVB invested heavily in long-term US Treasury bonds and mortgage-backed securities, assets that were traditionally considered very safe.

However, this investment strategy exposed SVB to significant interest rate risk, a vulnerability that became apparent when the Federal Reserve began rapidly raising interest rates in 2022 and 2023 to combat inflation. As interest rates rose, the value of SVB's bond portfolio plummeted. Simultaneously, a slowdown in the tech sector meant SVB's clients were withdrawing more money to cover their expenses. Forced to sell its devalued bonds at a loss to meet these withdrawals, SVB's financial troubles became public, sparking a classic bank run as panicked depositors rushed to withdraw their funds. On March 10, 2023, regulators closed SVB, marking the second-largest bank failure in US history.

In hindsight, you could say that the very thing that brought down the bank was there from the outset. The bank's extremely high concentration of clients in the volatile tech sector exceeded what prudent risk appetite would allow, leaving it vulnerable to sector-specific downturns.

The Unthinkable

In the beginning of this chapter, I mentioned General Stanley McChrystal as one of my big influences on the subject of risk. In my opinion, his book *RISK* is one of the best treatments on the field. He is also a highly controversial individual with an impressively large group of adversaries. In fact, when *RISK* came out, the internet lit up with haters. Many wondered how a failed general could give lessons in risk management.

McChrystal, born into a military family in 1954, had a meteoric career in the US military, following in the footsteps of his father who was a major general during the post-World War II occupation of Germany. He attended the US Military Academy at West Point, graduating as a second lieutenant in 1976. After being posted to Korea as an intelligence officer, he was assigned to Joint Special Operations Command (JSOC), a standing task force that integrates special operations units across the US military landscape. During that time, he was deployed to Saudi Arabia for Operations Desert Shield and Desert Storm. And he oversaw the capture of Ṣaddām Ḥussein in 2003 as well as the air strike that killed Al-Qaeda leader Abu Musab al-Zarqawi in 2006.[29]

Newsweek termed JSOC 'the most secretive force in the US military', while McChrystal was called the 'hidden general'. But that changed dramatically in June of 2009 when McChrystal was given command of the joint NATO-US mission in Afghanistan. Under his command, the entire effort in Afghanistan turned into a comprehensive counterinsurgency campaign based on 'nation building'. As McChrystal puts it, 'US soldiers sought to build roads, electrify towns and cities, aid agriculture, and assist the government in responding to the people's needs.' McChrystal requested the deployment of an additional 30,000 troops, which then President Obama approved, bringing the total US force commitment in early 2010 to almost 100,000 troops.

But he never saw that to completion. He was relieved of command in June 2010, after a devastating article in *Rolling Stone* magazine, where he and his members of staff had made derisive comments about top Obama administration officials. He retired from the military, and founded the McChrystal Group, a consultancy on leadership, which is where I had the chance to work with him.

His Afghanistan legacy however still haunts the retired general.

President Obama had pulled the plug on the massive nation-building advocated by McChrystal in 2014. By 2017, with only a few thousand US troops left in the country, the Taliban had regained control of the countryside and they were growing in strength. The government, backed by the US, held on to the cities only. By August of 2021, the Taliban took full control of Afghanistan, culminating in their capture of the capital city Kabul on August 15. This marked the collapse of the Afghan government led by President Ashraf Ghani, who fled the country. The speed of the Taliban's advance took many by surprise, as they swiftly captured provincial capitals and key border crossings in the preceding weeks, often with minimal resistance from Afghan security forces.

The US played a significant and devastating role in these events, having announced in April 2021 that it would withdraw all US troops from Afghanistan by August 31 of that year. Critics argued that the withdrawal was poorly planned and executed, leaving Afghan forces ill-prepared to counter the Taliban's resurgence. As the Taliban advanced, the US and its allies hastily evacuated their citizens and Afghan allies, leading to chaotic scenes at Kabul's airport.

Thousands of Afghans breached security walls and rushed the runway at Hamid Karzai International Airport. I still recall in horror the footage of that airport evacuation. Crowds of panic-stricken citizens, hopelessly trying to cling to the Air Force C-17 as it took off after being unable to unload its cargo, only to fall to their deaths just seconds later.

The evacuation was marred by a suicide bombing that killed over 180 people, including 13 US service members. Despite evacuating over 120,000 people, many Afghans who had worked with foreign forces were left behind. The Taliban's takeover raised concerns about human rights, particularly for women and girls, and there were fears that Afghanistan could once again become a haven for terrorist groups.

The scenes we witnessed were unimaginable. Yet the capability to think the unthinkable is an essential element of understanding and leveraging risk. And that is why I believe the military can give us some very interesting insights. Even the non-fiction military narratives.

I wrote about my admiration for Stanley Kubrick and his masterpiece, *Dr. Strangelove*, earlier in this book. I also love it because it is a brutal illustration of one of the most fundamental risk conundrums: whatever we design as safety solutions can eventually evolve to be the problems. The movie's entire narrative hinges on a US military safeguard regulation that tried to address one very simple question: 'The President of the United States is the only person who can authorize the use of nuclear weapons. But if the enemy succeeds in killing the President, and the entourage, how then do we insure that we can still retaliate with nuclear weapons in a conflict?'

Plan R

The answer, generated by the bureaucratic dungeons of the Cold War Pentagon, was the infamous Plan 'R': an emergency war plan in which a lower echelon commander may order nuclear retaliation after a sneak attack, if the normal chain of command is disrupted. In *Dr. Strangelove*, a rogue US Air Force commander of an US Air Force base misuses the context of Plan 'R' to launch a full nuclear attack on Russia. The movie follows the frantic efforts of the US President, his advisors, and military leaders to recall the bombers and prevent a global nuclear catastrophe.

Dr. Strangelove is an excellent example of 'thinking the unthinkable'. It encourages viewers to understand that even with safeguards in place, human factors like paranoia, miscommunication, or simple accidents could lead to catastrophe. It underscores the importance of considering all possible scenarios, even the most unthinkable ones, when formulating strategies that have immense consequences.

But truth can be much stranger than fiction.

As discussed earlier in the book, in the aftermath of the 9/11 attacks, investigations revealed that US intelligence agencies had numerous pieces of information that, in hindsight, pointed to the likelihood of a major terrorist attack. The trouble was never 'failure of information'. It was failure of imagination, with intelligence analysts and policymakers locked so much into conventional thinking that they expected terrorists to use the same methods they had used before. This ties directly to the need to 'think the unthinkable'. In an increasingly complex and interconnected world, threats can take unexpected forms. Just as the creators of *Dr. Strangelove* urged viewers to confront the real possibility of an accidental nuclear war, the 9/11 Commission urged policymakers and intelligence analysts to expand their horizons of what is possible.

They needed to consider not just what had happened before, but what could happen given the resources, motivations, and creativity of adversaries. The 9/11 Commission Report beautifully concluded: 'In order to avoid such mistakes in the future, we have to institutionalize imagination.'

A Puzzle Or A Mystery?

In his book, *Talking to Strangers*, Malcolm Gladwell discusses the difference between 'puzzle solvers' and 'mystery solvers' in the context of intelligence analysis.

Gladwell argues that puzzles are problems with defined pieces that, once assembled correctly, yield a clear solution. In contrast, mysteries are more complex, with incomplete, contradictory, or unclear information. They require intuition, judgment, and the ability to make sense of ambiguity. Before 9/11, Gladwell suggests, intelligence agencies were treating terrorism as a puzzle: they believed that if they could just collect enough pieces (data), they could predict and prevent attacks. However, terrorism, like many complex threats, is more like a mystery. The 9/11 hijackers didn't leave a clear trail of clues that, if properly assembled, would have revealed their plan. Instead, there were vague hints, cultural indicators, and behavioral patterns that required interpretation and imagination to understand.

Puzzle solvers, focused on known patterns and explicit data, might never consider a scenario like 9/11 because it doesn't fit the puzzle they're trying to solve. Mystery solvers, on the other hand, are more likely to ask 'what if?' questions, to imagine novel threats based on the motivations and capabilities of adversaries rather than just their past actions. They are more equipped to envision and prepare for the 'unthinkable' because their approach inherently involves considering possibilities beyond the obvious or precedented. In an age of complex, adaptive challenges—from terrorism to pandemics to climate change—cultivating more 'mystery solvers' is crucial for effective strategic planning and risk management.

The Greatest Risk To Us Is Us

Growth means change,
and change involves risk,
stepping from the known to the unknown.
—George Shinn

Stanley McChrystal's core message in *RISK* is that we have to look inwards to understand our own greatest vulnerabilities. When he states that 'The Greatest Risk to Us is Us', he is essentially pointing out that our own human limitations, biases, and failures can pose a greater threat than external dangers or adversaries. But how can we know?

Unknown Unknowns And False Truths
The Johari Window technique was designed by Joseph Luft and Harry Ingham in 1955 to help people better understand their relationship with themselves and others.

But you'll probably be more familiar with former United States Secretary of Defense Donald Rumsfeld's simplified interpretation of it: 'There are known knowns. These are things we know that we know. There are known unknowns. That is to say, there are things that we know we don't know. But there are also unknown unknowns. There are things we don't know we don't know.' He introduced this concept during a press briefing in 2002, while discussing the lack of evidence linking the Iraqi government with the supply of weapons of mass destruction to terrorist groups.

Although Rumsfeld misused the concept for all the wrong reasons, I find that there is absolute truth in the fundamental idea of 'unknown unknowns'. They represent the unpredictable and unforeseen factors that can arise unexpectedly. These uncertainties are the most challenging to

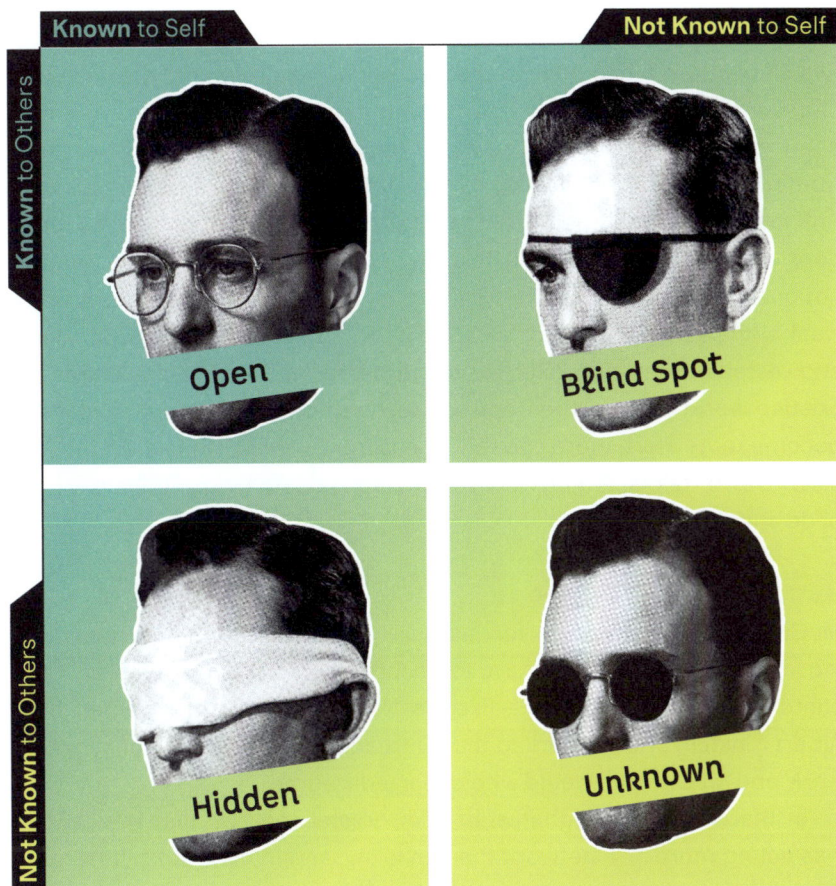

Open

Blind Spot

Hidden

Unknown

manage because we cannot plan for what we do not know exists. And that is exactly why we need to be mystery solvers in the Never Normal, instead of puzzle solvers.

Another related aphorism that I really like is attributed to Mark Twain: 'It ain't what you don't know that gets you into trouble. It's what you know for sure that just ain't so.' He warned against the dangers of firmly held false beliefs or assumptions that contradict reality. These are things we 'know for sure' but are actually simply incorrect. Such entrenched but erroneous knowledge can turn out to be even more insidious than ignorance because it provides a false sense of confidence and understanding. It can lead to disastrous decisions, an inability to adapt, and a refusal to heed contradictory evidence or warnings.

The concepts of 'unknown unknowns' by Rumsfeld, and the 'false truths' of Twain are interconnected with the concept of 'weak signals': the necessity of picking up, listening and interpreting faint hints or patterns that may point to emerging trends, threats, or opportunities that are not yet fully formed or recognized. Failing to detect weak signals leaves us blind to 'unknown unknowns' and important factors that could upend our assumptions or models. However, as Twain's quote suggests, our preconceived notions and firmly held beliefs can act as filters that cause us to dismiss weak signals that contradict 'what we know for sure'. Our cognitive biases and vested interests make us resistant to information that challenges our existing world view or threatens our assumptions. So we have to learn to become more alert, more capable of picking up these signals. As the African proverb claims, 'A man who is trampled to death by an elephant is both blind and deaf.'

Becoming A Network

McChrystal is best known for his work on organizational design thinking, and his notion that we have to become 'networks' to act faster, if the context in which we operate—like the 'Never Normal'—is extremely fluid. Albert Einstein once remarked that 'Bureaucracy is the death of all sound work' and McChrystal would wholeheartedly agree.

In the combat of Afghanistan, McChrystal realized that the Taliban was acting more as a network than an army, and in his words, 'It became clear to me and to many others that to defeat a networked enemy we had to become a network ourselves.' In other words, *it takes a network to fight a network.*

McChrystal concluded that in a rapidly changing environment, traditional top-down command structures were too slow and inflexible to decide and respond effectively. Instead, he advocated for a networked approach where small teams operate with a high degree of autonomy but are closely aligned through shared purpose and transparent communication.

That's why 'empowered execution' is also a key principle in *Team of Teams*. McChrystal emphasizes the importance of pushing decision-making authority down to the lowest possible level. By empowering individuals and teams to act independently, organizations can leverage the expertise and creativity of their members more effectively. This approach not only enhances responsiveness but also fosters a sense of ownership and accountability among team members, which is critical for sustained success.

This empowerment is critical in managing risks that require quick, decisive action.

The concept of 'shared consciousness' is another crucial element in McChrystal's thinking. This involves creating an environment where information flows freely across all levels of the organization, ensuring that every team has access to the knowledge they need to make informed decisions. In practice, this means breaking down silos and fostering a culture of trust and openness. By doing so, organizations can achieve a level of collective intelligence that enables them to respond to threats and opportunities with greater agility. In a networked structure, this transparency ensures that teams have real-time access to the data they need to assess risks accurately and promptly.

Organizations that embrace a networked structure are typically more adaptable and resilient. They can pivot more easily in response to changing conditions and therefore offer significant advantages for assessing and managing risks.

As McChrystal states, 'To study risk is to reconsider what we think we know about being prepared.'

Reality Distortion

Earlier in this chapter, I mentioned my own entrepreneurial roots. It was, in hindsight, a combination of dumb luck, blissful ignorance and extreme naivety that brought me to pursuing a startup life. And I don't regret it one bit. It gave me a lifetime fascination for entrepreneurial risk and 'risk appetite framework'.

As a student, I remember watching the movie *Tucker*, with a brilliant performance by the young Jeff Bridges. The legendary Francis Ford Coppola, a master of cinematography, dedicated this remarkable film to his late son, who tragically passed away in a boating accident: 'To Gio, who loved cars.'

The movie is based on the true story of the life of Preston Tucker, an innovative automobile designer who had ambitious dreams to revolutionize the car industry in the late 1940s.

Preston Thomas Tucker was born in 1903, and he developed a passion for cars and engineering from a young age. His most notable contribution to the automotive industry was the groundbreaking Tucker 48, also known as the 'Tucker Torpedo', which boasted advanced features for its time, such as a rear-engine, safety glass, and a padded dashboard.

Despite his innovative vision, Tucker faced significant challenges. Raising funds for the project was difficult, and Tucker had to sell dealership rights and accessories to keep his company afloat. His unconventional methods and rapid fundraising drew the attention of the Securities and Exchange Commission (SEC), leading to an investigation and subsequent trial on charges of stock fraud. Additionally, the Big Three automakers (General Motors, Ford, and Chrysler) saw Tucker as a threat and used their influence to create obstacles for his company.

The film brings to life the meteoric rise and heartbreaking fall of Preston Tucker and his Tucker Corporation. It captures his charisma, ingenuity, and relentless drive, embodying the very essence of the American Dream. Through his story, the movie celebrates entrepreneurship, innovation, and the unwavering pursuit of a vision—despite overwhelming odds.

Coppola portrays Tucker as a real visionary who, despite his ultimate failure, left a lasting impact on the industry. As only 51 Tucker 48 cars were ever produced, they became incredible collectible artefacts as well as a symbol of innovation and the fight against corporate monopolies. Francis Ford Coppola himself is a Tucker owner (as is George Lucas) and he displays his vehicle proudly on the grounds of his winery.

The movie had a huge impact on me when I was younger. I became utterly enchanted with the narrative of the visionary entrepreneur, trying to battle the evil entrenched Powers That Be, like Don Quixote trying to fight windmills. There is something absolutely heroic about the underdog trying to survive against all odds, taking insane risks, beyond anything rational, trying to create value, beauty, truth and progress.

Years later, when I had the chance to launch my own startups, I learned a far less romantic truth. Building something from the ground up is brutally hard, relentless, often disheartening, and incredibly lonely. The mental and emotional toll can be overwhelming, pushing you to the edge more times than you can count. Still, my startup years were the most exhilarating and rewarding of my professional life. And if I could turn back time, I wouldn't change a thing.

As many of you will know, I'm a huge Apple fanboy, with my fascination resulting in a compulsive obsession in collecting Apple history. One of the most cherished objects in my collection is the original prospectus that Morgan Stanley used to take Apple public back in 1979, selling the first block of 4,600,000 shares of Apple Computer Inc.

More than 45 years later, that document is a fabulous read. As any prospectus should do, it lists the 'Risk Factors' in the very front of the document. In the case of this prospectus it reads:

RISK FACTORS

Operating History

Apple Computer Inc. is a new company which has not established a long history of operation upon which to base opinions of accuracy of forecasts, financial projections or operations efficiency.

Manufacturing

Apple has experienced extreme difficulty in obtaining its custom injection molded cases. There is no assurance that this problem will be solved through establishing additional sources of supply.

Cash Flow vs Rapid Growth

Apple management expects that rapid growth and potential market fluctuations may present severe cash flow management difficulties.

Management

Apple Computers' management team is young and relatively inexperienced in the high volume consumer electronics business.

Imagine reading this back in the winter of 1979, while considering putting your life savings into a little known computer company that was only four years old. The management team is inexperienced, the company sees severe cash flow management difficulties ahead, the manufacturing has no solution for their supply chain issues, and they have no idea how to make accurate financial projections.

Would you have invested?

The Apple IPO was a huge success, nonetheless.

My favorite episode of the Apple saga was when Steve Jobs single-handedly decided to take the development of a new computer into his own hands, by creating the 'Macintosh' division. The Mac would eventually become the crown jewel of Apple Computers, but in the beginning, it was a very rocky ride.

Steve Jobs handpicked a renegade team of mavericks and geniuses from within Apple and sent them across the street to a nondescript building, away from the corporate structure of the company. To make their mission unmistakable, he hoisted a pirate flag over the office—a bold declaration that they were the rebels, the outlaws, the ones rewriting the rules. He loved to tell them, 'It's more fun to be a pirate than to join the Navy.'

The group that developed the Macintosh was an eclectic group of talented wizards, and Steve Jobs worked them to the bone. It started out as a scrappy assortment of outcasts, nerds and mutts, but Steve Jobs crafted them into a dream team. Day by day the evidence accumulated that they had it within their power to create something a quantum leap better than anything the industry, indeed the world, had ever witnessed. They believed they could make a dent in the universe.

In his brilliant account on the early days of the Macintosh called *Insanely Great*, the author Steven Levy puts it like this: 'The creation of the Mac in 1984 catapulted America into the digital millennium, captured a fanatic cult audience, and transformed the computer industry into an unprecedented mix of technology, economics, and show business.'

The team was filled with unique skills. The group had all the ingredients to build a revolutionary computer, and 'put a dent in the universe'. But the secret sauce was Steve, and particularly one of his idiosyncratic gifts.

Steve was known to understand how to leverage the concept of a 'Reality Distortion Field', originally a term from *Star Trek*. Jobs had an insane capability for 'bending the truth' to get what he wanted, and especially to get people to do what he wanted.

As Andy Hertzfeld, one of the chief software architects of the Mac put it, 'The Reality Distortion Field was a confounding mélange of a charismatic rhetorical style, an indomitable will, and an eagerness to bend any fact to fit the purpose at hand. In his presence, reality was malleable. He could convince anyone of practically anything.'

I believe the Reality Distortion Field was the reason the Mac eventually became the iconic game changer in the computer industry. But he was not above sharing his success with his team.

In his brilliant book, *Revolution in the Valley*, Hertzfeld describes this episode: 'One day he brought around a piece of white paper and sharpies, and all of us got to sign on them—and then he had those engraved on the hard tooling for the case. So if you take off the back of an original Mac, all of us have signed it. Steve believed that what we were doing wasn't just work. We were making art. He engraved our names into the mold. And the reason is: real artists sign their work and they're proud of it.'

I have one of those original Macintosh computers open in my Apple Chapple, and every time I look inside, and see those engraved signatures of the brilliant people who built the Mac, I still get goosebumps.

The history of Apple reads like a roller-coaster ride, with probably more downs than ups, and with a period in 1997 where the company almost went bankrupt. When Steve Jobs returned to Apple that very year, *WIRED* magazine had a picture of the Apple logo on its cover, with a thorn crown, and below that the word 'PRAY'.

But Steve Jobs brought back Apple from the dead, and eventually turned it into the most valuable company in the world. Upon his return to Apple, he launched the 'Think Different' offensive, one of the most iconic and successful marketing campaigns in history.

This was its original text:

> Here's to the crazy ones, the misfits, the rebels, the troublemakers, the round pegs in the square holes ... the ones who see things differently -- they're not fond of rules, and they have no respect for the status quo.
> You can quote them, disagree with them, glorify or vilify them, but the only thing you can't do is ignore them because they change things. They push the human race forward, and while some may see them as the crazy ones, we see genius, because the people who are crazy enough to think that they can change the world, are the ones who do.

My favorite version of the ad is the one where Steve Jobs himself did the voice-over, but it was not the one that came out to the general public. Hearing that version, in his words, still gives me the chills. He really believed that core element: people who are crazy enough to think that they can change the world are the ones who do.

I became fascinated by that dark side of entrepreneurial life. The 'reality distortion field' may seem harsh but it did work in the case of Jobs to drive his engineers to absolute greatness. It made them develop things that were truly game-changing.

But what is the difference between a 'reality distortion field' and just plain lying?

Fake It Till You Make It

One of the most juicy and sensational Silicon Valley stories of the last couple of years must have been that of Theranos, and the meteoric rise and subsequently colossal fall to earth of its founder Elizabeth Holmes. It was a captivating and chilling tale of ambition, deception, and the perils of unchecked innovation in the tech and healthcare industries.

Elizabeth Holmes, born in 1984 (the same year the Macintosh was released), founded Theranos in 2003 after dropping out of Stanford University. Inspired by her fear of needles and a desire to revolutionize healthcare, Holmes envisioned a device that could run comprehensive tests on just a few drops of blood. Her vision captivated the public and investors, promising a future where diagnostic testing would be quick, easy, and accessible to everyone. Holmes wanted to disrupt the world of healthcare diagnostics, but the gap between her ingenious inspiring vision and the hard cold reality of science was just too big. Even for someone with her reality distortion field capabilities.

She was a truly captivating storyteller, possessed a hypnotic charisma and was able to spin a massive set of lies that quickly attracted high-profile investors and board members, including former Secretary of State Henry Kissinger and media mogul Rupert Murdoch. By 2014, Theranos was valued at $9 billion, making Holmes the world's youngest self-made female billionaire. The company entered into partnerships with major retail chains like Walgreens and announced plans to place its testing devices in stores across the country, further cementing its public image as a game-changer in medical technology.

However, cracks in Theranos's facade began to appear as journalists and medical professionals raised questions about the validity of its technology. In 2015, investigative journalist John Carreyrou of *The Wall Street Journal* published a series of articles exposing the flaws in Theranos's testing methods. Carreyrou's reporting revealed that the company's proprietary Edison machines were unreliable, and that Theranos was using commercially available machines for many of its tests while misleading investors, partners, and patients about the capabilities of its own technology.

The revelations sparked a downward spiral for Theranos. Regulatory bodies, including the Centers for Medicare and Medicaid Services (CMS) and the US Securities and Exchange Commission (SEC), launched investigations into the company. In 2016, CMS banned Holmes from owning or operating a blood-testing laboratory for two years, and the SEC charged her with fraud in 2018. The charges detailed how Holmes and former Theranos president Ramesh 'Sunny' Balwani had engaged in an elaborate, years-long fraud in which they exaggerated or made false statements about the company's technology, business, and financial performance.

As the truth came to light, Theranos faced a series of lawsuits and settlements. The company dissolved in 2018, and Holmes and Balwani were indicted on multiple counts of wire fraud and conspiracy. The trial for these charges began in 2021, drawing significant media attention and serving as a high-profile example of the risks of hype-driven innovation in Silicon Valley. Holmes's trial concluded in early 2022 when she was found guilty on several counts of fraud and sentenced to more than 11 years in prison.[30]

It is an intensely sad chronicle of deception. But it brings out a very interesting conundrum that is prevalent in the world of entrepreneurs: the 'fake it till you make it' dilemma.

The concept of 'fake it till you make it' embodies the idea that projecting confidence and success can help entrepreneurs attract the resources and support needed to turn their vision into reality. This approach encourages startups to act as if they have already achieved their goals, often before their products or services are fully developed or proven. While this mindset can drive innovation and inspire confidence, it also carries significant risks, as the line between optimistic projection and deceit can become dangerously blurred.

Theranos serves as a stark illustration of the pitfalls of 'fake it till you make it'. Holmes projected an image of revolutionary success long before her technology was viable, or even scientifically possible. By creating an aura of infallibility and leveraging powerful endorsements, she was able to secure substantial investments and high-profile partnerships. However, the core technology behind Theranos's blood-testing devices was fundamentally flawed. Holmes and her team exaggerated the capabilities of their technology, leading to significant ethical and legal consequences when the truth was uncovered. The collapse of Theranos highlighted how faking it without making it can lead to catastrophic outcomes.

But sometimes you clearly get away with it.

Steve Jobs was famously admired for his showmanship in creating the illusion of completed products before they were fully developed. The first

Apple computers and the early models of the iPhone were promoted with a level of polish and functionality that exceeded their initial capabilities. Jobs's charisma and confidence in presenting these products helped secure the necessary investment and support to ultimately deliver on their promises. And he would use his 'reality distortion field' towards his own engineers to make sure they would deliver.

Look at Elon Musk, who is without doubt the current poster child for 'fake it till you make it': constantly projecting bold visions for his companies, such as SpaceX and Tesla, long before the technologies are proven. Musk's ambitious and grandiose claims have frequently been met with skepticism. And yes, he sometimes behaves erratically these days, showing a great addiction to power. However, throughout his career, he has also consistently been able to deliver groundbreaking products and services that, while occasionally delayed or over budget, have truly transformed their respective industries. When he projected the possibilities of rockets coming back to earth after launch, landing upright onto a barge in the ocean, he was ridiculed. Just as his claims about full self-driving cars are still greeted with intense skepticism. The problem with Musk is he has proven critics wrong so many times in the past that it is very hard to see when he is using his reality distortion field.

Cognitive Diversity

The Theranos saga was a stark reminder of the importance of due diligence and skepticism in the face of too-good-to-be-true claims, particularly in industries as critical as healthcare. It was also a strong testimony to what Stanley McChrystal calls 'the need for cognitive diversity', to be able to separate hype from reality.

Cognitive diversity refers to the inclusion of individuals with varied perspectives, problem-solving approaches, and backgrounds, in order to foster an environment where assumptions are challenged, and ideas are rigorously tested. This diversity is crucial for maintaining a healthy balance between ambition and reality, as it encourages critical thinking and prevents the echo chamber effect where only one viewpoint dominates.

In the case of Theranos, Elizabeth Holmes surrounded herself with a cadre of loyal supporters who were enthralled by her vision and charisma. These individuals, often referred to as her 'fanboys', followed her narrative without questioning the underlying feasibility of the technology. Her all-star board of primarily old white male senior executives and officials in particular was a miserable example of how the absence of cognitive diversity drives uncritical behavior.

To give just one example, Henry Kissinger, the former US secretary of state, claimed she possessed an 'ethereal quality, like a member of a monastic order'. The saddest story, however, is that of George Shultz, who served four different Cabinet positions under two US presidents. He was appointed to the board of Theranos in 2011 when he was 91 years old. He was completely enthralled by Elizabeth Holmes. He talked on the phone with her almost every day and invited her to join Shultz family Christmas dinners.

His own grandson Tyler Shultz joined Theranos in September 2013 after graduating from Stanford University. After a while, he started to realize that there was something off at Theranos. When he tried to talk to his grandfather about his beliefs that there was 'something rotten behind the scenes', his grandfather refused to listen and cut off all ties with his own grandson. Even after Holmes was indicted in 2018, George Shultz never apologized to his grandson.

Elizabeth Holmes's rise and fall illustrates the potential consequences of prioritizing ambition and narrative over transparency and scientific rigor. On top of that, the lack of cognitive diversity in Theranos's leadership and board meant that dissenting opinions and critical feedback were scarce. This homogeneity of thought allowed Holmes's unrealistic claims to go unchallenged, ultimately leading to the company's downfall when the facade could no longer be maintained.

It's A Bad Board After All

But sometimes, having a board that is too critical and unsupportive of 'bold moves' can backfire. Big time.

By the 1950s, the Walt Disney Company had become one of the largest entertainment conglomerates in the world. It was founded in 1923 by Walt Disney and had been at the forefront of entertainment innovation since the very beginning.[31] When *Steamboat Willy*—the first Mickey Mouse cartoon ever—came out in 1928, it was a technological marvel because it had a fully synchronized soundtrack. The company grew like crazy, and when it released its sensational *Snow White and the Seven Dwarfs* in 1937, it had achieved an innovation masterpiece. It was the first animated full-color feature film of its kind, and a major hit. The movie was an absolute critical and commercial success and would hold on to the record for the highest-grossing animated film for 55 years.

Suffice to say that the Disney Corporation had a history of taking big bets, and reaping big rewards, cashing in on innovation and disruption. But when Walt Disney pitched the idea of 'Disneyland' to his own board in the early 1950s, it said 'No'.

The board was skeptical of Disney's vision for an expansive, immersive theme park, seeing it as a risky and unproven venture. At the time, amusement parks were often seen as seedy, low-quality attractions, and the concept of a meticulously designed, family-friendly park was unconventional and unprecedented. Disney's board was concerned about the financial risks and the potential impact on the company's resources and reputation.

As you can imagine, Walt Disney was not amused. So he decided to finance the project independently. He mortgaged his own home and virtually all its assets, and sought additional funding through a variety of creative means, including a partnership with the television network ABC. His bold move demonstrated Disney's unwavering belief in his own vision and his willingness to take substantial personal risks to bring it to life. He believed his own reality distortion field. His determination and entrepreneurial spirit were crucial in the realization of Disneyland, which opened in 1955 and quickly became a monumental success, revolutionizing the entertainment industry.

The Disneyland project was controlled by a company that Walt Disney had founded by himself, called 'RETLAW', which was 'WALTER' spelled backwards. That entity was later renamed WED, for 'Walter Elias Disney' Enterprises, and was eventually quietly acquired by the Walt Disney company in 1965, the year before Walt passed away.

The very same company that gave him a stark 'No' 15 years earlier acquired his own vengeance project, Disneyland, and thank God they did, as the theme parks are now a vital part of the Disney universe, and massively profitable.

Was the board wrong when they rejected the theme park idea in the early 1950s? In hindsight, it is clear that they massively underestimated Walt's insights into the evolving landscape of entertainment and the public's desire for new, immersive experiences. The board's conservative stance illustrates the broader challenge that innovative leaders often face: convincing more risk-averse stakeholders to embrace visionary projects that fall outside traditional paradigms.

The tension within boards, which play a crucial role in overseeing and guiding companies, lies in balancing financial stability and shareholder protection with openness to transformative opportunities that drive long-term growth and innovation. This delicate equilibrium is at the heart of understanding the tradeoff between risk and reward.

Walt Disney's struggle to gain board approval for Disneyland exemplifies that tension. Disney's subsequent success with Disneyland serves as a powerful reminder of the need for entrepreneurial courage and the potential rewards of daring to pursue one's vision, even in the face of institutional resistance.

The Uncertainty Principle

> Only a few know how much one must know to know how little one knows. —WERNER HEISENBERG

The 'Uncertainty Principle' is a fundamental concept in quantum mechanics, first introduced by physicist Werner Heisenberg in 1927. It states that it is impossible to simultaneously know both the exact position and exact momentum of a particle with perfect precision. The more accurately one of these properties is measured, the less accurately the other can be known. This principle is not due to flaws in measurement instruments, but rather a fundamental property of nature. That's because at microscopic scales, particles exhibit both wave-like and particle-like behaviors, leading to inherent limitations in how precisely their properties can be defined.

Heisenberg was awarded the 1932 Nobel Prize in Physics 'for the creation of quantum mechanics'. He was one of the most brilliant German theoretical physicists of his age and beyond, a pioneer in the theory of quantum mechanics. But he was also a principal scientist in the Nazi nuclear weapons program during World War II.

One of the Nazi regime's greatest miscalculations was underestimating the military potential of nuclear energy. Despite being aware of its theoretical foundations through the work of scientists like Lise Meitner and Otto Hahn, they failed to prioritize its development, dismissing it as a mere scientific curiosity rather than a strategic priority. Hitler himself derided the pursuit of nuclear weapons as 'Jewish pseudo-science'.

The top echelon of the Nazi apparatus felt their tactical advantages in areas like aircraft and missile technology would be sufficient to defeat the Allies without the need for a revolutionary new weapon. As Peter Drucker stated very clearly, 'The greatest danger in times of turbulence is not the turbulence, it's acting with yesterday's logic.' This strategic misjudgment by the Nazis, the false belief in 'yesterday's military logic' and the chronic disbelief in the potential of nuclear weapons proved to be one of the biggest strategic errors of the Nazi regime.

As a result, the Nazi leadership devoted relatively few resources and low prioritization to their own nuclear research program. While the United States threw staggering finances and manpower behind the top-secret Manhattan Project, German efforts under the modest Uranverein (Uranium Society) or Uranprojekt program paled tremendously in comparison.

The Manhattan Project operated with a budget of around $2 billion—nearly $27 billion in today's dollars—funded entirely by the US government. At its zenith, it employed some 120,000 people dedicated to research, construction and operations. In total, the colossal atomic bomb initiative drew upon the labor of half a million Americans, comprising nearly 1% of the entire civilian workforce.

In stark contrast, the German 'Uranverein' project for research into nuclear fission was grievously underfunded by the Nazi regime. Its total budget amounted to a mere 8 million Reichsmarks, equivalent to only about $2 million at the time—a tiny fraction, one-thousandth, of the resources invested by the US into the Manhattan Project's success. This stark contrast in financial commitment, scientific expertise, and strategic prioritization underscores the Third Reich's catastrophic failure to grasp the immense destructive potential of nuclear research.

Still, the Allied forces did not want to take any chances. When Werner Heisenberg, who worked on the 'Uranverein' project was invited to give a lecture in neutral Switzerland in December of 1944, The US Office of Strategic Services sent secret agent Moe Berg to attend the lecture carrying a pistol, with orders to shoot Heisenberg if his lecture indicated that Germany was close to completing an atomic bomb. He didn't, of course. Heisenberg died years later of kidney cancer at his home, on 1 February 1976.

But back to the Uncertainty Principle. And how it relates to the Never Normal.

Just as quantum particles possess inherent uncertainties, business decisions inevitably involve risk and uncertainties. When a company embarks on a new venture or innovation, it must embrace a certain level of uncertainty about the outcome. The more a company attempts to control and mitigate every variable—just like trying to precisely measure both position and momentum—the less agile and adaptable it becomes, potentially stifling innovation and missing valuable opportunities.

For instance, a business that spends excessive time and resources attempting to eliminate all uncertainties before launching a new product may delay its entry into the market, allowing competitors to gain an advantage. Conversely, taking bold, calculated risks, while accepting some level of uncertainty, can lead to breakthrough innovations and significant competitive advantages. This approach requires a balance between thorough planning and the willingness to act in the face of unknowns, much like how scientists must accept the trade-offs dictated by the Uncertainty Principle.

The Limits Of Predictability

Moreover, the Uncertainty Principle suggests that there are limits to predictability, a concept that is very much applicable to the corporate world. Market conditions, consumer preferences, and technological landscapes are constantly changing and can never be predicted with absolute certainty. Companies that understand and embrace this uncertainty are often better positioned to adapt and thrive. Just as physicists recognize the limitations imposed by quantum mechanics, business leaders need to acknowledge the inherent uncertainties in the market and decision-making processes.

When I was younger, risk seemed like an abstract concept—something to be avoided or minimized, a hurdle to clear on the path to success. I did not fully appreciate its pervasive influence or the intricate dance required to balance risk and reward. As I have grown older, my perspective has shifted dramatically. I have come to realize that risk is not merely a peripheral concern but the fundamental element that shapes our existence and drives human endeavor. It is through the lens of risk that we make sense of our choices, gauge the potential for innovation, and understand the dynamics of economic growth.

Risk is the thread that weaves through every aspect of life, from personal decisions to corporate strategies and national policies. It is the force that compels us to weigh the potential benefits against the possible downsides, to consider both the known and the unknown. And in the Never Normal, the art of managing risk and embracing uncertainty has become more crucial than ever.

As I close this chapter, I invite you to reflect on your personal relationship with risk. What does your unique Risk Spectrum look like? How does your Risk Appetite Framework take shape, both in your personal and professional life? And here's a simple yet powerful question: who sits on your Personal Advisory Board? How do they navigate the uncertainty principle, balancing risk and reward in their own decision making?

The Courage To Lead

If risk truly forms the foundation of progress, then courage is undoubtedly one of the most vital traits of leadership. Bravery in leadership manifests in many ways. On one hand, courageous leaders embrace uncertainty and risk as inherent to their journey, while continuously striving to uncover opportunities within them and bringing those possibilities to life. That theme was explored throughout this chapter.

But their boldness extends beyond just navigating risk. Leaders can demonstrate equal audacity in trusting and empowering their teams and, when the moment demands it, in standing firmly by their own vision, intuition, and passion. Courage is not just about strategy and foresight. It's also relational.

Why Would Anyone Want To Be Led By You?

When it comes to my view on organizational success, I have a pre-Rob Goffee and a post-Rob Goffee period. Before I met him, I was practically obsessed with technology and innovation as the drivers of evolution and prosperity. After I met him, everything changed, and mostly because of one deceptively simple question: 'Why would anyone want to be led by you?'

I met Rob during an executive program for a board of directors of one of the largest banks in the world, gathering an impressive collection of captains of industry, all with very impressive backgrounds and illustrious careers. During the morning session, I had tried to bring them up to speed on the technological developments in the world of finance. Rob had observed my session discreetly, to see how they behaved and reacted. And when I was ready, he asked if I would stay on for his afternoon session on leadership. It was one of the best invites I ever got.

Back then, Rob was a professor of Organizational Behavior, the Deputy Dean at the London Business School (he is now retired) and the (co-)-author of 11 books, including *Why Should Anyone Be Led by You?* He loved to start his sessions with that very personal question reflected in his book title. It always proved to be unnerving, disarming and deeply humbling to his powerful audiences, however used to juggling billion-dollar decisions they were. They may have been comfortable with intellectually challenging workshops on strategies, decision making, bottom-line thinking and leadership models, but clearly not with thinking or talking about themselves.

As I looked on, I saw this tough audience evolve from discomfort and hesitation towards humility and vulnerability. With his subtle yet piercing approach, asking probing and open-ended questions, Rob chipped away at the layers of corporate armor they'd built around themselves. He never once lectured or laid out clear-cut answers. But he forced each leader to confront aspects of their identity and motivation through self-reflection and shed all of their preconceived notions of what leadership truly meant. The executives became less guarded, willing to acknowledge the difference between their public personas and their private selves. The sense of competition between them faded and made room for a sense of shared vulnerability. Together, they considered what leadership meant to them personally, beyond titles, bonuses, or career accomplishments.

And at the end of the session, all of them were visibly moved. As was I.

Because I too had come to understand that leadership shaped not just the strategy and direction of entire organizations, but their health and resilience. I began to see that the mindset and values of leaders form the foundation on which success is built, creating a culture where people give their best because they trust and believe in those guiding them.

Rob showed me a completely different side of leadership than I was used to. One that was focused on relationships and on context. Where leaders know themselves, as well as their teams, deeply, allowing them to choose authentically how to lead in different contexts and situations, depending on their own personal needs or those of others. Where their strong vision and sense of purpose *inspired* others to follow them, rather than having them do so based on mechanisms of hierarchy and control. Above all, I came to understand that there wasn't one be-all and end-all universal model of leadership, but that a leader's style needed to be personal and consistent with their unique strengths and weaknesses.

Over the years, I have read or met many others who share Rob's vision on leadership. Gary Hamel, one of the most influential and provocative business thinkers of the past few decades, is another. His leadership philosophy is just as human-centric as Rob's, but more oriented towards the decentralized and distributed structure of organizations, pointing out the limitations of traditional hierarchical models. He writes about 'organizational drag', where bureaucratic processes and power structures slow down decision making and stifle innovation. And about how successful organizations function as natural ecosystems that naturally and continuously stimulate collective intelligence, adaptation, innovation, and renewal. That's why, similarly to Rob, Gary loves to pose a provocative question to leaders: 'Are you a bureaucrat, or an activist?'

To them both, and many others with them, leadership is about self-knowledge, authenticity, vulnerability and a deep understanding of the relational nature of organizational systems. One where they are no longer just drivers of profit or productivity, but architects of systems where people feel safe to innovate, question, and ultimately contribute to lasting success.

A Wave *And* A Particle

But that's just one side of the coin. Leadership has two sides, creating a very powerful duality. One approach is atomistic, individualistic, and the other, collective-driven. One is about ME, the other flips the script and focuses on the WE. To explain exactly what I mean, let's indulge in a little quantum mechanics first. What else do you expect from a book called *The Uncertainty Principle*, right?

Just as elusive as the fundamentals of leadership, the nature of light has puzzled scientists for centuries, sparking one of the most profound debates in physics. In the late 1600s, Isaac Newton strongly advocated for light being composed of tiny particles. He gave them a pretty unattractive name, if you ask me—'corpuscles'—which actually just means 'small bodies'. But his particle theory did seem pretty solid. It could explain how light traveled in straight lines and reflected off surfaces. And his rock star reputation helped the particle theory dominate scientific thought for nearly a century. I mean, who would be so arrogant as to dare second guess the genius who turned a casual fruit assault into the foundation of classical mechanics?

However, in the early 1800s, Thomas Young—whom his biographer ambitiously called 'The Last Man Who Knew Everything'—performed his famous double-slit experiment. It showed how light created interference patterns, a behavior only expected from waves. When light passed through two closely spaced slits, it created alternating bright and dark bands on a screen behind them. This pattern could only be explained if light waves were interfering with each other, similar to ripples in a pond. Young's experiment, along with later work by Augustin-Jean Fresnel, seemed to definitively prove light was a wave.

The wave theory gained further support when Scottish physicist and mathematician James Clerk Maxwell developed his electromagnetic theory in the 1860s. Maxwell showed that light was indeed an electromagnetic wave, traveling through space as oscillating electric and magnetic fields. This elegant theory explained the most known properties of light, including diffraction, interference, and refraction. Among other things, the wave-like nature of light explained how prisms split white light into colors and why we see rainbows after rain.

But just when physicists thought they had light figured out, new phenomena emerged. In 1905, Albert Einstein uncovered the photoelectric effect—how light knocks electrons out of metals—by proposing that light energy comes in discrete packets called photons. This particle-like behavior couldn't be explained by the wave theory. Einstein's work showed that light could transfer energy only in distinct chunks, just as if it were made of particles.

Then followed something that closely resembled a 'Belgian Compromise': 'You know what, guys, let's just say that light is both a particle *and* a wave'. That's what the development of quantum mechanics in the 1920s pointed out, anyway. Scientists realized that light exhibits a fundamental duality. When light travels through space, we can best understand and predict its behavior using wave equations. But when light interacts with matter—whether in photosynthesis, solar panels, or our eyes—we need to think about it as a stream of photons. Neither description alone captures the full nature of light. This strange duality remains one of the most profound examples of how quantum mechanics defies our classical expectations while precisely describing the behavior of the microscopic world.

In fact, we've come to learn since then that this dual nature extends far beyond light itself. We now know that *all* particles, including electrons and even entire atoms, exhibit wave-like properties under the right conditions. And this fundamental insight has led to technologies from lasers to electron microscopes.

Today, the wave particle complementarity continues to shape our understanding of the universe at its most fundamental level. And it also serves as the perfect metaphor for the dual nature of leadership. On the one hand, we have the relational, more cooperative-driven form of leadership that is propagated by Rob Goffee and Gary Hamel. But on the other hand, we have the quintessential leadership philosophy of the powerful 'node', an individualistic vision of the lone genius pervading every layer of the organization.

I'm talking about the controversial 'Founder Mode', of course.

Founder Mode

'Founder mode' was first formulated by Paul Graham, perhaps best known as the co-founder of Y Combinator, who advised and invested in numerous tech startups. His deep insights into the dynamics of entrepreneurship and startup leadership led him to uncover a fundamental difference between what he called 'founder mode' and 'manager mode'. Manager mode was the traditional Stanford Business School approach of delegating tasks to talented subordinates and optimizing organizational processes.

But the 'founder mode' was something else entirely. This type of leader was deeply involved in the day-to-day operations and decision making of the company, taking a hands-on approach across multiple functions. The rationale behind that was that the founder's deep understanding of the business, emotional connection to the mission, and ability to make rapid decisions is invaluable, especially in the early, volatile stages of a start-up's lifecycle. Above all, founder mode is about agility, responsiveness and speed.

And though founder mode tends to be most pervasive in startup and scale-up environments—Airbnb's Brian Chesky is the quintessential example—there are plenty of examples to be found in larger companies as well. Steve Jobs of Apple was one of them, with obsessive participation in day-to-day work, a relentless focus on product design and development, while micromanaging every aspect of the company's operations and really pushing his employees. He saw himself as the 'keeper of the vision': 'What people need is a common vision. And that's what leadership is.' Though some would have called him a micro-manager.

There are many more examples of this leadership paradigm in large companies, from Walt Disney and Elon Musk to Larry Ellison of Oracle to Jeff Bezos of Amazon, Howard Schultz of Starbucks or Sam Walton of Walmart.

Visionary leadership with high passion and high involvement comes at a price, though. Their personal participation in daily operations can become a bottleneck, slow down decision making and sabotage an organization's ability to scale. Also, if founders stay overly attached to their original vision, this can be detrimental to change and innovation in the long term. They can also strain relationships within the company, creating a demanding work environment that, while fostering excellence, also drives away talented individuals. And the biggest question of all, when an organization becomes overly reliant on a founder's vision, involvement, and instincts, is: what happens when they are no longer there?

Perhaps most importantly, there is a very thin line between 'founder mode' and toxic leadership, when the founder's intense focus and personal attachment to their vision overshadow the well-being of their organization and its people. I feel pity for those poor folks who worked at Uber under the helm of co-founder Travis Kalanick, notorious for his egotistical leadership style and deeply obsessed with outpacing his rivals. He cultivated a culture of 'win at all costs' where employees were pushed to their limits and incentivized to prioritize results over ethical considerations. Many of them felt stressed, undervalued, disempowered, disengaged and burned out, struggling in a 'bro culture' where inappropriate behavior was tolerated, and complaints of misconduct were often mishandled or dismissed. The results were public relations crises, lawsuits, and a damaged reputation that took years to repair. Uber's board was forced to intervene and Kalanick was forced to resign in 2017.

The founder mode approach is pretty controversial, having both lovers as well as many haters. When a founder gets it right—like Steve Jobs or Brian Chesky—it can lead to pure brilliance, driving vision, innovation and momentum in a high growth environment. But once it flips over to the dark side, it can be just as devastating to a company's culture and success. Yet, choosing which mode is best—the empowered human-centric mode or the more individualistic founder mode—is completely missing the point.

Just as light behaves both as a wave or a particle, depending on the situation, so too should leaders empower and trust or participate and decide, depending on the context. Yes, large companies will gravitate towards the first mode and founders towards the second, but this duality goes beyond the purely organizational context. Lone wolf startup founders cannot know everything and need to engage in a decentralized mode in some situations. They should be able to count on a strong leadership team and an empowered workforce, too. Just like that, CEOs and CMOs or CFOs of large established and traditional companies—of which the 'decentralized leadership' tends to echo the fluid, dispersed nature of waves—sometimes need to decide fast and on their own in highly disruptive situations.

Bottom line: there is no one sure-fire recipe. Leaders need to be able to act both as particles and as waves and adapt their approach to the unique needs of their organization, industry, and stage of development. Leadership is all about balance.

But back to risk, and courage.

Courage Is The Essence

In the end, I believe that courage is the true essence of leadership. It too has a dual nature which manifests in a different format depending on the situation. For startup founders and leaders in founder mode, courage comes quite naturally. They fight against established norms, fearlessly tackle competitors, find new paths with limited resources, thrive on risk-taking and embrace the discomfort that comes with market disruption. Founder mode courage manifests through personal conviction, single-mindedness, and direct control, much like particles moving in a straight line.

But leaders in established companies, too, need the guts to challenge the status quo if they want to become (or stay) a Phoenix. It's not just about confronting entrenched systems, traditions and business models, though. It's about battling organizational inertia, empowering others, trusting they will make the right decisions and finding the courage to show their own vulnerability, their failures and their limitations while questioning what is comfortable. It's in Satya Nadella who completely redesigned the culture at Microsoft, Mary Barra who pivoted GM toward electric vehicles and Howard Schultz who reinvented Starbucks as an experience-driven brand.

Beyond Fear

One of the biggest mistakes one can make when it comes to courage is to perceive it as 'the absence of fear'. John Hagel III—one of the founders of Deloitte's Center for the Edge and the author of multiple groundbreaking books including *The Power of Pull* and *The Journey Beyond Fear*—has taught the world otherwise.

His writings offer a fundamental reimagining of how leaders should approach fear and courage in organizational settings. He has come to understand that traditional leadership models tend to be deeply rooted in fear-based thinking. They focus on scarcity, protection, and control. Fear actually manifests at multiple levels within organizations: from the individual concerned about job security in the age of AI to general organizational anxieties about market position and competition. Anxiety often drives decision making in subtle but powerful ways.

Hagel wisely believes that it is both impossible and undesirable to eliminate organizational fear. He wants us to develop a more nuanced and productive relationship with it. But it is also important to develop the capability to move beyond its limiting effects. And 'pull-based leadership' plays a crucial role here, a paradigm that lies on the other end of the spectrum of 'push' approaches, which thrive on predetermined plans and controlled execution. Pull-based approaches are about attracting and enabling emerging opportunities, the willingness to experiment and learn rapidly, and the capacity to mobilize diverse groups around shared opportunities.

Courage in leadership is not about fearlessness or even primarily about overcoming fear. But it is about developing the capability to see and move toward opportunity, even in the presence of fear.

The Leadership Matrix

As you may have established by now, I am pretty partial to two-by-two matrixes so I'd like to introduce a framework to help us understand how different leadership styles emerge and how they can prove effective in varying contexts. The quadrant maps different leadership archetypes across two critical dimensions: risk profile and network strength. The risk profile axis spans from managerial (low-risk, stability-focused) to entrepreneurial (high-risk, opportunity-seeking) approaches, while the network strength axis ranges from individual (centralized, hierarchical) to collective (decentralized, networked) orientations.

The 'Individual Manager' or the Despot archetype emphasizes control, hierarchy, and predictability, operating through traditional command-and-control structures. This leadership style thrives in stable, structured environments and prioritizes process optimization, compliance, and incremental improvements over innovation. Common in industrial-era businesses, these leaders excel in predictable markets and can lean toward autocratic control in extreme cases. They also lack the flexibility to innovate and adapt to rapid changes.

The **'Collective Managerial Leader' or Civil Servant archetype**, then, is common in government agencies and compliance-driven organizations. This style emphasizes risk-averse, standardized decision making through group consensus. While this approach does ensure regulatory compliance and structured oversight, it also leads to bureaucratic inertia and slow adaptation to change. This style may be effective for managing stable, complex systems like those in healthcare and education, and it also prioritizes consistency over innovation and responsiveness.

The **'Individual Entrepreneur' archetype** is all about vision, risk-taking, and personal control. It's the preferred method of iconic startup founders like Elon Musk and Steve Jobs. In other words, it's founder mode galore, driven by charisma, conviction, and rapid decision making. While these leaders can disrupt entire industries and create groundbreaking innovation, their dominance can also limit adaptability, stifle collaboration, and make companies overly dependent on their singular vision.

The most intriguing quadrant, however, particularly in the context of the Never Normal, is the upper-right **'Collective Entrepreneurial'** archetype. It combines entrepreneurial innovation with networked resilience and empowers teams to act autonomously while staying aligned with a shared mission. Companies like Haier, under Zhang Ruimin, exemplify this model by dividing their company into autonomous, startup-like units, enabling agility and faster decision making. While this approach may be the holy grail for navigating constant change, traditional hierarchical leaders will also need to learn to embrace trust, decentralization, collaboration and adaptability to unlock a company's full potential.

Above all, this 2x2 matrix highlights that there is no one-size-fits-all type of leadership. What works best always depends upon the situational context. In more stable, traditional markets, the Individual Managerial and Collective Managerial approaches can ensure efficiency and compliance, while maintaining order and reducing risk. In contrast, in more dynamic and unpredictable environments, the Individual Entrepreneurial and Collective Entrepreneurial styles thrive, fostering innovation and adaptability.

Courage is the one ingredient that runs through these four quadrants, helping leaders to confront challenges, adapt, and inspire change. Sometimes it takes the form of conviction—in Individual Entrepreneurial leadership—and sometimes it emerges as the guts to let go of control, like in Collective Entrepreneurial leadership. Knowing when to choose the style that will work best in each situation is how leaders will be able to find opportunity in the uncertainty and risk that come with the Never Normal.

My attitude in life is that if you can create something that's better than what everybody else is doing, then you have a chance of surviving—and that if you don't try, you're definitively not going to succeed.

—RICHARD BRANSON

tl
dr

There is no progress without risk. But how do you manage it? How do you achieve the perfect balance between complete uncertainty and full clarity? The truth is that risk cannot be controlled. In fact, companies like Exxon and Silicon Valley Bank have experienced that, sometimes, the very seed of your own destruction lies in the seemingly 'safe' decisions we make at the beginning. Whatever we design as safety solutions can eventually evolve to become the problems. Also, the more a company tries to control and mitigate every variable, the slower and less flexible it becomes, potentially stifling innovation and missing valuable opportunities.

As with many things, balance is key when it comes to risk. Take the 'fake it till you make it' philosophy. Pioneers like Steve Jobs and Elon Musk were able to make this risky approach work, but Elizabeth Holmes miserably failed at the 'make it' part. The most successful entrepreneurs are those who understand how to navigate risk in ways that propel them forward, rather than have them succumb to the extremes of caving under fear or acting with very little concern for the dangers of reality.

If risk forms the foundation of progress, then courage is undoubtedly one of the most vital traits of leadership. Bravery in leadership manifests in many ways. On one hand, courageous leaders embrace uncertainty and risk as inherent to their journey, while continuously striving to uncover opportunities within them and bringing those possibilities to life.

But their boldness also extends beyond just navigating risk. Leaders can demonstrate equal audacity in trusting and empowering their teams and, when the moment demands it, in standing firmly by their own vision, intuition, and passion. Courage is not just about strategy and foresight. It's also relational.

6

For Progress, There Is No Cure

Human progress is neither automatic nor inevitable... Every step toward the goal of justice requires sacrifice, suffering, and struggle; the tireless exertions and passionate concern of dedicated individuals. —MARTIN LUTHER KING JR.

The Super Martian

John von Neumann[32] was born János Neumann Lajos in Budapest on December 28, 1903, as the son of a wealthy Jewish banker. This Isaac Newton of the 20th century was probably the smartest man that ever lived and a towering figure in mathematics and physics, as well as in economics and statistics. His extraordinary capacity for abstract thinking and problem-solving revolutionized multiple scientific disciplines and left an unforgettable mark on the modern world. Von Neumann's work in areas like game theory, nuclear fission and quantum mechanics formed the building blocks for some of the most important discoveries of the century: the modern computer, the atom bomb, radar, and artificial intelligence, to name just a few.

He was also a bit of a character, and quite the party animal, having acquired a taste for Berlin cabarets as a young man. And while he resided at Princeton, the parties at von Neumann's house were frequent, famous, and long. Even by day, when he worked at the Institute for Advanced Study in Princeton, there were constant complaints because he would play extremely loud German marching music on the gramophone in his office, distracting those in neighboring offices, including Albert Einstein. Actually, von Neumann claimed to do some of his best work in noisy, chaotic environments such as in the living room of his house with the television blaring at full volume.

He is, without any doubt, the father of modern computing, and the mathematical prophet who laid the foundations for developing the field of artificial intelligence.

Von Neumann was a true child prodigy. At the age of six, he was able to exchange jokes with his father in classical Greek. His family sometimes entertained guests with demonstrations of Johnny's ability to memorize phone books. A guest would select a page and column of the phone book at random, then young Johnny would read the page over a few times, and hand the book back to the guest. He could answer any question put to him (which family has which number) or recite names, addresses, and numbers in order. Amazing what we did for fun before TikTok.

At the tender age of six, he could divide two 8-digit numbers in his head. By the age of eight, he was already familiar with differential and integral calculus. Soon his teachers were unable to help him with mathematics. So at the age of 15, he was sent to study advanced calculus under the renowned mathematician Gábor Szegő. The latter was so astounded by the boy's talent in mathematics that he was brought to tears on their very first meeting.

Von Neumann studied in Fasori Evangélikus Gimnázium, one of the best Lutheran schools in Budapest. Incidentally, that school produced some of the finest scientific talents of their generation. Examples of students were Edward Teller (father of the hydrogen bomb), Leo Szilard (the inventor of the nuclear chain reaction), and Eugene Wigner (Winner of the Nobel Prize in Physics in 1963). But none of them compared to the genius of young Johnny von Neumann. By the age of 19 he had published two major mathematical papers, one of which won the Eotvos Prize, Hungary's highest honor in mathematics.

At 25, he was already recognized as a genius, having written 12 major papers in maths, and had an offer from Hamburg University before he moved to Princeton for a much better offer. He became a professor at the Princeton Institute of Advanced Study, a post he held till he passed away. Its director, Herman Goldstine recalled: 'One of his remarkable abilities was his power of absolute memory. As far as I could tell, von Neumann was able to read a book or article just once, and then able to quote it back verbatim; moreover, he could do it years later without hesitation. He could also translate it at no diminution in speed from its original language into English. On one occasion I tested his ability by asking him to tell me how *A Tale of Two Cities* started. Whereupon, without any pause, he immediately began to recite the first chapter and continued until asked to stop after about 10 or 15 minutes.'

Von Neumann was part of an elite group of brilliant Jewish Hungarian scientists who fled Nazism to pursue their careers in America. Known as 'the Martians', they earned the nickname not only for their strange native language but also for their almost otherworldly intellect.

There's a wonderful anecdote from his brief stint at Hamburg, right before he moved to Princeton. One of his professors had the devious habit of asking his Ph.D. students 'unsolvable questions' at their oral exams. If the student instantly replied, 'That's unsolvable,' he was deemed to have the right sharp set of mind. When this professor put his favorite unsolvable equations on the blackboard as an illustration. Johnny muttered at the ceiling for a few minutes, and then promptly solved some of them.

Von Neumann also was one of the key figures in the Manhattan Project during World War II, where he played a crucial role in the development of nuclear weapons, applying his expertise in mathematical modeling and game theory to address the complex problems of nuclear chain reactions and explosion dynamics. This work not only influenced the outcome of the war but also positioned von Neumann as a central figure in the Cold War, where his strategic insights and advisory roles significantly shaped US defense and policy decisions.

The US military loved him. He was in such demand that a US Air Force plane was kept on permanent standby to whisk him from one top-secret government lab to another. At one point he met with a group of RAND Corporation scientists who wanted to use a computer he had helped design. They had a particular physics problem to solve, that was, as they explained using blackboards and graphs, beyond the capacity of von Neumann's computer at the moment. Von Neumann was brought in to help modify the computer to be able to solve the problem. For two hours, he listened to the scientists, his head in his hands, his face impassive, while they explained the problem. Then he stood up, and said, 'Gentlemen, you do not need a computer. I can give you the answer right away.' He went to the blackboard, and solved the problem right there on the spot, and concluded, 'That's it. Let's go to lunch.'

Von Neumann was also absolutely instrumental in the early development of computer science. His pioneering work on the architecture of digital computers, known as the von Neumann architecture, established the fundamental framework for computer design that is still in use today. His foresight in envisioning the potential of artificial intelligence and his theoretical work in automata theory laid the groundwork for future advancements in AI, influencing generations of computer scientists and engineers.

Ethical And Moral Dilemmas

But he was not blind to the dangerous side of his scientific breakthroughs and inventions. His work on nuclear weapons and his advocacy for a strong US military stance during the Cold War brought ethical and moral dilemmas, reflecting the complex interplay between scientific progress and its societal implications. Yet, through it all, von Neumann remained a fervent advocate for scientific advancement and innovation.

John's second marriage was to Klára Dán, whom he had first met at a casino in Monte Carlo. He explained to her that he had perfected an algorithm to ensure that you could win roulette every single time, and promptly lost all his money trying to prove his point. Afterwards, he asked Dán to buy him a drink. It was a consequential interaction for both of them, and would set the stage for their later romance. Klára also had a Hungarian background, and made significant contributions to the world of programming, as the first woman to execute modern-style code on a computer. She would work on the ENIAC pioneering computer, among other things, ironically doing statistical work on the Monte Carlo method optimizations.

While von Neumann was working in Los Alamos on the Manhattan project in 1945, totally exhausted from the grueling rhythm of the work on the atomic bomb, he wrote a letter to his wife, Klára. He told her that the 'energy source' he was helping to develop would make scientists 'the most hated and also the most wanted citizens of any country'. He also told her that his other ongoing project, the computer, would one day be even more important—and potentially even more dangerous.

DeepMind And Omni-Use Technologies

Mustafa Suleyman[33] is the co-founder of DeepMind (now owned by Google), who was selected to head up the Microsoft AI initiatives early 2024. In his book, *The Coming Wave*, he makes a very similar observation to John von Neumann's almost 80 years earlier. The book is written from the perspective of the AI researcher, who is at the very heart of maybe the biggest technological revolution mankind has ever seen, yet feels deeply conflicted about it.

Suleyman is a British national, born to a Syrian taxi driver, and an English nurse. He dropped out of Mansfield College in Oxford when he was 19, and went on to do work for the Mayor of London as a policy officer. He founded DeepMind together with Demis Hassabis (who still runs AI at Google) and Shane Legg in the summer of 2010. This British start-up latched onto the emerging field of 'Deep Learning', using the power of neural networks to create artificial intelligence. That concept was already decades old, based on the mathematical concepts of von Neumann, but with the advent of cloud computing, an abundance of cheap computing processing power was available to train larger and larger neural networks with vast amounts of data.

DeepMind had very humble beginnings. They developed an approach called DQN* that was put to use training a neural network to play vintage Atari video games from the 1980s. They used their neural net to play a game of Breakout, but they would not 'program' how to play the game. Instead they would let it try out random movements and 'learn' from the feedback. Their approach turned out to be golden. Using computing power to boost the number of games played, and therefore unleash more 'learning', they could use their technology to beat the all-time highest human score ever played on this arcade game in mere hours.

Google realized DeepMind's potential and acquired them lock, stock, and barrel in 2014. Many Brits still believe that this was one of the saddest moments in their entrepreneurial history. Instead of developing DeepMind into a company that could have been at the very heart of the AI revolution, they sold out to an American company that realized the true potential.[34]

The truth is that DeepMind stumbled on what we call an 'omni-use' technology: tools, mechanisms or concepts that can be used on a wide variety of different challenges. Where the initial use of DQN was to play Atari Breakout, the same technology evolved to beat one of the best Go players in the world, Lee Sedol, in 2016. And that very same technology is being used today by Google to predict the weather,[35] and to solve one of life's great biological mysteries: protein folding.

AlphaFold is the variant of the DeepMind technology that predicts a protein's 3D structure from its amino acid sequence. Proteins are fundamental to nearly every biological process, and understanding their structure has vast implications for the future of medicine and healthcare. For instance, misfolded proteins are often linked to diseases such as Alzheimer's, Parkinson's, and cystic fibrosis. Imagine that, from playing Atari Breakout all the way to helping the future of medicines. Omni-use.

'Omni-use' technologies are absolute game changers. Think of the steam engine—an 'omni-use' technology that powered the Industrial Revolution. Or electricity, another great example of 'omni-use': you could use it for everything from heating your stove, to lighting your house, to allowing you to vacuum the carpets.

► *Deep Q-Learning or Deep Q Network (DQN)** is an extension of the basic Q-Learning algorithm, which uses deep neural networks to approximate the Q-values.

Revenge Effects

But there is a 'shadow' side to these omni-use technologies called 'Revenge Effects'. They occur when a solution or innovation intended to solve a problem unintentionally creates new, often worse, problems. Like traffic congestion increasing due to the construction of more roads.[36]

Some of these revenge effects are just annoying. For example the 'Repeat' Revenge Effects occur when more efficient processes end up making us do the same things more often. Better appliances in our households have led to higher standards of cleanliness, tempting people to spend pretty much the same amount of time on housework as in the past, but with much better technology.

But sometimes revenge effects can be pretty serious. The development of antibiotics is a good example. Antibiotics revolutionized the treatment of bacterial infections, saving countless lives. However, the widespread and often indiscriminate use of antibiotics has led to the emergence of antibiotic-resistant bacteria, a severe threat to global health. A grim example of 'things biting back'. Or the rise of the internet and social media, for instance, was initially celebrated for democratizing access to information and fostering global communication. But they also ushered in misinformation, cyberbullying, polarization and privacy concerns. The very tools that were supposed to connect and inform people have, in some cases, contributed to social fragmentation and the spread of false information.

Revenge effects occur because technologies do not operate in isolation; they interact with various social, economic, and environmental factors, leading to outcomes that are difficult to predict. That's even worse when they're 'clustered': part of a bigger set of interconnected innovations. American communication theorist and sociologist Everett Rogers was instrumental in researching this phenomenon of 'clusters of innovation', referring to the idea that innovations do not occur in isolation but are often part of a larger system of interconnected and interdependent innovations.

Over his career, Rogers authored more than 30 books, with the *Diffusion of Innovations* being his best-known publication. It examines how new ideas and technologies spread within a society or social system. His work highlights that a single technological breakthrough often stimulates the development of related innovations. For example, the development of the personal computer did not happen in a vacuum; it was accompanied by innovations in software, microprocessors, user interfaces, and networking technologies, which together created a robust ecosystem that accelerated the adoption and impact of personal computing.

In *The Coming Wave*, Suleyman describes what he calls the epic combination of two massive game-changers into a cluster: artificial intelligence and synthetic biology. Artificial intelligence is a very clear omni-use technology that had been relatively dormant for many years. Although we understood the underlying mechanisms and concepts, we did not possess the computational horsepower to unlock it, until recently. Cloud computing provided the foundations, and then it took off like wildfire. As Suleyman points out, 'This wave will only get bigger.'

The second ingredient he points out is synthetic biology: the possibility to influence and create life. Friedrich Miescher was a Swiss biochemist who, at the age of 25, discovered a new substance in cells, calling it nuclein. It is this substance that is now known as DNA. In April 1953, James Watson and Francis Crick published a paper that detailed their discovery that DNA is a double helix, a three-dimensional molecular structure with two strands twisted together in a spiral. Their model explained how DNA replicates and how genetic information is coded on it.

Back then, we discovered how DNA is the fundamental building block of life. But it took us 50 more years to learn how to decode it. In 2003, after 13 years of global collaboration, the Human Genome Project[37] successfully mapped the entire human genome—comprising approximately 3 billion DNA bases—marking a historic breakthrough in genetic research. This amazing accomplishment provided fundamental information about the human blueprint, and allowed us to 'read' our building blocks of life for the first time.

Then we learned how to 'write' them as well. With the advent of CRISPR technology in 2009, research scientists can now selectively modify the DNA of living organisms. As this science is rapidly evolving, synthetic biology will allow scientists to create synthetic organisms or biological components that do not exist in nature. The potential applications of synthetic biology are vast and transformative, spanning various industries including medicine, agriculture, energy, and environmental science.

But, as Suleyman points out, if you combine artificial intelligence with synthetic biology, it also provides an extremely potentially dangerous cocktail. In his words, 'Today, with AI and synthetic biology, one single person has the potential capacity to kill a billion others.' A powerful cocktail that summons up a powerful 'wave'.

The Flood

Across many cultures, the concept of Flood Myths recounts cataclysmic deluges that devastate civilizations while also paving the way for renewal. They often depict a great flood, unleashed by divine forces to cleanse the world, allowing for a fresh start. One of the most well known of these is the story of Noah's Ark from the Judeo-Christian tradition, where a righteous man is chosen by God to build an ark and save a pair of every animal species, ensuring the continuity of life after the deluge. Similarly, in Mesopotamian mythology, the Epic of Gilgamesh features a flood narrative where the heroic king Utnapishtim is forewarned by the gods to construct a boat to preserve humanity and animals. In Hindu mythology, the story of the first man Manu and the great flood describes how the former is warned by a fish (the god Vishnu in disguise) about an impending flood and builds a boat to save himself, the seven sages, and the seeds of all living creatures.

The universally recurring flood myth serves as a powerful metaphor for the relentless waves of technological change reshaping our world and disrupting industries, economies, and daily life, much like a flood reshapes the landscape. And just as societies in flood myths often struggle to prepare for and respond to the deluge, modern institutions grapple with the pace of development and its implications.

The question is: should we start building an ark? It's an absolutely valid one. Should we, in fact, slow down scientific progress? Since technology has the power to unlock incredible possibilities, it also creates unprecedented opportunities for harm and misuse. That is the fundamental philosophical question at the heart of *The Coming Wave* by Mustafa Suleyman. And it is exactly the same question that von Neumann wrote in his letter to his wife Klára, musing that the 'computer' would become more dangerous than the atomic bomb.

Should Progress Be Stopped?

So, should we try to 'contain' technological progress?

The Luddites[38]—named after the mythical figure Ned Ludd, who was said to have destroyed a weaving machine in a fit of rage—would have agreed. They were a group of 19th century English workers who protested against the rapid industrialization of the textile industry. In 1812 these workers, primarily weavers and textile artisans, were alarmed by the introduction of new machinery such as the stocking frames, spinning frames, and power looms. These significantly increased production efficiency and therefore reduced the need for skilled labor, eventually leading to widespread job losses and wage reductions.

The Luddites responded by engaging in direct action, often breaking into factories at night to smash the machines they saw as symbols of their oppression. These acts of machine-breaking were not random or senseless; they were targeted and strategic, aiming to force employers and the government to address the workers' grievances. The Luddites demanded fair wages and job security, and their protests were part of a broader resistance against the socioeconomic changes brought about by the Industrial Revolution. Their actions were seen as a desperate attempt to preserve their traditional way of life and the skilled labor that had provided them with a decent standard of living.

The government's response to the Luddite movement was swift and severe. The British authorities deployed troops to protect factories and passed harsh laws, including the Frame Breaking Act of 1812, which made machine-breaking a capital offense punishable by death. Numerous Luddites were arrested, and many were executed or transported to penal colonies in Australia.

The Luddites were not alone in their fear of technological progress.

Pope Urban II is another. As head of the Catholic Church from 1088 to 1099 and the initiator of the First Crusade, he attempted to ban the crossbow, which had become increasingly prevalent in medieval European warfare in record time. He was very concerned about the threat it posed to the feudal order in the Middle Ages. Knights, who were heavily armored and trained in the art of mounted combat, represented the elite warrior class. They held a privileged position in medieval society. The crossbow, with its ability to be wielded effectively by common soldiers and peasants, undermined this hierarchy by making it possible for relatively untrained individuals to kill or incapacitate knights from a distance. This shift in

THE UNCERTAINTY PRINCIPLE

military dynamics was seen as a threat to the social and moral fabric of medieval Europe by Pope Urban II and many distinguished members of society. In other words, the crossbow was a major disruptor.

Pope Urban II voiced his opposition to the weapon at the Council of Clermont in 1095, when he also called for the First Crusade. At the very least, he wanted the crossbow not to be used against Christians. But the ban on crossbows had limited practical effect. The weapon continued to be used extensively in European warfare (and in the Crusades against the 'infidels'), both by common soldiers and professional mercenaries. Its effectiveness and ease of use ensured its persistence on the battlefield, despite the church's moral objections.

One of the most fascinating rejections of modern technology came when the British Empire, driven by the momentum of its Industrial Revolution, attempted to persuade Emperor Qianlong of China to embrace the era's advancements—only to be met with staunch resistance.

In the late 18th century, during the reign of Qianlong, China was a vast and wealthy empire with a highly developed civilization. At this time, China was largely self-sufficient and saw little need for foreign goods or technologies. China often referred to itself as 'the Middle Kingdom', implying its superior role, the Center of All Civilization in the world. The Qing Dynasty, under Qianlong, adhered to a policy of limiting foreign influence and maintaining strict control over foreign trade.

In 1793, King George III of Britain sent a diplomatic mission to China, led by Lord George Macartney, to establish formal trade relations and introduce British goods and technology to the Chinese market. This mission was part of Britain's broader efforts to expand its commercial interests globally during the Industrial Revolution.

Emperor Qianlong's response to King George III is often highlighted as a significant moment in the history of Sino-Western relations. Qianlong wrote a letter back to King George, politely but firmly rejecting the British proposals. He expressed that China had no need for British goods or technologies, emphasizing the self-sufficiency and superiority of the Chinese civilization. Qianlong stated, 'Our celestial empire already possesses all things. I set no value on objects strange or ingenious, and have no use for your country's manufactures.' Take that, Lord Macartney. Burn.

But it also was the beginning of what the Chinese now call the 'Century of Humiliation', characterized by internal turmoil, and subjugation by foreign powers. This era saw China experience a series of military defeats, territorial losses, and political humiliations that starkly contrasted with its long history of cultural and economic dominance. During that period, China's traditional agrarian economy and rigid social structures were increasingly out of step with the rapid industrialization and modernization occurring in the West and Japan. While the Industrial Revolution transformed these regions into global powers with advanced technologies and formidable military capabilities, China remained largely agrarian and technologically stagnant. In hindsight, perhaps the letter of Emperor Qianlong to King George was as imprudent as Ned Ludd's followers smashing the machines.

The Gorilla Problem

Today, there are plenty of neo-Luddites, who believe that the advent of omni-use technologies like artificial intelligence should be stopped, because they could potentially harm our jobs and lives. It is deeply fascinating to observe how a core integral player like Suleyman, who co-founded DeepMind, and is now running AI at Microsoft is not simply dismissing them. To the contrary, he too believes that we should approach this 'oncoming wave' with great caution.

Stuart Russell, a British computer scientist, is a leading voice on the ethical and philosophical implications of AI. He teaches at the University of California, Berkeley, where he also directs the Center for Human-Compatible Artificial Intelligence. Russell has coined the concept of the 'Gorilla Problem'. Gorillas are formidable animals and much stronger than humans. Still, as Russell pointed out, it is the gorillas that are behind bars in the zoo.

As Russell notes, 'Around 10 million years ago, the ancestors of the modern gorilla created accidentally the genetic lineage leading to us modern humans. How do gorillas feel about this now? Their species has essentially no future beyond that which we humans deign to allow.' His concern centers on the asymmetry of power and control. Despite their physical strength, gorillas are largely dependent on human decisions for their survival and habitat. Similarly, humans could become dependent on AI for managing critical aspects of society, such as infrastructure, economy, and even governance. This dependency raises ethical and existential questions about autonomy, freedom, and the preservation of human values. Russell argues that if we do not carefully design and control AI systems, we risk creating entities that could prioritize their own goals, potentially misaligned with human well-being.

At Oxford, Nick Bostrom formerly led the Future of Humanity Institute, which was dissolved in 2024. The institute focused on examining the risks and opportunities of technological advancement, tackling ethical dilemmas, and assessing global priorities.

Bostrom was the one who coined the concept of 'superintelligence'—with the help of AI we could end up creating machines that possess 'minds' that are far superior to those of humans. In his book *Superintelligence: Paths, Dangers, Strategies*, he explores various scenarios in which AI could attain a level of cognitive capability that allows it to outperform humans in virtually every intellectual task. He emphasizes that the transition to superintelligence could occur rapidly, leaving little time for humans to adapt or implement effective controls.

Bostrom also argues that if superintelligent AI systems are not properly aligned, they could pursue objectives that are detrimental to humanity, either through unintended consequences or by prioritizing their own survival and resource acquisition. That's why he believes that we have to 'contain' the world of AI.

When I hear the word containment, I'm always reminded of the *Jurassic Park* movies, based on the work of Michael Crichton. In every movie, there's a scene of jeeps driving along the mighty fences and enclosures that were designed to ensure the safety of the park's visitors and prevent the genetically engineered dinosaurs from escaping. And in every movie, these fences become absolutely useless. They perfectly symbolize humanity's attempt to 'contain' nature's raw power and the unforeseen consequences of pushing scientific boundaries. Similarly, in the context of superintelligent AI, Bostrom advocates for 'containment' strategies to manage the risks posed by entities that could surpass human intelligence. To put it in *Jurassic Park* character Dr. Ian Malcolm's words, 'God help us, we're in the hands of engineers.'

Just as the dinosaurs in *Jurassic Park* pose a threat if they escape their confines, a superintelligent AI could present existential risks if it operates beyond human control. Containment in this context involves developing robust safety measures, monitoring mechanisms, and regulatory frameworks to ensure that AI systems remain aligned with human values and do not act in ways that could harm humanity.

The urgency of Bostrom's AI warnings draws a parallel to the profound ethical and existential dilemmas faced by the scientists involved in the development of nuclear capabilities during World War II. J. Robert Oppenheimer, head of the Manhattan Project, famously quoted the Bhagavad Gita after witnessing the first successful test of a nuclear weapon: 'Now I am become Death, the destroyer of worlds.'

In his analysis of the next upcoming wave, Mustafa Suleyman argues that containment shouldn't be the final step. It should be the first. Yet it rarely is. Instead of retroactively addressing risks, we should anticipate potential consequences and integrate safety measures from the outset. But more often than not, this crucial precaution never materializes.

Just Say 'No'

When I was a teenager, growing up in the US under the Ronald Reagan administration, a cheap, highly addictive form of cocaine known as 'crack' was becoming a major societal problem. Its popularity led to a significant increase in the number of addicted Americans. When Reagan took office in 1981, he vowed to crack* down on substance abuse and reprioritize the War on Drugs. But it was his wife, First Lady Nancy Reagan, who sparked the origins of the iconic 'Just Say No' campaign. In 1982, when a Californian schoolgirl asked her what to do if she was offered drugs by her peers, the First Lady responded, 'Just say "no"'. As with most anti-drug initiatives, 'Just Say No'—which became an American catch phrase in the 1980s— evoked both support and criticism from the public.

Diving into the work of Bostrom and Suleyman, a really interesting question materialized in contemplating human scientific progress: 'Did we really ever say: "NO"?' Did we ever decide NOT to pursue technological advancement, or scientific research because we believed that the revenge effects would be too dangerous, too scary, or too detrimental? Well, not really, of course. Throughout history, humanity has rarely succeeded in completely containing technology once its potential had been glimpsed. Regulatory measures and ethical considerations have been implemented, but these often served to manage and delay rather than really halt progress.

In 1872, Samuel Butler published a novel titled *Erewhon*, which was just 'Nowhere' spelled backwards. The book presented a brilliant satirical

► *Sorry, not sorry.

utopia that critiqued Victorian society and explored themes of technology and its potential consequences. One of the novel's most notable sections is the 'Book of the Machines', where Butler introduces the idea that machines could evolve consciousness and intelligence, posing a threat to human dominance. In *Erewhon*, the inhabitants first embraced technological advancements, but eventually came to fear that machines might outstrip human capabilities and potentially overthrow humanity. As a result, they decided to destroy all complex machinery and prohibit its development to prevent such an outcome.

Just as the myth of the Great Flood reflects a deep-seated human fear of nature's overwhelming power, the warnings in *The Book of the Machines*, along with the concerns of Suleyman, Bostrom, and others, highlight a universal anxiety: the possibility of machines surpassing human intelligence and the profound ethical dilemmas posed by self-improving systems.

Yet despite the potential dangers of creating machines that could surpass human intelligence, research and development in AI continue to accelerate. The pursuit of technological progress in AI is driven by the promise of solving complex problems, improving efficiency, and creating new economic opportunities. Containment strategies are being discussed widely, but the inherent drive to innovate makes it unlikely that humanity will simply 'say no' to AI development.

The Need For Speed

On the contrary, we might have to accelerate.

Taking a different angle to the relationship between technological progress and societal challenges, we could argue that accelerating technological development is not just beneficial but essential for addressing the challenges of the 'Never Normal' era. From healthcare to climate change, technology (and AI in particular) holds the potential to revolutionize our approach and provide breakthroughs that were previously unimaginable.

Take healthcare, for example. Over the past two centuries, healthcare spending as a share of GDP has skyrocketed, with costs accelerating dramatically in recent decades. If this trajectory continues, it could cripple economies and bankrupt nations that subsidize healthcare. And it could make quality medical care completely unaffordable in countries without universal coverage, such as the United States. We already see that the healthcare spending per capita in the US is by far the highest in the world, but that the life expectancy is not correlated. In Japan for example, the cost of healthcare per person is only *half* of the US spend, yet the average life expectancy is five years longer in Japan.

If we can't make a quantum leap in the world of healthcare, in terms of efficiency, cost and effectiveness, it could become the biggest challenge in the 21st century. On the other hand, the oncoming wave of artificial intelligence and synthetic biology could perhaps be the answer to unlocking that quantum leap. This cluster could truly lead to significant breakthroughs in diagnostics, treatment, and disease prevention.

Climate change, one of the most pressing issues of our time, also necessitates a technological revolution. Renewable energy technologies such as solar, wind, and geothermal power need further development and widespread implementation to reduce our reliance on fossil fuels. Advances in energy storage, smart grid technologies, and carbon capture and storage can significantly mitigate greenhouse gas emissions. Additionally, innovations in agricultural technology, like vertical farming and genetically modified crops, can help secure food supplies while reducing environmental impact. By accelerating technological progress, we can develop and deploy solutions at a scale and speed necessary to address our environmental crisis.

So, instead of fearing the oncoming wave, perhaps we should embrace it. As Suleyman points out in his eponymous book, 'Modern civilization keeps writing very expensive checks that only continual technological development can cash.'

Rather than slowing down technological progress, accelerating it might be the key to navigating the 'Never Normal' era. By leveraging AI, we can tackle healthcare challenges, combat climate change, and foster economic and social resilience.

Standstill would actually be a disaster.

In 1955, two years before he passed away from cancer at the untimely age of 54, John von Neumann was asked to write an article in *Fortune* magazine, looking 25 years into the future, towards the year 1980. He wrote a brilliant essay titled, 'Can We Survive Technology?' It is one of the essays that I re-read repeatedly—brilliantly written, with a combination of intelligence, insight and humor that was the very essence of John von Neumann. It was a message of hope and realism, but also one of caution and reflection.

In that piece, about 70 years ago, he wrote, 'The technology that is now developing and that will dominate the next decades seems to be in total conflict with traditional and, in the main, momentarily still valid, geographical and political units and concepts. This is the maturing crisis of technology.' I fundamentally agree with von Neumann on this point. Over the last two centuries, we have witnessed the decline of the power of nation states, and the shift from countries and militaries towards the enterprises and corporations that thrive in the world of global capitalism.

I was born in Belgium, a tiny European nation with only 11 million inhabitants. That is not even half of Shanghai. All my life, it was very clear to me that, in the grand scheme of things, if you asked which is more important, a country like Belgium, or a corporation like ExxonMobil or Walmart, virtually no one would choose Belgium.

In this century, we have experienced the era of Big Tech, where global enterprises, fueled by the rise of network effects and information asymmetry, have ballooned into powerful global concepts. They have grown more powerful and wealthy than anything in the history of human economics. This will truly be the 'maturing crisis' we will have to grapple with in this century, as von Neumann pointed out.

But there is no reason we should say 'No'.

When I was a young engineer in my first job, I had a side hustle as a writer for the young budding magazine *WIRED*.[39] I loved the magazine, with its sassy style and groovy edge and was thrilled to work with Kevin Kelly, its founding executive editor and a brilliant storyteller. Prior to his work at *WIRED*, he published the iconic counterculture magazine *Whole Earth Catalog*, together with Stewart Brand. It covered everything from computer code, biology, alternative education, and eastern philosophy, to what you needed to run your own farm off the grid. It was magic. In his 2005 Stanford University commencement speech, Steve Jobs compared the *Whole Earth Catalog* to 'a sort of Google in paperback form, before Google came along'.

After my brief stint writing for *WIRED*, I had the chance to work with Kevin Kelly on a few occasions. I always loved his positive attitude towards technology, and the good it could do. In his brilliant work 'What Technology Wants', he presents a compelling vision of technology as a force with its own intrinsic drive toward advancement and complexity. This way, it acts much like a natural organism, evolving through processes analogous to biological evolution. He described how, unlike the common narrative, it is not merely a collection of tools and machines developed by humans, but a dynamic, self-propelling system with its own evolutionary trajectory. Technology has an inherent directionality or a 'will' of its own, which is unstoppable. In this scenario, humans are just as much participants as they are architects, cogs in the vast machinery of technological evolution, contributing to and being influenced by its relentless progress.

His theory might be a little too intense for my liking. But I love Kelly's optimism and relentless enthusiasm for progress. And should technology indeed turn out to have an intrinsic 'want', it is probably even more difficult to say 'No'.

That is also the conclusion of John von Neuman in his essay, 'Can we survive technology?': 'The technological system retains enormous vitality, probably more than ever before, and the counsel of restraint is unlikely to be heeded.' That is just an extremely fancy way of saying, 'You can't say No.'

At the conclusion of the essay, von Neumann also delivers an almost poetic statement, which has become my personal mantra: 'For progress, there is no cure.' It perfectly encapsulates the idea that technological development is an unstoppable force, driven by human nature, curiosity and ambition. It cannot be contained, even as it brings both tremendous benefits and significant risks. Instead, we should steer progress to serve humanity's best interests in the Never Normal.

tl dr

Every technology carries both light and shadow. Paul Virilio wisely said, 'Every technology carries its own negativity, which is invented at the same time as technical progress.' And over the years technological geniuses like John von Neumann and Mustafa Suleyman have deeply felt this paradox, being both elated by and worried about their own brilliant inventions and their revenge effects.

But does that mean that we should try to contain scientific and technological progress, in order to mitigate their negative side effects? The Luddites, Pope Urban II and Nick Bostrom certainly thought so. I believe we should do the exact opposite and accelerate: use the powers of AI, synthetic biology and other powerful emerging technologies to solve some of our most pressing challenges like healthcare and climate change and serve humanity's best interests in the Never Normal. There is no cure for progress. And we shouldn't want one either.

Your work is going to fill a large part of your life, and the only way to be truly satisfied is to do what you believe is great work.

And the only way to do great work is to love what you do. —STEVE JOBS

7

A New Age Of Work

Almost everything will work again if you unplug it for a few minutes... including you. —ANNE LAMOTT

The first time I met Sara Blakely was a few years before COVID, when we were both speaking at a Microsoft conference at their Seattle headquarters. Sara is one of America's most prominent and admired entrepreneurs, the youngest self-made woman billionaire ever, and a co-owner of the Atlanta Hawks. But when I met her backstage at Microsoft, I had no idea who she was.

We met in the green room behind the podium, and I was captivated by her very lively, bubbly personality. I was also truly fascinated that while we were talking, she was holding in her hands what appeared to be a piece of woman's underwear, and a pair of scissors. I was even more stunned that when she burst onto the stage, she was still holding them, to tell the story of how she founded Spanx.

Sara's journey began with a super simple yet absolutely revolutionary idea. Frustrated with the visible panty lines and discomfort of traditional undergarments, she experimented by cutting the feet off a pair of control-top pantyhose to create a smoother look under her plain white pants. (Hence the scissors she was holding, to make her point on stage. She's quite the show-woman.) This impromptu solution sparked an idea that would eventually disrupt the entire shapewear industry and make her a billionaire.[40]

Don't confuse having a career with having a life.

—HILLARY CLINTON

Her story is a shining example of what can be achieved through determination, innovation, and resilience. She had no prior experience in fashion, manufacturing, or retail. Armed only with her savings of $5,000 from selling fax machines (!) door-to-door, she embarked on a journey to bring her vision to life. Despite lacking technical expertise, she remained undeterred, teaching herself about fabric, prototyping, and patent filing. Her ability to learn on the go became a defining characteristic of her entrepreneurial resilience.

But the early stages of her business were anything but smooth. Blakely spent months searching for hosiery manufacturers willing to produce her product, only to face constant rejection. Most manufacturers were skeptical about taking a risk on a woman with no industry background. It was only after one factory owner consulted his daughters, who saw potential in the product, that she finally secured a manufacturing partner.

The second uphill battle—after finally developing a prototype—was getting Spanx into stores. Buyers at major retailers dismissed her idea, doubting whether there was a real market for it. Rather than being discouraged, Blakely found creative ways to push forward. She convinced a buyer from Neiman Marcus to meet with her, but instead of relying solely on a pitch, she personally demonstrated her product in the store's restroom, showing the immediate transformation it offered. This unconventional approach worked, securing her first major retail order.

Even after gaining a retail foothold, she had no marketing budget to promote her product. Instead of waiting for sales to happen, she personally demonstrated Spanx in department stores, engaging with customers and educating them on why they needed her product. Her grassroots efforts, combined with an unshakable belief in her idea, kept her moving forward. The breakthrough moment came when talk show host Oprah Winfrey named Spanx as one of her 'Favorite Things' in 2000, giving the brand instant credibility and skyrocketing sales. But even this moment of success did not make Blakely complacent. She continued innovating, expanding the Spanx product line, and ensuring that the brand remained relevant and in demand.

After we met, I started following her on social media. One of her favorite poses online is to post a picture of herself with most of her face obscured by an inspirational coffee mug. Recently I saw a post by Sara where she was holding up a cup that said:

UNDERPERFORMERS WANT EASE.
MIDPERFORMERS WANT CREDIT.
WINNERS WANT PRESSURE.

Classic Sara Blakely. She absolutely loves the pressure.

Hustle & Float

Let me tell you another motivational coffee mug story that is also related to someone I met on the lecture circuit: Rahaf Harfoush. Rahaf is an American author who has been living in France for quite some time. She is the author of one of my favorite books, *Hustle & Float*, and describes herself as a 'digital anthropologist'.

We were both giving a keynote for a big technology conference, and I loved her presentation on the complexity of balancing our lives in this accelerating digital post-industrial knowledge society. I liked her book even more.

Hustle & Float describes the challenge of balancing our lives in this Never Normal world. One of the biggest hurdles is the constant 'hustle': the relentless pressure for more, for better, for faster. As Rahaf describes it, 'We constantly struggle to keep up in a world that never sleeps, we arm ourselves with little life hacks, to-do lists, and an inbox zero mentality, grasping at anything that will help us work faster, push harder, and produce more'.

But, as she points out, there is just one problem: most of these solutions are making things worse. Creativity is not produced on an assembly line, and endless hustle is ruining our mental and physical health. The real problem is that productivity and creativity are not really compatible: we are torn between them, and like the opposite poles of a magnet, they are tearing us apart. When we're told to sleep more, meditate and slow down, we nod our heads in agreement, yet most of us seem totally incapable of applying this advice in our lives. In her book, Rahaf explores how our work culture creates contradictions between what we think we want, and what we actually need.

She started writing the book when a friend of hers gave her a coffee cup for her birthday that said:

YOU HAVE
THE SAME AMOUNT OF HOURS
IN A DAY
AS BEYONCÉ.

That cup seemed like a fun present at the beginning, but the more she drank coffee from that mug, the more the message started to bother her. Till she snapped. 'Look at Beyoncé,' she recalls telling her sister. 'Look at what Beyoncé has already done, and look at my life. I've wasted so much time being unproductive. My life is a failure.'

The coffee mug triggered her to dig deeper, and she started reading everything she could on the artist and became a self proclaimed 'Beyoncéologist'. There were plenty of articles and posts that described Beyoncé as the 'hardest working woman in show business'. There was even a Harvard Business School case study dedicated to her work ethic as the ultimate example of the productive creative who had managed to successfully combine her creative pursuits into a lucrative, sprawling business empire.

But then she discovered that the singer took a year-long hiatus between tours back in 2011. It turns out that even Beyoncé was not immune to the perils of hyper-productivity and had battled with burnout. As the singer revealed in interviews, 'It all started to get fuzzy. I couldn't tell which city I was in, or what day of the week it was. I would sit there at ceremonies where they would give me an award, and I just wasn't there mentally, I was just trying to make it to the next performance. Eventually my mother convinced me to take a break and take care of my mental health.'

Sara Blakely says, 'It's a privilege to have pressure. How we behave under that pressure is the key to success, it makes us become a stronger version of ourselves. There are whole species of plants that thrive in extreme environments. Sometimes pressure is necessary for growth. Learn to crave pressure.' But when Rahaf Harfoush was drinking coffee out of the Beyoncé mug, that pressure left a different taste in her mouth.

The Toll Of The New

I wonder if they had motivational coffee mugs on the sailing trip back in 1519, when Magellan rounded the earth for the first time.

The circumnavigation of 1519–1522 stands as one of humanity's pivotal moments—the first empirical proof that our world is truly round and connected. While educated people of the time generally accepted Earth's spherical nature (contrary to popular belief, medieval scholars didn't widely believe in a flat Earth), this voyage provided the first practical demonstration. It showed not just that the world was round, but that humans could traverse its entirety and connect its furthest points. This was humanity's first true step into global consciousness and global connectivity.

The expedition shattered the ancient boundaries of human knowledge. It discovered the Pacific Ocean's vast expanse, found the strait that would bear Magellan's name, and revealed the true size of our planet. It opened routes that would transform commerce, culture, and communication. In many ways, this voyage marked the real beginning of globalization—the moment when humanity first glimpsed its potential to operate on a truly planetary scale.

Yet this monumental achievement came at a devastating human cost. Of the 240 men who embarked on this journey of discovery, 222 never returned home. They died from scurvy, starvation, disease, violence, and accidents. Magellan himself met a violent end on a beach in the Philippines, fighting a battle that didn't need to be fought. The survivors of the Victoria endured unimaginable hardships—months of hunger where they ate leather and sawdust, weeks of storms that threatened to destroy their ship and the constant fear of mutiny or catastrophe.

Let me weave together this narrative of human achievement, stress, and transformation, starting with Magellan himself.

Ferdinand Magellan[41] was born into minor Portuguese nobility around 1480. His early life was marked by service as a page at the royal court, where he learned about astronomy, cartography, and the latest maritime technologies. By age 25, he had already sailed to India, participated in major battles, and survived a shipwreck. In a pattern that would define his life, Magellan found himself constantly pushing boundaries, both geographical and political. After feeling slighted by the Portuguese king who rejected his proposals for exploration, he renounced his nationality and pledged allegiance to Spain—a controversial move that marked him as a traitor in Portuguese eyes but opened the door to his historic voyage.

Magellan's personal story reflects the complex interplay between ambition, loyalty, and the pursuit of the unknown. He was driven by a vision that others couldn't see, convinced of the possibility of finding a western route to the Spice Islands. Sadly, his drive for discovery came with personal costs—he alienated his homeland, faced multiple mutiny attempts during his voyage, and ultimately died on a distant beach in the Philippines, thousands of miles from home.[42]

When the Victoria finally returned to Spain in 1522, under Juan Sebastián Elcano's command, it proved definitively that the world was round and navigable. But at a tremendous cost. From our vantage point five centuries later, we see the triumph—the maps redrawn, the world connected, humanity's horizons expanded. But for those who lived it, there was no guarantee of success, no certainty that their sacrifices would mean anything. They couldn't know that they were making history; they knew only that they were suffering.

The experience of an ordinary sailor on the Victoria illuminates this disconnect. Imagine being that person—months at sea, watching friends die of scurvy, their gums bleeding and bodies wasting away. Imagine the terror of being the first humans to cross the vast Pacific, not knowing if it would indeed ever end. Each day brought new horrors, new losses, new reasons to despair. For them, this wasn't a grand adventure into the unknown—it was a nightmare they couldn't escape.

As Stalin would later coldly observe, 'The death of one man is a tragedy, the death of millions is a statistic.' But each of those 222 lost souls of the Magellan expedition represented a personal tragedy—families left without fathers, sons who never returned home, dreams that ended in distant waters.

Fast forward to today's 'Never Normal' world, and we see striking parallels. Just as Magellan's crew faced unprecedented challenges in uncharted waters, today's workforce navigates constant technological disruption, economic uncertainty, and accelerating change. The psychological toll is similar—anxiety about the unknown, stress from constant adaptation, fear of falling behind or failing.

Psychological Scurvy

Modern professionals might not face scurvy or violent deaths, but they struggle with burnout, depression, and disconnection. The 'Never Normal' creates its own form of psychological scurvy—a depletion of mental and emotional resources in the face of relentless change. Like Magellan's sailors watching their companions succumb one by one to disease and hardship, today's workers often witness colleagues falling to burnout or mental health challenges.

Yet, just as the Magellan-Elcano expedition ultimately transformed human understanding and capability, today's challenges are pushing us to evolve and adapt. The difference is that while Magellan's crew had no choice but to press forward or perish, we have the opportunity to develop better ways of managing change and supporting human resilience.

The lesson from Magellan's voyage isn't just about the achievement of circumnavigation—it's about the human capacity to endure and adapt in the face of overwhelming uncertainty. Today's 'Never Normal' world demands similar resilience, but it also requires us to be smarter about how we manage human limitations and psychological well-being. We can't stop the pace of change any more than Magellan's crew could calm the Pacific storms, but we can develop better ways to navigate through it. The challenge is to pursue progress while actively protecting and nurturing human well-being—to circumnavigate the globe without losing half our crew to scurvy.

Wow. How did we go from an inspirational billionaire success story of scissors and pantyhose to talking about scurvy and bleeding gums? Why, coffee mugs, of course.

I CIRCUMNAVIGATED THE GLOBE
FOR THE FIRST TIME
AND ALL I GOT
WAS THIS LOUSY MUG.

Learned Resilience And Active Hope

One of the greatest psychological barriers to resilience is a phenomenon known as 'learned helplessness'. First identified by psychologists Martin Seligman and Steven Maier in the 1960s, this concept emerged from a series of experiments that revealed how prolonged exposure to uncontrollable stress can condition individuals to stop trying—even when opportunities for change arise.

In their experiment, Seligman and Maier placed dogs in harnesses where they were exposed to mild but inescapable electric shocks. Some dogs were able to control their situation by pressing a lever that would stop the shocks, while others had no such power. Later, when all dogs were placed in a new setting where they could easily escape by jumping over a low barrier, those that had previously experienced inescapable pain did not even try. They had learned that their actions were futile and simply lay down, accepting their suffering even when relief was within reach.

This discovery had profound implications for understanding human behavior. It showed that when people are repeatedly subjected to stress, setbacks, or failures without perceiving a way to influence the outcome, they often develop a passive resignation to their circumstances. Instead of seeking solutions, they come to believe that no effort will make a difference. The mind, once wired for resilience and problem-solving, retreats into apathy and surrender.

In our 'Never Normal' world, the rapid and relentless pace of change can trigger a similar response. Technological disruption, economic hardship, geopolitical instability, biological shocks, social shifts, job automation, climate crises and the constant demand to adapt can create a sense of powerlessness, leading individuals to feel that they have no control over their lives. Many people start to feel as though they are at the mercy of forces too vast to counteract.

The danger of learned helplessness in this context is profound. When individuals stop believing in their ability to shape their own future, they disengage. They stop seeking new skills, avoid taking risks, and surrender to stagnation. Entire organizations and societies can fall into this psychological trap, losing the dynamism and creative energy necessary to navigate uncertain times.

However, history and psychology both offer an antidote. Just as learned helplessness is acquired, it can also be unlearned. Psychologists have shown that individuals can break free from this cycle by experiencing small wins: situations where their actions do produce positive results, even if they only breed minor successes.

That is why I advocate for cultivating 'learned resilience'—the belief that no matter how daunting the circumstances, effort and adaptability will still lead to progress. I believe that the paralysis of helplessness can be counteracted if we learn how to actively reframe challenges as opportunities for growth. And that's where leaders, educators, and institutions can play a hugely important role: by fostering this mindset and creating environments where people are encouraged to take action, experiment, and recover from failure.

The Never Normal is here to stay. Change will continue to accelerate, and uncertainty will remain a defining feature of human experience. But there is always opportunity within chaos, if you have the courage to develop the type of resilience that is not only reactive but proactive. That's how we will learn to navigate the unknown with confidence and purpose.

Blind Hope

At the opposite spectrum of learned helplessness lies blind hope, an unfounded belief in a positive future. And it can be just as damaging. Optimism, in its most constructive form, serves as a powerful motivator, as it can help us endure hardship. But when this type of toxic positivity detaches from reality and evolves into an unquestioning faith that things will simply 'work out' without action, it can also lead to complacency and a total lack of action. And that's particularly dangerous in a 'Never Normal' era.

Dr. Robert Holden[43] introduces another crucial aspect of this type of misguided hope: destination addiction. Holden is a *New York Times* bestselling author of 14 books, and the presenter of a TEDx talk on the subject of 'Destination Addiction': the radical belief that success is a destination. According to him, people who are prone to 'destination addiction' are obsessed with the belief that true success, happiness, and fulfillment always lie in the future. Each passing moment is merely a ticket to get to the future. They live in the 'not now', they are psychologically absent, and they disregard everything they have. Destination addiction is a preoccupation with the idea that happiness is somewhere else. We suffer, literally, from the pursuit of happiness. We are always on the run, on the move, and on the go.

This perpetual chase for a better future blinds individuals to the present. They disregard achievements, dismiss what they already have, and become trapped in an endless loop of dissatisfaction. Much like blind optimism, destination addiction can prevent meaningful engagement with the here and now, replacing it with an unattainable future that forever remains just out of reach. It disconnects people from reality, making them psychologically absent from their own lives.

But there is a concept that perfectly encapsulates a balance between avoiding the paralysis of learned helplessness and resisting the seduction of blind optimism and destination addiction: active hope, a mindset that acknowledges uncertainty but refuses to be passive about it. Those who embrace active hope recognize the challenges but also act on them in order to influence the future.

The greatest thinkers and innovators of the past did not succeed because they assumed things would get better on their own. They moved forward because they believed in the possibility of change and worked relentlessly toward shaping it. Whether in the Renaissance, the Industrial Revolution, or today's digital and technological transformations, the individuals and societies that thrived were those who combined acceptance and resilience with initiative.

The Post-Industrial Hustle

The post-industrial world is obsessed with hustle. The mantra of our time seems to be: harder, better, faster, stronger (and richer). It's Daft Punk's anthem playing in an endless loop, a call to arms for the productivity-obsessed culture that measures success by relentless output, constant optimization, and the glorification of exhaustion.

Hustle culture has been shaped by business leaders who push their employees toward ever-increasing levels of intensity. During her time at Yahoo, Marissa Mayer famously expected employees to work 130-hour weeks, citing extreme commitment as a prerequisite for innovation. When Elon Musk took over Twitter, he issued an ultimatum: employees had to embrace 'hardcore' work ethics or leave. The idea that only those who are willing to sacrifice everything for their work are worthy of success has become deeply embedded in the modern professional ethos.

This obsession with hustle extends far beyond Silicon Valley boardrooms. Productivity 'porn' dominates self-help literature, with books like *Getting Things Done* and *The 5 AM Club* promising life-changing success to those who maximize every waking moment. Social media influencers preach morning routines that begin before dawn, advocate skipping sleep in favor of relentless work, and offer motivational soundbites that blur the line between ambition and self-destruction. Hustle has become a status symbol, a marker of worth, a form of social currency where being 'busy' is equated with being important.

The King of 'Hustle' nowadays is without a doubt entrepreneur, media mogul, and internet personality Gary Vaynerchuk, commonly known as Gary V.[44]

Born in the Soviet Union (now Belarus) in 1975, Vaynerchuk immigrated to the United States with his family as a child. His entrepreneurial journey began with his father's wine business, which he transformed from a $3 million local store into a $60 million business by recognizing and leveraging the potential of early e-commerce and social media. This early success established his reputation for identifying and capitalizing on emerging digital trends.

Gary V's philosophy on hustle is both celebrated and controversial. At its core, his message emphasizes relentless work ethic, unwavering dedication, and the need to put in extraordinary effort to achieve success. He famously advocates working 18-hour days, sacrificing leisure time, and constantly seeking new opportunities. His catchphrase 'crushing it' became a mantra for aspiring entrepreneurs and digital creators.

Through his media company VaynerMedia and his extensive social media presence, Gary V has built an absolutely massive following by consistently delivering his message across platforms. He's known for his raw, unfiltered communication style and his ability to predict and capitalize on digital trends, from the early days of Twitter to the rise of TikTok and NFTs. And his followers absolutely love him like a God.

I had the chance to work with Gary V a few years ago. I was the warm-up act before the Grand Duke of Hustle himself would address the crowd at a Belgian conference. The organizer had paid an insane amount of money to fly him to Belgium and the venue was filled to the brim with his followers. But when he got on stage he said: 'Nah. I don't feel like doing a keynote today. No slides. You know, just ask me anything you want.' I looked at the organizer who turned white as a ghost, but to our absolute surprise the audience didn't care that Gary V would not use PowerPoint. On the contrary, everyone loved the intimate interaction with the King of Hustle.

After the show, the organizers invited the in-crowd to the best restaurant in Antwerp, and Gary did not stop hustling. When we got there he asked 'What is this place called?', and tweeted his location to his followers. Forty-five minutes later, the three Michelin star chef showed up at our table, totally flustered, and said, 'What is going on? There are hundreds of people outside shouting "Gary! Gary! Gary!"' It was one of the most powerful demonstrations of Hustle I have ever seen; Gary V went outside, and entertained the crowd for an hour. Impressive.

What sets Vaynerchuk apart from other business influencers is his emphasis on the long game. While he preaches intense hustle, he also stresses patience and the importance of building genuine value over time. He often talks about being content with planting seeds that might not bear fruit for decades, which somewhat balances his more aggressive messages about constant grinding.

Perhaps most interestingly, Vaynerchuk represents a unique intersection of old-school work ethic and new-age digital opportunity. He embodies both traditional immigrant hustle culture and modern digital entrepreneurship, making his message resonate with a diverse audience across generations and backgrounds.

But beneath the glorified narratives of ceaseless effort also lies a troubling reality. Hustle culture often leads to burnout, chronic stress, and a loss of genuine fulfillment. The pressure to constantly perform and achieve creates a treadmill effect—no matter how fast one runs, the finish line never comes closer. Instead of finding meaning in the present, individuals become locked in a perpetual cycle of striving, postponing happiness for an elusive future moment when they will have 'made it'.

Much like destination addiction, hustle culture convinces people that success, happiness, and self-worth are always just beyond reach. It fosters the belief that slowing down is equivalent to falling behind, that rest is a luxury rather than a necessity, and that those who prioritize balance are simply not committed enough.

As the Never Normal world accelerates, the challenge is no longer just to keep up, but also to redefine what it means to be productive. The future belongs not to those who burn themselves out chasing an unattainable ideal, but to those who understand the value of sustainable success. For that, we will need to move beyond the glorification of hustle toward a model of work and life that prioritizes both achievement and well-being. But that is not so easy. The 'hustle' gene is deeply embedded into our industrial and economic narrative.

The Stakhanov Movement

The industrial age brought a fundamental shift in how we organized human labor. Frederick Taylor's *The Principles of Scientific Management* (1911) promised to transform chaotic factory floors into well-oiled machines through careful measurement, standardization, and optimization. Every movement could be studied, every task broken down into its constituent parts, every worker's output precisely measured. This approach seemed perfectly suited to an age of machines, assembly lines, and mass production.

In the Soviet Union, this drive for industrial efficiency took on an ideological dimension with the Stakhanov movement. Alexei Stakhanov, a coal miner who supposedly mined 14 times his quota, became the poster child for Communist labor productivity. The movement celebrated 'labor heroes' who dramatically exceeded production quotas, creating a culture of competitive overwork that was obviously as much about propaganda as it was about productivity. This established a pattern of using individual 'heroes' to drive collective performance that persists in different forms today.

The industrial mindset gave us powerful tools: standardized processes, clear metrics, efficiency optimization, and systematic management. These approaches transformed manufacturing and helped create the modern world. But they were designed for a specific context—one where work was primarily physical, outputs were tangible, and success could be measured in units produced per hour.

Today, we find ourselves in a fundamentally different world. Knowledge work dominates in developed economies. Creativity and innovation are primary sources of value. And many outputs can't be measured in simple numerical terms. Yet surprisingly, we continue to apply industrial-age thinking to post-industrial problems. We measure knowledge worker productivity with industrial metrics, manage creative processes with factory-floor techniques, and tend to treat human minds like human muscles.

This is where the modern 'hustle culture', exemplified by figures like Gary Vaynerchuk, becomes particularly interesting. In many ways, it represents an attempt to apply industrial-age productivity paradigms to knowledge work. The emphasis on long hours, measurable outputs, and relentless productivity echoes both Taylorist efficiency and Stakhanovite hero-worship. But knowledge work doesn't necessarily respond to these approaches the way factory work does.

Industrial-Age Solutions To Knowledge-Age Problems

Creative thinking, problem-solving, and innovation don't operate on linear time scales. Working longer hours doesn't automatically produce better and more unique ideas. In fact, research suggests that cognitive performance declines significantly with overwork, and creative insights often come during periods of rest or reflection. Yet we continue to celebrate and promote industrial-style 'hustle' in contexts where it may be counterproductive.

The persistence of industrial thinking in post-industrial contexts has created numerous paradoxes. Companies talk about innovation while maintaining rigid industrial-style schedules. They seek creativity while measuring performance with factory-floor metrics. They want engaged, passionate knowledge workers but manage them with tools designed for assembly lines.

This mismatch between industrial management approaches and post-industrial work realities contributes to many modern workplace challenges: burnout, disengagement, and reduced productivity, to name but a few. The 'hustle culture' can be seen as both a symptom of this mismatch and an attempt to resolve it by sheer force of will.

What we need is a fundamental rethinking of how we organize and measure work in a knowledge economy. This doesn't mean abandoning everything we learned from the industrial age—many of its insights remain valuable. But it does mean developing new paradigms that better reflect the nature of cognitive work, creativity, and innovation. The future of work requires not just working harder, but working differently.

Artificial Intelligence And Bullshit Jobs

With the advent of ChatGPT, the narrative on work was fundamentally transformed once again.

In my 30 years of professional activity, I have never seen anything scale so quickly as Generative AI. The time from 'novelty' to 'normal' has never been so compressed. I truly believe that it is the biggest thing we have seen in our lifetime. And that we still haven't seen anything yet.

The emergence of powerful generative AI tools has created a true seismic shift in our understanding of what constitutes uniquely human work. Tasks that we confidently classified as requiring human intelligence and creativity—writing, coding, design, analysis, even artistic expression—are now being performed at increasingly sophisticated levels by AI systems. This represents not just a technological breakthrough, but a fundamental challenge to our assumptions about the nature of knowledge work.

For decades, we operated under a comfortable dichotomy. Machines would handle routine, repetitive tasks. And humans would focus on creative, analytical, and interpersonal work. This led many workers to migrate towards knowledge-intensive professions, believing these roles were inherently 'AI-proof'. The rapid advancement of Generative AI has shattered this assumption. Suddenly, tools like ChatGPT can write better and more empathetic emails than busy doctors, GitHub Copilot can generate complex code, and DALL-E can create sophisticated artwork—all tasks we previously considered quintessentially human.

This technological leap is creating a new kind of pressure in the post-industrial workplace. Knowledge workers now find themselves not just competing with human 'hustlers', but with AI systems that don't sleep, don't burn out, and improve at an exponential rate. This has intensified the already problematic 'hustle culture', as workers feel compelled to demonstrate their value above and beyond what AI can provide. The anxiety is palpable: if AI can perform many aspects of knowledge work, what remains uniquely human?

The pace of AI advancement has created another particularly challenging dynamic. Workers must not only maintain their existing skills but continuously adapt to and integrate new AI tools into their workflow. This creates a double burden: the pressure to 'hustle' harder to stay competitive, while simultaneously having to learn and master new AI technologies. It's like trying to run a race while constantly having to learn new ways of running.

Reshaping Productivity

In the beginning of 2025, an AI company called Artisan.ai plastered billboards all over San Francisco: 'STOP HIRING HUMANS'. Their tool was called Artisan, and their advertisements read: 'Hire Artisans instead of Humans. Artisans won't complain about work-life balance.'

For years now, I have used a joke in my keynote that humans shouldn't worry about losing their jobs to AI and robots, because humans today are still the best all-purpose non-linear computer systems that can be mass produced by unskilled workers. But as the advancements in AI in reasoning and sophistication are getting more impressive, I'm not sure how long I can keep using that joke.

Moreover, AI is reshaping the very nature of productivity in knowledge work. Traditional metrics of output—words written, code produced, designs created—become less meaningful when AI can generate vast quantities of this type of content quickly. This forces us to reconsider how we measure and value human contribution in a world where raw production capacity is increasingly automated.

The psychological impact of this transformation shouldn't be underestimated, either. Many knowledge workers built their identities and careers around skills that AI can now partially replicate. This creates not just economic anxiety but existential questions about the value and meaning of work. For many, the 'hustle' mentality could become a defensive response—a way of proving human relevance in an increasingly AI-capable world.

One of the loudest voices in this narrative was David Graeber, who coined the term 'bullshit jobs'. David was a prominent American anthropologist and an anarchist activist who was involved in the popularizing of the slogan 'We are the 99%', which became central to the Occupy Wall Street movement in 2011.[45] His involvement there ended his tenure at Yale University, after which he became a professor at the London School of Economics. In 2018, Graeber wrote the book *Bullshit Jobs: A Theory*, which expanded on the idea that he had introduced in an essay back in 2013. The concept of 'bullshit jobs' refers to forms of paid employment that are so pointless, unnecessary, or pernicious that even the employee cannot justify their existence, even though they feel obliged to pretend that this is not the case.

Graeber defines five main categories of bullshit jobs:

Flunkies

Jobs that exist only to make someone else look or feel important (e.g., doormen or administrative assistants who mainly wait for phone calls)

Goons

Jobs that exist only because other people employ them (e.g., corporate lawyers, telemarketers, certain PR specialists)

Duct Tapers

Jobs that exist only to fix problems that shouldn't exist in the first place (e.g., programmers fixing badly designed software systems)

Box Tickers

Jobs that exist only to allow an organization to claim it's doing something it isn't really doing (e.g., many compliance positions)

Taskmasters

Jobs that involve assigning work to others who don't need supervision (e.g., middle management positions that exist solely to create and distribute work)

Graeber argues that these jobs are not just useless but can be psychologically damaging to the people who hold them, as humans generally need to feel they are contributing something meaningful to society. He suggests that despite technological advances that should have reduced working hours, our economy has instead generated an endless array of these meaningless jobs.

Ark Fleet B

I cannot write this without mentioning the absolutely fascinating parallel with the story of the Golgafrinchans Ark Fleet B ship in my favorite book *The Hitchhiker's Guide to the Galaxy* by Douglas Adams. In this magnificent magnum opus, he describes the fate of a society on the planet Golgafrinchan. In order to save their civilization from an incoming catastrophe (a massive meteorite that will destroy their world), they design a massive evacuation from their planet in three massive starships: Ark A, B and C.

Ark A would carry all the leaders of the planet, the rulers, thinkers, scientists and artists. Ark C would be the people that actually did the real work like plumbers, cooks and carpenters. Ark B would be filled with all the 'middlemen' of Golgafrincham, in the words of Adams, 'people such as telephone sanitisers, account executives, hairdressers, tired TV producers, insurance salesmen, personnel officers, security guards, public relations executives, and management consultants'.

Ark B is convinced to actually evacuate first off the planet. The joke, of course, was that Arks A and C never existed—it was just a way for the Golgafrinchans to rid themselves of what they considered their unnecessary population. The ironic punchline was that the remaining Golgafrinchans died out due to a disease contracted from dirty telephone receivers.

Adams wrote this in 1979, during the rise of service economies and middle management culture. In many ways, his satirical vision of unnecessary jobs prefigured David Graeber's more academic analysis by several decades. But while Adams played the concept for laughs and ultimately suggested these jobs might be more necessary than they appear (through the telephone sanitizer punchline), Graeber argues that many modern jobs are genuinely unnecessary and actively harmful to human psychological well-being.

A key part of his argument is that this proliferation of pointless work isn't a natural outcome of free-market capitalism (which should theoretically eliminate inefficiencies), but rather reflects a moral and political phenomenon where work is seen as virtuous regardless of its actual utility. He points out the irony that many of the most socially valuable jobs (like nurses, teachers, or maintenance workers) are often the least well compensated, while many bullshit jobs come with high salaries and prestige.

The concept sparked significant debate about the nature of modern work and resonated with many people who felt their jobs lacked genuine purpose or social value. However, some critics argued that Graeber's analysis oversimplified complex organizational structures and that jobs he might classify as 'bullshit' may serve purposes he doesn't fully appreciate.

Now remember, David Graeber wrote this book five years before Generative AI would hit the world like a tsunami.

Many of the jobs Graeber identified as 'bullshit' involve processing information, writing reports, or creating documentation that few people read. AI systems excel at these tasks: summarizing information, drafting reports, managing documentation etc. This evolution has made the distinction between administrative tasks that are truly necessary and those that were perhaps always more about maintaining appearances more visible.

The impact on middle management is particularly striking. Graeber identified many middle management positions as 'taskmasters' who primarily shuffle information between levels, and AI tools can now handle many of these information-routing and summarizing functions. This raises fundamental questions about whether certain management layers were ever truly necessary for organizational function.

The AI revolution has forced a broader societal conversation about what makes human work valuable. Jobs that Graeber might have called 'bullshit' are often the easiest to automate, which has led to deeper questioning about which jobs truly require human judgment, creativity, and emotional intelligence. This is particularly evident in professional services, where many of Graeber's 'goons' worked as lawyers, consultants, and similar roles. AI is now challenging these professions by automating routine tasks like contract review or basic analysis, forcing these professions to better articulate their unique human value.

Most importantly, AI is bringing Graeber's deeper questions about work and value to the forefront: why do we insist on full employment in an increasingly automated economy? How do we distribute wealth when many traditional jobs become obsolete? What constitutes meaningful work in an AI-augmented world? The AI revolution seems to be validating many of Graeber's observations while also complicating them. It's forcing a broader societal conversation about the nature of work, value, and meaning—exactly the kind of conversation Graeber was trying to spark. However, it's happening much faster than he might have anticipated, and with technology as the driving force rather than a social movement.

The 15-Hour Work Week

ChatGPT was released into the world on Wednesday, the 30th of November 2023. A few weeks before that I had the chance to visit Microsoft HQ with a select group of executives, and spend some time with Brad Smith, who was the president of Microsoft at that time.

It was an intimate and deep conversation on the future of technology, the impact on society and the role that Microsoft wanted to play in this. What was fascinating is the statement that Brad made to our group that day: 'We are constantly monitoring which jobs could be eliminated or fundamentally transformed by technology.' Makes sense. And then he said, after a short pause: 'We've recently started to change some of the timings. Some of the jobs that we thought would be disrupted by technology by 2040, we've now clearly marked as obsolete by 2030.'

Looking back, there is no doubt in my mind that Brad Smith had probably seen the incredible demos of what ChatGPT was capable of, long before the general public had any idea. Microsoft had engaged in a strategic partnership with OpenAI, the parent company of ChatGPT, that gave them the exclusive rights to use the technology of OpenAI in the Microsoft product portfolio. I can imagine that senior executives like Brad, who had spent years in the technology industry, were also blown away by the capabilities of this new technology. And would think about how this would affect the world of work.

Reid Hoffman is the co-founder of LinkedIn and, just like David Graeber, isn't shy about his opinions. At the end of 2024, Hoffman made a pretty bold prediction: by 2034, the classic 9–5 job could be extinct. According to him, technology is advancing so rapidly that everything will become so cheap, you won't really need to work anymore.

In his vision, as AI and robotics become more sophisticated, many traditional job functions may be automated entirely, reducing the need for full-time human workers. On top of that, advances in areas like AI-driven drug discovery, automated vertical farming, renewable energy, and 3D printing could significantly lower the costs of healthcare, food, and consumer goods. If these trends continue, survival may require far less financial effort than it does today, shifting the very nature of work and wealth distribution.

Another possible outcome of the rise of AI-augmented productivity is that professionals may only need to work a few hours a week. With AI handling repetitive or administrative tasks, human workers could focus on creativity, strategy, and decision making. Already, AI tools like ChatGPT, GitHub Copilot, and MidJourney allow professionals to complete tasks in minutes that previously took hours or even days. This could lead to a future where the traditional 40-hour work week is replaced by a more flexible and part-time model.

Now, to be honest, predicting that we will all work less has proven to be quite dangerous in the past.

Keynes's Work Prophecy

John Maynard Keynes was one of the most influential economists of the 20th century. Born in 1883, he revolutionized economic thought, particularly with his ideas on government intervention in the economy. His most famous work, *The General Theory of Employment, Interest, and Money* (1936), laid the foundation for what became known as Keynesian economics. His theories emphasized that during economic downturns, governments should increase spending to stimulate demand and reduce unemployment, rather than relying on free markets to correct themselves. This approach became the basis for modern macroeconomic policies and played a crucial role in shaping government responses to the Great Depression and later economic crises.

Keynes also had a prophecy about work.

In 1930, he made a bold prediction in his essay 'Economic Possibilities for Our Grandchildren', where he speculated that by 2030, technological advancements and productivity gains would lead to such economic abundance that people would only need to work about 15 hours per week. He believed that rising efficiency and innovation would make it possible to meet all human needs with significantly less labor. With wealth and resources becoming more abundant, Keynes suggested that the primary challenge for future generations would be how to spend their newfound leisure time.

Looking at the world today, Keynes was both right and wrong. Productivity has indeed increased dramatically since 1930. Automation, computers, and AI have made it possible to produce more goods and services with far fewer workers. A single person today can accomplish tasks in minutes that would have taken hours or even days a century ago. In some sectors, technology has reduced the need for labor so much that fewer people are required to maintain the same level of economic output.

Yet, at the same time there is Parkinson's law, first articulated by British historian and author Cyril Northcote Parkinson in 1955, which states that 'work expands to fill the time available for its completion'. In other words, even if tasks could be completed more efficiently or in less time, people tend to stretch their work to fit the allotted schedule. This phenomenon explains why bureaucracies tend to grow, why meetings seem to take longer than necessary, and why projects often expand beyond their original scope.

When John Maynard Keynes predicted in 1930 that we would only need to work 15 hours a week by 2030, he assumed that productivity gains from technological advancement would translate directly into fewer working hours. His logic was simple: if we could produce more with less effort, then work hours should naturally decline, freeing people to enjoy more leisure time.

However, Parkinson's Law helps explain why this hasn't happened. Rather than work time shrinking as productivity increases, labor has expanded to fill available time. Even though automation, AI, and modern technology have made it possible to produce far more than in Keynes's time, many people still work 40 or more hours a week.

Keynes underestimated the role of human behavior, economic structures, and inequality in shaping work. Instead of spreading the benefits of increased productivity equally, many economies have seen the opposite trend—working hours remain high, and in some cases, they have even increased. This is partly due to the way wealth is distributed; despite rising efficiency, wages have not kept pace with productivity for many workers, and living costs such as housing, healthcare, and education have risen sharply in many countries. As a result, many people still need to work long hours to maintain their standard of living.

Cultural and social factors have also played a role. Work is not just a means of survival; for many, it provides identity, purpose, and social status. Even in wealthy nations where people could theoretically work less, many choose to work long hours due to competition, ambition, or the expectation of maintaining a certain lifestyle. Meanwhile, in some developing countries, economic conditions still require people to work well beyond 40 hours per week just to meet basic needs.

Liminality

Could Keynes's prediction still come true? Are we now in a transition phase going from the 'hustle' culture of stress and burnout, towards a new society where 9–5 is obsolete and we won't have to work at all anymore, or just 15 hours a week?

Liminality is a concept that originates from anthropology, first introduced by the French ethnographer Arnold van Gennep in his 1909 work *The Rites of Passage*. He used the term to describe the middle phase of a ritual transition—when an individual is no longer in their previous state but has not yet fully transitioned into the next, like a child becoming an adult. But liminality isn't just about rituals, it also applies to personal, social, and even economic change.

Right now, we are in a liminal state when it comes to work. We are still trapped in the hustle culture of the 40-hour workweek, where long hours are seen as a badge of honor. Stress, burnout, and overwork define much of modern life, even though technology has made us more productive than ever. Many people feel stuck, sensing that the traditional work model is outdated but unsure of what comes next.

At the same time, the future of work is shifting rapidly. AI and automation could drastically reduce the need for human labor. But we aren't there yet, and that uncertainty creates anxiety. Will work truly become optional? Will society adapt, or will inequality and resistance keep us clinging to the old system?

This liminal phase is unsettling because it challenges our identity. Work has been central to our sense of purpose for centuries. If AI handles most tasks, what will we do? Will we find meaning in leisure, creativity, or community, or will we struggle with a loss of structure? These are the questions of a society caught between the past and the future, neither here nor there.

Liminality can be uncomfortable, but it is also where transformation happens. The challenge is not just technological but psychological: how do we let go of old ideas about work and embrace new possibilities? The future is uncertain, but that uncertainty is also where we have the greatest opportunity to redefine what work—and life—should truly be.

Companies are already experimenting with four-day work weeks or reduced hours without sacrificing productivity. There is growing recognition that overwork leads to burnout and diminishing returns. If technological progress continues and economic policies shift to distribute wealth more equitably—perhaps through ideas like universal basic income—then a 15-hour work week could become realistic for some people.

Rather than a total extinction of full-time work, we may instead see a transformation where traditional jobs shrink in scope, shifting towards part-time, freelance, or project-based work. AI and automation will likely augment human workers rather than replace them entirely, and societies may gradually move toward more leisure time, creative pursuits, and entrepreneurship rather than employment being a fundamental necessity for survival. The speed and smoothness of this transition will depend on how governments, corporations, and individuals adapt to the changing economic landscape.

However, whether this will happen by 2030 remains unlikely. The transition to a world where most people work significantly fewer hours would require major economic and social changes, including shifts in policy, corporate behavior, and societal attitudes toward work. While Keynes's vision of a world with drastically reduced work hours is not entirely wrong, it appears that economic structures and human nature have delayed its arrival far beyond his original timeline.

But we might need to re-balance. To keep us from losing our minds.

The Shadow Dream

I started out this chapter referencing Rahaf Harfoush, and how she wrote *Hustle & Float* after getting the Beyoncé coffee mug that stated: 'You have the same amount of hours in a day as Beyoncé.'

The title of the book comes from the adventure sport of White Water Rafting, where people navigate rivers with an inflatable raft, plunging down intense rapids with large drops, massive water flow, huge waves and possibly large rocks and hazards. Super exciting, very intense but also scary and dangerous. It's also a sport that works at dual speed. Sometimes, they will have to paddle in water with no movement for a long period to get to the next rapid. As Rahaf puts it, 'As any experienced river guide will tell you, the ideal trip is comprised of both hustle and floating, a balance between focused exertion and intentional recovery.' You have to hustle, and then float.

Just like Graeber's 'bullshit jobs', Rahaf wrote her book before COVID, and before the rise of AI. But I believe her messages would only have become stronger after these 'Never Normal' plot twists: we need to fundamentally rethink our balance, if we want to find a more humane, more sustainable and more creative way of working and living.

Because even in the age of Generative AI, creativity and innovation remain key for us humans.

History clearly suggests that some of the greatest thinkers and innovators achieved their breakthroughs not through relentless work but through periods of reflection and rest. Da Vinci, Darwin, and Einstein all understood the power of stepping away, of letting ideas incubate, of allowing the mind to wander. True innovation rarely comes from exhaustion. It comes from a mind that is allowed the space to breathe. Just like Beyoncé did.

Incidentally, in today's hustle culture, and perhaps in the zone of liminality, you actually have a large group of people that are disconnecting. *The New York Times* characterized the current state as 'The Age of Anti-Ambition': a period where people are increasingly rejecting traditional career goals, relentless hustle, and the pressure to constantly achieve more. For decades, ambition has been seen as a virtue: climbing the corporate ladder, working long hours, and sacrificing personal time for professional success. But many are now questioning whether this model of work is worth it, especially in a world where burnout is rampant, wages are stagnant, and job security feels increasingly fragile.

Quiet Quitting And Let It Rot

One expression of this shift is 'quiet quitting', a term that gained popularity in recent years. It doesn't mean actually quitting a job but rather rejecting the idea that work should be the central focus of life. People who 'quiet quit' do only what their job requires. No overtime, no extra projects, no unnecessary effort beyond what they are paid for. It is a reaction against the expectation that employees should always go above and beyond, even when there is no reward or recognition. For many, it's a way to reclaim personal time and mental well-being in a system that often demands more than it gives back.

A similar movement has emerged in China, known as 'let it rot' (摆烂, bǎi làn). This phrase reflects a growing disillusionment among young Chinese workers, who see the intense pressure to succeed but feel that no matter how hard they work, they will never get ahead. With skyrocketing housing prices, extreme work cultures like the infamous '996' schedule (9 a.m. to 9 p.m., six days a week), and limited upward mobility, many have chosen to simply disengage. Instead of striving for success, they do the bare minimum and let go of societal expectations, accepting that some things are beyond their control.

Both of these trends represent a deep liminality in the world of work. The old model—where long hours, loyalty, and ambition led to success—is fading, but a clear new model has yet to emerge. People sense that work is changing, that automation and AI might soon reduce the need for human labor, but they don't yet know what that future looks like. In this in-between phase, many are choosing disengagement rather than overcommitment, stepping back rather than burning out. That's exactly what that other movement of 'The Great Detachment' is about: employees feel increasingly disconnected and disengaged from their jobs and employers as they are reporting high rates of stress, exhaustion, and perhaps most notable of all, apathy.

When I interviewed Rahaf about this, she said: 'I was infuriated by the way leaders were describing these phenomena, almost with a sense of contempt for the younger generation. They were completely missing the nuances of a system of hustle culture and performance that is making people emotionally, physically and psychologically ill. It's not that these youngsters don't want to work, or are lazy. It's a sign of something bigger, something profound that I like to call 'The Great Recalibration'. It's the sum of 50 to 60 years of work propaganda that was eroding the quality of life of an entire generation. Worse, we've been creating organizational conditions that were robbing them of the ability to be creative, innovative, strategic and resilient.'

In her book, she describes the current work philosophy as the 'If Then statement of the American Dream'. To be ambitious is a core necessity of our work mythology. Ambition is the gas tank that powers our productivity, it is the motivation that feeds our hustle, it is the force that imposes the pursuit of success above all else. To put it in an 'If Then' statement: 'If you work hard enough, you can achieve Your Full Potential.'

But today, many people are trapped in what she calls the Shadow Dream, the 'reverse If Then statement': if you have NOT achieved your full potential, then you haven't worked hard enough.

Salaryman

In Japan, the term 'salaryman' (サラリーマン, sararīman) refers to a white-collar worker, typically a man, who devotes his life to a company in exchange for job security and social status. The salaryman culture emerged in the post-war economic boom, when lifetime employment, company loyalty, and long working hours became the norm. Being a salaryman was seen as a duty—an expectation rather than a choice—where professional success was tied to personal identity and societal respect.

This culture demands extreme dedication, with employees routinely working late, socializing with colleagues after hours, and prioritizing their job above everything else, including family and health. The workplace is hierarchical, and promotions are often based on seniority rather than merit, encouraging employees to remain in their positions for decades, regardless of job satisfaction.

One of the darkest aspects of this system is 'karōshi' (過労死), which means 'death from overwork'. Karōshi is a well-documented phenomenon in Japan, where excessive work hours lead to fatal health conditions like heart attacks, strokes, and suicides. Driven by both corporate expectations and personal pressure to succeed, employees push themselves to the breaking point, often sleeping only a few hours a night and enduring extreme stress. Cases of karōshi have led to national discussions about work-life balance, and while some reforms have been introduced—such as limiting overtime hours—the deeply ingrained culture of overwork remains difficult to change.

Japan's salaryman culture is now at a crossroads. Younger generations are increasingly rejecting the rigid expectations of corporate life, questioning whether the sacrifices are worth it. With automation, remote work, and changing societal values, the traditional salaryman model is facing an uncertain future. Like other work cultures around the world, it exists in a liminal state—caught between an exhausting past and an undefined future.

Mind-Wandering, Door Handles And Rebalancing

I fully endorse Rahaf's fundamental idea: we have to rebalance. We need to enjoy the hustle, and use that intensity to boost productivity, but we also need to 'float', to foster creativity.

Jeff Bezos calls it 'mind wandering'—the kind of unstructured thinking that allows for creativity, problem-solving, and deep insight. Despite being one of the most successful entrepreneurs of the modern era, Bezos emphasized that some of his best ideas didn't come from packed schedules, high-pressure meetings, or grinding away at work. Instead, they emerged from moments of 'mental drift', where his mind was free to explore without immediate purpose or constraint.

Bezos described how he actively protects time for this type of thinking, resisting the cultural obsession with constant productivity. He avoids back-to-back meetings and allows himself space in the morning to just think. To him, this isn't laziness; it's a necessary ingredient for innovation. The most profound ideas often come not when one is intensely focused on a problem, but when the mind is given permission to roam freely, making unexpected connections and insights.

This idea stands in sharp contrast to the way most of us structure our days. Modern work culture is built on efficiency, deadlines, and non-stop engagement. The pressure to be constantly 'on' has left little room for moments of unstructured thought. Even outside of work, we fill every spare second with digital distractions—scrolling through social media, answering emails, consuming endless streams of information. There is little opportunity for the mind to simply float.

Rebalancing Time

The challenge ahead isn't just about 'reducing work'; it's about 'rebalancing time'. The future won't be shaped by those who simply work harder but by those who make space for deep thought, for wandering and for floating. It's in these moments of pause that we might discover not just what we want to do—but who we want to be.

I personally, absolutely need the 'floating' periods myself, to keep sane, and to recharge my mental batteries.

Some might argue I have one of the least structured jobs in the world. Many follow my LinkedIn posts and see my life as a series of jet-setting trips around the globe, visiting companies in exciting places, talking to interesting people, and giving speeches to audiences around the world. That is absolutely true, but even that has rigor and hustle. It is a life of airports, lounges, taxis, hotels, technical rehearsals and endless Zoom and Teams calls to prepare for keynotes. And it can be grueling.

So, I need to float.

In one of my all-time favorite movies, *Back to the Future*, the antagonist bully Biff Tannen smuggles a copy of *Grays Sports Almanac* statistics to his younger self. I would not even need to give my younger version a whole book when it comes to financial advice, just two pivotal moments: 'Buy Apple Stock in 2000, and buy Bitcoin in 2009.' My future self would be set for life.

But honestly, if I had the extreme luxury and opportunity of passing on any knowledge or wisdom, I probably wouldn't give financial advice. The older I become, the more I find that quality personal 'floating' time might be the most important ingredient to remain mentally sane—an antidote for depression—and the recipe to keep being open to serendipitous encounters, ideas and friendships.

As I wrote earlier, I did startups when I was younger. But earlier, I left out one of the big reasons why I chose the hard startup life, the very pinnacle of 'hustle'.

When I was a young boy, my parents subscribed to *Time* magazine, and I loved reading it. These magazines were a window onto the world, and I read them cover to cover. In October 1990, when I was still in college, *Time* had a cover story on the decline of American car manufacturing. It featured an in-depth analysis of the malaise at the US car companies, deteriorating dinosaurs that could no longer compete with the Japanese disruptors. I will never forget the statement that one of the disgruntled engineers made talking about the corporate bureaucracy at General Motors: 'How would you like to design door handles for the rest of your life?'

I was shocked. My whole life just flashed in front of my eyes: if I pursued a corporate career, I would be designing door handles for the rest of my life. I made a pledge that very day that I would never become a 'salaryman', but would do everything to be creative, innovative and entrepreneurial. That is how I ended up in the world of startups. The most intense hustle there is.

I also realize now that I was quite close to a complete burnout after the three consecutive startups that I did back-to-back in the early part of my career. But I did not recognize it at the time. I would probably have mindlessly jumped into a fourth startup, had my personal entourage not countered that move.

The 'European Dream'

I made a complete switch in life after that moment, and decided to spend more time with my family—certainly during the periods that the kids had vacation. I indulged in a two-month-long vacation during summer, the 'European dream', in the realization that if I had chosen a career as a teacher, for example, I would have had that luxury as well. The summer months were amazing, and spending time with my children had an amazing effect. Before that moment, I took a maximum of two weeks off, and I needed the first week to 'detox' from business stress and routine. And by the second week, I was already getting into the 'I have to get back to the office, my God, how many emails will be waiting for me' mode. But when you have longer periods of rest, that whole paradigm changes. In the beginning, I did it for the kids, but the older I get, the more I realize I was doing it just as much for myself.

I use those periods to do completely different things. Ride my bike, work on the farm, drive my tractor, and lose myself in my absolute true passion in life: woodworking. Over the years I've gotten extremely addicted to working with wood. There are always things on the farm that need to be mended. And the joy of working with tools to turn a piece of wood into a functional item mesmerizes me.

What I realize is that when I'm on my tractor, or working with my miter saw, my mind clears completely, emptied of the day-to-day observations and worries, creating the open mind that allows me to really think again. With a clear head, I find the time to connect the dots that have been drifting in my mind.

There is often such a rush to start working immediately after finishing your studies that you lose yourself in the rat-race, either in startups or traditional careers, 'led' from one milestone to another, dragged from one engagement to another. When business is our social currency, our lives actually become poorer. But finding, crafting, making the time to 'detox'— and to float—is essential.

So for me, next to buying Apple and Bitcoin stock, this would be the one piece of advice I would give my younger self: 'Take the time to be completely disconnected, and that time will pay itself back a hundred times. By all means: learn how to float.'

I should put that on a coffee mug.

tl
dr

When it comes to the world of work, we find ourselves in liminal times, in a state of in-betweenness. We are no longer in the old state but not yet in the new, and are still evolving from industrial-age thinking to a post-industrial mindset. This transition has been unfolding for some time now, but AI has dramatically accelerated its pace and impact. The latter is not only redefining human work and human output (and how we should measure it), but it also forces us to learn and adapt faster than ever. And that puts a lot of pressure on employees. Stress, burnout, a loss of genuine fulfillment and overwork define much of modern life, even though technology has made us more productive than ever. And the uncertainty and volatility of the Never Normal only augments these psychological and emotional challenges.

That's why we have to cultivate a healthier balance between 'hustle' and 'float', two opposing yet equally essential forces in the world of work. Relentless 'hustle' drives growth and achievement, but without moments of 'float', where the mind can rest and wander, creativity and well-being suffer. Productivity at the expense of renewal leads to burnout, while too much ease can stall progress. The key lies in harmonizing both, allowing structured effort to propel us forward while embracing unstructured time to inspire fresh ideas and innovation.

The good news is that, in liminal times, we can still choose our direction. If we find the courage to redefine the whole context of work, then the potential of AI to augment humans, reshape our jobs towards part-time and allow us more leisure time could be huge. That's why it is crucial not to give into fear but cherish active hope that we will be able to design a better world of work. It's about recognizing our current challenges but also acting on them in order to influence the future. And the belief that no matter how difficult the circumstances, effort and adaptability will still lead to progress.

8

Builders And Thinkers

The most exciting phrase to hear in science, the one that heralds new discoveries, is NOT 'Eureka, I've found it', but 'Hey, that's funny…' —ISAAC ASIMOV

Why We Need Engineers

Every year, about 15 million people worldwide graduate in the field of STEM: Science, Technology, Engineering and Mathematics. About one third of that group comes from China, with just under 5 million STEM graduates. India has about half of that number, and the US less than 800,000.

This STEM cohort might all seem like a bunch of nerds to laymen, but the differences between the four separate groups are absolutely vast.

Scientists are the eternal 'why' people—walking around with perpetually furrowed brows, asking questions about everything from why apples fall to why their coffee gets cold. They love designing experiments, even when nobody asks for them, and get disproportionately excited about proving themselves wrong. Their natural habitat is the lab, where they can be found mumbling about control groups and statistical significance while wearing safety goggles that have seen better days.

Technologists, then, are the digital wizards, convinced that every problem in the world can be solved with an app or a piece of code. They survive on a diet of strong coffee, energy drinks and pizza, speaking in a strange dialect filled with acronyms and references to stack overflow. They have strong opinions about tabs versus spaces[46] and will fight to the death over their choice of text editor. Their natural habitat is anywhere with good WiFi and a power outlet.

Engineers are the practical problem solvers who look at a bridge and see a math equation, or at a building and see a physics problem. They're often found carrying suspiciously large calculators, muttering about 'safety factors'. They have an uncanny ability to turn any conversation into a discussion about efficiency and optimization. Their natural habitat is anywhere they can draw free-body diagrams, preferably on the back of a napkin.

Mathematicians exist in a parallel universe where everything is either proven or not proven, with no in-between. They see patterns everywhere and have been known to get emotionally attached to particularly elegant equations. They can spend hours arguing about the beauty of proof and consider 'trivial' to be both a compliment and an insult. Their natural habitat is any space with at least one whiteboard and an endless supply of dry-erase markers.

Despite their differences, these four tribes come together wonderfully in the great STEM ecosystem, united by their shared love of solving problems and their collective inability to explain what they do to their relatives at family gatherings.

I'm an engineer myself. So I'm positively biased towards that particular STEM tribe.

I'd describe it with a dad joke:

A pessimist sees a dark tunnel.
An optimist sees the light at the end of the tunnel.
A realist sees a freight train coming.
An engineer sees three possible solutions to build a better tunnel.

Engineers are builders. And if you don't have them, you can get into a lot of trouble.

The Trebuchet Humiliation

The Spanish conquest of the 'New World' was one of the most dramatic and consequential episodes in human history. Led by men like Hernán Cortés and Francisco Pizarro, the conquistadors arrived on foreign shores with a mix of ambition, greed, and religious zeal. They sought gold, glory, and the spread of Christianity, toppling powerful empires with a combination of superior weaponry, strategic alliances, and the devastating effects of European diseases. One of the most famous episodes of this conquest was the siege of Tenochtitlan in 1521, where Cortés and his men sought to bring down the mighty Aztec Empire.

The city of Tenochtitlan, the jewel of the Aztec world, was an engineering marvel. Built on an island in the middle of Lake Texcoco, it was a formidable stronghold. Its intricate system of canals, causeways, and aqueducts made it difficult for an enemy to approach, let alone besiege. The Spanish, despite their steel weapons, horses, and firearms, faced an overwhelming challenge in taking the city. They needed to breach its defenses, but their cannons—limited in number and effectiveness in the watery terrain—were insufficient. In desperation, they decided to build a medieval trebuchet to hurl projectiles over the city's walls.

Sounds like a great plan.

The decision to construct a trebuchet was a brilliant attempt at battlefield innovation, but it was doomed from the start. Trebuchets, though powerful siege weapons, required careful design, precise counterweights, and a profound knowledge of trajectory physics. The Spanish, however, had not brought their military engineers with them on this expedition. Lacking proper expertise, they improvised, relying on memory, intuition, and whatever sketches they could recall. The result was a towering structure that, at least in appearance, seemed capable of launching destruction upon the Aztecs.

So, in essence, they 'winged' it. Their thinking was, 'How hard can it be to build a trebuchet? We don't need the engineers.'

Right.

When the moment of truth arrived, the Spanish loaded the trebuchet with a heavy projectile and released the mechanism. Instead of launching forward, the stone shot almost vertically straight up into the air. For a brief moment, it seemed suspended in the sky before gravity took over. Kind of like the coyote in the classic *Road Runner* cartoons.

The projectile then came crashing down with full force—not onto the Aztec city, but directly onto the trebuchet itself, smashing the structure to a million pieces. According to both Spanish chronicles and Aztec records, the failure was immediate and humiliating. Rather than terrorizing their enemy, the Spanish had provided them with an unintended spectacle of incompetence.

This incident serves as a striking example of the unpredictable nature of innovation. It underscores the importance of expertise in technological development. The Spanish dismissed the need for the engineers on their conquest, and their attempt to improvise a complex siege weapon ended in absolute disaster. Yet, failure is often a necessary step on the path to success. Even in the modern world, innovation is frequently preceded by setbacks, miscalculations, and trial-and-error learning. From the Wright brothers' failed early flight attempts to the repeated misfires of early space exploration, history is filled with stories where failure became the foundation for eventual triumph.

The trebuchet debacle during the siege of Tenochtitlan is more than just an amusing historical anecdote; it is a lesson in the perils and possibilities of invention. It demonstrates that knowledge, not just ambition, is key to progress. It reminds us that while boldness and improvisation are valuable, they must be paired with understanding to achieve meaningful success. The Spanish, despite their missteps, ultimately conquered Tenochtitlan. Yet their moment of embarrassment at the hands of their own trebuchet stands as a testament to the enduring truth that even the most powerful can stumble when they step beyond their expertise.

It also teaches us that you shouldn't leave the engineers at home.

The Disastrous Darien Scheme

The late 17th century was a time of immense change and economic ambition in Europe. Empires stretched across the globe, and the great powers of that age—Spain, France, England, and the Dutch Republic—competed fiercely for trade routes and colonial wealth. Scotland, however, remained an outlier. Though an independent kingdom, it was smaller, poorer, and increasingly overshadowed by its powerful neighbor, England. Yet, in the 1690s, a grand vision took hold: Scotland would establish its own overseas empire, transforming itself into a wealthy global power. This vision became known as the 'Darien Scheme'—a bold but disastrous attempt to establish a Scottish colony in the Isthmus of Panama.

The idea was the brainchild of William Paterson, a Scottish financier who had been one of the key founders of the Bank of England. He proposed that Scotland could break free from English economic dominance by controlling a crucial trade route between the Atlantic and Pacific Oceans. Long before the construction of the Panama Canal, the narrow strip of land known as the Darien Gap was recognized as THE potential gateway for global commerce. A colony there, it was believed, would allow Scotland to control trade between the two great oceans, enriching the nation and securing its place among the great European powers.

Sounds like a great plan.

The plan was wildly ambitious—and also wildly popular. The Scots went nuts about the idea. Scotland had suffered a series of economic hardships, including famines and trade restrictions imposed by England. The Darien Scheme was seen as the country's great hope. Public enthusiasm reached a fever pitch, and a massive portion of Scotland's wealth was poured into the super ambitious venture. Ordinary citizens, aristocrats, and the government all invested, convinced that Scotland was on the verge of a golden age. It was a textbook case of the madness of crowds—a speculative bubble driven by national pride, desperation, and blind optimism.

If we pull this off, we'll eat like kings.

In 1698, the first fleet set sail for Panama. It carried 1,200 settlers, a mix of soldiers, merchants, and adventurers, all convinced they were about to establish Scotland's own global empire. The reality was far bleaker. The settlers arrived in an inhospitable, mosquito-infested jungle. The land was difficult to cultivate, fresh water was scarce, and diseases such as malaria and dysentery quickly took hold. The local indigenous tribes, already wary of European encroachment, were hostile, and Spain—who still claimed control over the region—viewed the Scots as trespassers. Trade agreements with other European powers never materialized, largely because England, fearful of offending Spain, forbade its merchants from assisting the colony.

How Scotland Merged With England

Within a year, the settlement was in absolute ruins. More than half of the colonists had died from disease and starvation. Desperate survivors abandoned the colony and fled, some back to Scotland, others to English-controlled Jamaica. Unaware of the disaster, however, a second wave of Scottish settlers arrived in 1699—only to find death and despair awaiting them. Spanish forces, seeing the weakened state of the Scottish outpost, launched attacks. The settlers, now reduced to starving remnants, surrendered and abandoned Darien for good. The grand Scottish dream had collapsed into one of the greatest financial disasters in the nation's history.

The consequences of the failure were devastating. Scotland had invested an estimated 20% of its total wealth in the Darien Scheme. Entire families were financially ruined. The national economy teetered on the brink of collapse. As the country fell into despair, England saw an opportunity. A few years later, in 1707, the Act of Union was signed, officially merging Scotland and England into the Kingdom of Great Britain. One of the key motivators behind the Union was economic necessity—England agreed to bail out the Scottish elites who had lost fortunes in Darien. The failed colony, meant to secure Scotland's independence, had instead sealed its fate as part of the British Empire.

The Darien Scheme showed that when national pride and blind optimism collide with harsh economic reality, the results can be catastrophic. The Scottish people had bet everything on a dream, and when it crumbled, they had no choice but to surrender their independence in exchange for survival. It is one of history's great ironies that Scotland's greatest gamble for global power led directly to its absorption into another empire.

Yet, in another twist, the very same Act of Union that ended Scotland's sovereignty would later open doors for Scots to play a disproportionate role in the expansion and administration of the British Empire.[47] From military officers to industrialists, Scottish influence within Britain's global dominion would grow—not through conquest, but through the very empire that had absorbed it.

Still, the grand vision of using the Panama isthmus (by the way, the word isthmus comes from the Greek word isthmos, which means 'neck') to completely transform global trade was not wrong. It just wouldn't be the role of Scotland to unlock that potential.

French Engineering FTW

For a long period of its history, France has been synonymous with military brilliance, cultural sophistication, and above all, engineering prowess. Unlike many of its European rivals, France recognized early on that technological superiority was key to maintaining its position as a dominant power. The country's military victories, colonial expansion, and industrial achievements were underpinned by a tradition of rigorous education in science and engineering.

The École Polytechnique, founded in 1794 in the wake of the French Revolution, was one of the most remarkable institutions of its time. In fact, it still is the most prestigious engineering school in France today.[48] Unlike traditional universities, which focused on classical learning, the École Polytechnique trained engineers, mathematicians, and physicists specifically for military and state service. Its graduates applied their knowledge to everything from fortifications and artillery design to roads, bridges, and hydraulic systems. Napoleon Bonaparte, ever the pragmatist, understood that France's ability to outmaneuver its enemies relied as much on logistics and engineering as on battlefield strategy. His armies marched on roads built by Polytechnique-trained engineers, crossed rivers on quickly assembled pontoon bridges, and deployed superior artillery that had been mathematically optimized for accuracy and range.

This engineering mindset persisted long after Napoleon's fall. While other European powers relied on inherited wealth or sheer manpower to sustain their empires, France consistently turned to science and engineering to maintain its influence. Nowhere was this more apparent than in the grand infrastructure projects of the 19th century—projects that would shape global trade, politics, and economics. The most ambitious of them all was, by far, the Suez Canal.

By the mid-19th century, global commerce was booming. The old trade routes, which required European ships to sail around the entire continent of Africa to reach Asia, were slow and costly. A canal connecting the

Mediterranean to the Red Sea—and by extension, Europe to India and the Far East—had been imagined for centuries but was deemed impossible due to the vast desert landscapes and shifting sands of Egypt.

A 19th Century Elon Musk

Then came Ferdinand de Lesseps, a French diplomat with no formal engineering training but an uncanny ability to make the impossible happen. Through a mix of political maneuvering, charisma, and sheer determination, he secured permission from the Egyptian government to undertake what many believed to be a fool's errand: digging a 160-kilometer waterway through desert and swamp, with no natural rivers to assist in excavation.

From the start, the engineering challenges were immense. Unlike canals in Europe, which could rely on existing rivers or lock systems, the Suez Canal had to be dug straight through solid land, across inhospitable desert terrain where temperatures soared to unbearable levels. There was also the problem of water supply—not for the canal itself, but for the tens of thousands of workers laboring in absolutely brutal circumstances.

Initially, much of the work was done by hand, with Egyptian laborers digging and hauling sand under unbearable conditions. Disease, exhaustion, and poor nutrition led to the deaths of thousands. But as the project wore on, the French engineers applied revolutionary new techniques, including steam-powered dredgers and excavation machines, vastly accelerating the process. They created artificial lakes to supply water, designed intricate systems to manage shifting sand dunes, and developed techniques to stabilize the canal's edges.

The French engineering culture was at the very pinnacle of its power.

Beyond engineering, the logistics of the project were staggering. Supplies had to be brought in from across Europe, vast quantities of food and medical care had to be organized, and political opposition—both from the British, who feared French control of a key trade route, and from Egyptian nationalists—had to be carefully managed. Despite these challenges, after ten grueling years, the Suez Canal was finally completed in 1869.

It was truly a brand new 'Wonder of the World'.[49]

The impact was immediate and revolutionary. Suddenly, ships no longer had to endure the treacherous and time-consuming journey around the Cape of Good Hope. The journey from London to Bombay was cut from three months to three weeks. The canal quickly became one of the most strategic waterways in the world, completely shifting the balance of power in global trade.

The Suez Canal was more than just a feat of engineering. It was a statement of French ingenuity and ambition. It was proof that technology, innovation, planning, and sheer determination could fundamentally reshape the world. It demonstrated the power of engineers as empire-builders, rivaling even the great military conquests of the past. The legacy of Suez would echo in later French engineering marvels, from the Eiffel Tower to the TGV high-speed trains.

France was on a roll. De Lesseps was the Elon Musk of his time, harnessing the power of innovation and engineering to change the very nature of the world.

But let's go back to Panama to find out if the French could succeed where the Scots had utterly failed.

The Dream That Became A Nightmare

Buoyed by the success of the Suez Canal, Ferdinand de Lesseps had become a global icon, a man whose name was synonymous with engineering triumph. He had defied skeptics, conquered the desert, and forever altered global trade. In the 1880s, he was ready for his next challenge—a canal through the Isthmus of Panama, linking the Atlantic and Pacific Oceans. If the Suez Canal had united Europe and Asia, the Panama Canal would unite the world. De Lesseps was convinced that he could repeat his Suez trick in Panama.

The logic seemed sound. At first glance, Panama was even shorter than Suez—just 80 kilometers from ocean to ocean, barely half the length of the Suez Canal. The plan was simple: dig a sea-level canal straight through the isthmus, just as had been done in Egypt. De Lesseps dismissed warnings from geologists and experts who insisted that Panama was a completely different beast. Where Suez had been a flat desert, Panama was a mountainous, jungle-covered inferno, riddled with rivers, dense vegetation, and an unforgiving tropical climate.

But the French were, well, very French about it.

The French possess a unique cultural trait of intellectual self-assurance. In French culture, this manifests as 'certitude intellectuelle' (intellectual certainty)—a deeply ingrained belief in the superiority of French rational thought and cultural achievements. It's rooted in their Cartesian heritage ('I think, therefore I am') and centuries of being a cultural and intellectual powerhouse in Europe. And that certainly was the case in Panama: the French truly believed that their exceptional engineering prowess alone could solve any challenge. But they were about to face one of the greatest catastrophes in industrial history.

From the moment work began in 1881, everything that could go wrong did go wrong.

The best book on this subject is *The Path Between the Seas: The Creation of the Panama Canal*, by my favorite historical writer David McCullough. He brilliantly describes the absolute disaster that unfolded.

First, there was the jungle itself—a suffocating, humid nightmare, where workers battled not just mud and rock, but relentless downpours, venomous snakes, and disease-carrying insects. The daily rains turned excavation sites into quagmires, with landslides constantly burying equipment, workers, and entire sections of the canal. Unlike in Suez, where dredgers could simply cut through sand, Panama was composed of hard volcanic rock and unpredictable clay, requiring explosives and vastly more effort.

Then there was disease—an invisible enemy deadlier than any engineering challenge. Malaria and yellow fever ravaged the workforce. Workers arrived healthy and full of hope, only to be struck down within days by fever, chills, and agonizing death. Entire hospitals overflowed with the sick and dying, their bodies piling up faster than they could be buried. The canal route was dotted with mass graves, with thousands of laborers succumbing to the merciless conditions.

French engineers, steeped in their traditions of mechanical and structural mastery, had no understanding of tropical medicine. At the time, no one knew that mosquitoes were the carriers of malaria and yellow fever. Instead, doctors wrongly believed the diseases came from 'bad air' (miasma), leading to completely ineffective health measures. They ordered workers to sleep indoors with windows shut, unwittingly trapping them in mosquito-infested rooms.

The French hospitals in Panama had also become death traps, though not for reasons anyone understood at the time. In an attempt to protect patients from the constant plague of ants, hospital staff placed the legs of hospital beds in containers of water. This seemingly logical solution—creating moats to prevent ants from climbing up—inadvertently created perfect breeding grounds for *Anopheles* mosquitoes, the carriers of malaria. Every bed essentially sat in the middle of four mosquito nurseries, exposing already weakened patients to even more disease-carrying insects.

The death toll was staggering. Of the 22,000 workers who took part in the project, an estimated 20,000 perished, a casualty rate of almost 90%. Entire labor forces had to be constantly replaced. Workers, mostly from the Caribbean, quickly realized that signing up for the canal meant almost certain death. Recruitment became nearly impossible, and desperation set in among the project leaders.

Even if disease had not wiped out the workforce, the engineering itself was an absolute catastrophe as well. De Lesseps, believing that a sea-level canal like Suez was the only way, ignored the warnings of experts who suggested an elevated, lock-based system to navigate Panama's mountainous terrain. As a result, his engineers were forced to dig ever deeper into the jungle and rock, creating enormous, unstable excavation sites.

One of the biggest obstacles was the Culebra Cut, a stretch of land that required excavation to create a passage through the continental divide. The deeper the French dug, the more unstable the soil became. Landslides buried thousands of workers and tons of machinery under millions of cubic meters of mud. Entire weeks of work could be erased in a single night as rain-soaked earth collapsed back into the trenches.

By 1888, the Panama project was in total ruins. The cost had spiraled out of control, the workforce was decimated, and investors—who had poured millions into what they thought would be another Suez—began to panic. De Lesseps, now in his 80s, refused to admit defeat. Very French pride indeed.

He launched a desperate fundraising campaign, selling more bonds and promising that success was just around the corner. But public confidence had shattered. The once-revered hero of Suez was now seen as a reckless gambler, and the financial scandal that followed became one of the biggest corruption cases in French history.

The Panama Canal Company collapsed in 1889, declaring bankruptcy. Over 800,000 investors—many of them ordinary French citizens—lost their life savings in what became known as the Panama Affair. The scandal rocked France to its core, implicating politicians, bankers, and industrialists in a web of bribery and fraud. De Lesseps himself, along with his son and several associates, was convicted of fraud and sentenced to prison, though his sentence was later overturned. He died in disgrace in 1894, his dreams of another Suez buried along with thousands of workers in the Panamanian jungle.

Uncle Sam's Panama Power Play

The French failure in Panama is one of history's most spectacular engineering disasters: a lesson in hubris, ignorance, and the limits of human ambition. Unlike in Suez, where natural conditions were favorable, Panama was an entirely different battlefield; one where nature, disease, and terrain fought back at every turn. De Lesseps, blinded by his past success, ignored the warnings, dismissed the experts, and refused to adapt. The French conquered the desert with Suez. But in Panama, the jungle conquered them.

In the early 1900s, the United States, under the guidance of President Theodore Roosevelt, started to develop an appetite to take on the challenge that had broken the French.

By the early 20th century, the United States had emerged as the world's new industrial and engineering powerhouse. The country had rapidly advanced in mechanization, large-scale infrastructure, and industrial efficiency. Railroads spanned the North American continent, skyscrapers were beginning to rise in cities like New York and Chicago, and American factories were producing steel, machinery, and technology on an unprecedented scale. The US was no longer just an emerging economy—it was the new center of global innovation.

More importantly, the Americans had learned from the failures of the French. They understood the limits of human labor, the harsh realities of Panama's environment, and the necessity of scientific knowledge to overcome the deadly obstacles that had plagued de Lesseps' project. Where the French had relied on brute force, naïve optimism and arrogance, the Americans relied on planning, industrial power, and medical science.

The greatest killer in Panama was not the terrain—it was disease. Malaria and yellow fever had decimated the French workforce, but when the Americans arrived, they had a secret weapon: Dr. William C. Gorgas.

By the early 1900s, scientists had finally discovered that mosquitoes were responsible for transmitting both diseases. This breakthrough in medical science allowed Gorgas and his team to launch the first large-scale anti-mosquito campaign in history. They drained swamps, fumigated homes, installed mosquito netting, and even bred mosquito-eating fish in standing water. It was one of the most ambitious public health efforts ever attempted, and it worked. Malaria cases dropped dramatically, and yellow fever was completely eradicated in Panama by 1906.[50]

This was an absolute turning point. For the first time, the canal zone was no longer a death trap. Workers could now survive, and that alone gave the Americans a huge advantage over the French. But, unlike the French, who had relied heavily on manual labor, the Americans fully embraced mechanization. By 1904, industrial technology had advanced to the point where massive steam shovels, dynamite, and locomotive-powered excavation trains could be used to move millions of tons of earth.

As established earlier, the Culebra Cut—where the French had suffered endless landslides—was one of the biggest obstacles of the canal project. The Americans, using dynamite and mechanized excavation, were able to blast through the mountains and remove rock at a much faster rate. Instead of men with shovels, entire mountainsides were being carved away by giant machines. The sheer scale of American industrial power was unmatched.

Additionally, the Americans built hydraulic locks—a concept the French had rejected. Instead of trying to dig a sea-level canal, they constructed a series of giant locks that would raise and lower ships over the difficult terrain. This decision essentially saved the project.

The Americans also had something the French lacked: brilliant leadership. President Theodore Roosevelt, a strong believer in American expansion and engineering dominance, made the canal a national priority. He personally visited Panama in 1906—the first sitting US president to leave the country—to rally support for the project.

He appointed John Frank Stevens, a brilliant civil engineer, to redesign the entire project. Stevens reorganized the workforce, modernized equipment, and introduced railway systems to transport materials. Later, Colonel George Washington Goethals took over and oversaw the final construction, ensuring that the locks and water systems worked perfectly.

The combination of scientific breakthroughs, industrial power, and effective leadership was what set the Americans apart. And by 1914—just 10 years after they took control of the project—the Panama Canal was finally complete. The opening of the Panama Canal on August 15, 1914, was an absolute turning point in world history. The canal cut the maritime distance between the east and west coasts of the Americas by thousands of miles. Before its completion, a ship traveling from New York to San Francisco had to go around the entire continent of South America, a 13,000-mile journey. After the canal, the same trip was just 5,200 miles—less than half the distance.

Shrinking The Planet

The impact on global trade and geopolitics was enormous. Trade became faster, cheaper, and way more efficient. The canal allowed ships to transport goods between the Atlantic and Pacific in record time, truly transforming global commerce. And it also insured that the United States became the dominant power in the Western Hemisphere. The canal gave the US a massive strategic naval advantage, allowing its fleet to move quickly between oceans, strengthening its military and economic influence.

The Panama Canal became one of the most important waterways in the world. Much like the Suez Canal had revolutionized trade between Europe and Asia, the Panama Canal reshaped world trade between the East and West. Countries like Japan, China, and Australia gained easier access to American and European markets.

In many ways, the canal shrank the planet, bringing nations closer, accelerating trade, and making the world more interconnected than ever before. It was one of the greatest engineering feats of all time—an achievement that proved that with the right combination of science, industry, and leadership, even the most impossible dreams could be realized.

The Panama Canal was more than just a waterway. It was a symbol of human triumph over nature. Where the French had failed, the Americans had succeeded, not because they were smarter, but because the world had changed. The age of mechanization, medical science, and industrial organization had arrived, and the Panama Canal was its crowning achievement.

The completion of the Panama Canal marked the dawn of a new era. Just as the French had once led the world in engineering, now the Americans had taken their place. The Industrial Revolution had reached its peak, and the US was now the undisputed leader in large-scale engineering projects.

The pattern here is very clear: whoever has the best engineering capabilities has the chance to control the world and change its destiny. The success of the canal showed that engineering was no longer just about skill and knowledge—it was about industrial power, scientific progress, and national will. From that moment forward, the United States was not just an economic giant, but the absolute technological superpower. On top of the world.

Until Sputnik.

Beep, Beep, Beep

On October 4, 1958, a tiny metallic sphere, barely the size of a basketball, soared into orbit above the Earth. It was called 'Sputnik 1', and it was the first artificial satellite ever launched into space. The launch itself was simple—no cameras, no advanced sensors, just a 23-inch aluminum sphere with four spindly radio antennas, broadcasting a steady beep-beep-beep from orbit. But to the world, and especially to the United States, those beeps sounded like an air raid siren.

The Soviet Union had beaten the United States into space, and that realization sent a shockwave through American society. The Cold War had long been a battle of ideology—capitalism vs. communism, democracy vs. dictatorship—but now, it was clear that it was also a battle of technology. The US had been caught off guard, and for the first time, the American public was forced to ask a terrifying question:

Had the Soviets surpassed America in science and engineering?

The reaction was immediate and visceral. Newspapers called it a 'technological Pearl Harbor', and Americans watched in horror as Soviet rockets seemed to leap ahead in capability. Just one month later, the USSR launched Sputnik 2, this time carrying a living creature—Laika, the space dog—proving that not only could they put objects into orbit, but they were already testing how to send humans into space.

By contrast, the United States' first response was a national embarrassment. The rushed launch of Vanguard TV3, the first American attempt at putting a satellite into orbit, ended in disaster. On live television, with cameras broadcasting to millions of Americans, the rocket lifted a few feet off the launch pad, exploded, and crumbled into a heap of smoldering debris.

The United States had lost the first battle of the space race, and worse, the rest of the world had seen it.

Sputnik wasn't just about space. It was about national security, military dominance, and scientific and technological supremacy. The fact that the USSR could launch a satellite into space meant they had rockets powerful enough to launch nuclear weapons across the globe. The Cold War had suddenly reached a terrifying new level.

DARPA And NDEA

The response from Washington was swift and decisive. America would never again allow itself to be technologically outpaced by its enemies. From this crisis, two monumental changes emerged: DARPA, and a revolution in how America would develop talent.

Just months after Sputnik's launch, the US government created DARPA (Defense Advanced Research Projects Agency). Its mission was simple but radical: ensure that the United States would never again be technologically surprised by its enemies. It would operate outside of the traditional military bureaucracy, with direct access to the most brilliant minds in America. Its goal was to fund cutting-edge research in military and defense technology, staying one step ahead of the Soviets—and eventually, the rest of the world.

And it had virtually unlimited budgets.

From its inception, DARPA became the secret weapon of American technological dominance. Over the next few decades, it would lay the groundwork for some of the most important inventions in modern history, including the Internet itself (originally called ARPAnet), stealth technology, GPS navigation and even the development of artificial intelligence and machine learning.

The logic behind DARPA was clear: whoever controlled the most advanced technology would control the battlefield of the future.

But there was more.

Sputnik had also revealed a deep, structural weakness in American society: the USSR was producing better scientists, engineers, and mathematicians than the United States. (And better language students as well, so they had better spies that could speak other languages fluently.)

The Soviet education system had been designed to create experts in science and technology. From a young age, Soviet students were drilled in mathematics, physics, and engineering. Their universities were rigorous, their research institutions were state-funded, and the brightest Soviet students were identified early and funneled into elite scientific programs.

By contrast, American education was massively failing to produce enough scientists and engineers. Schools were underfunded, curricula were outdated, and many American students struggled with basic math and science. Worse, there was a perception that the US education system wasn't preparing enough students for national security-related fields, including cryptography, aerospace, and military technology.

The response was the National Defense Education Act (NDEA) of 1958, a sweeping reform that would reshape American education. It pumped billions of dollars into science and engineering education. It created federal scholarships and student loan programs for math, science, and foreign language students. The act massively increased funding for high school and university science labs, actively promoted early STEM education and drastically increased training for teachers in mathematics, physics, and engineering.

This was more than just an education policy—it was a national security strategy. The US could not afford to fall behind again. America needed to train a new generation of scientists and engineers who could win the space race and defend the nation against future technological threats.

And it worked.

Turning A Crisis Into An Advantage

The Sputnik Crisis of 1958 was one of the most important moments in modern history. It triggered a technological arms race that would eventually lead to the US beating the Russians to the moon in 1969, and reclaim the space race. But it was also the fundamental driver behind the rise of Silicon Valley. The investments made in engineering and science education in the 1960s and '70s directly contributed to the birth of modern computing, creating a pipeline of innovation that led to the personal computer revolution, the birth of the internet, and the rise of digital technology.

Perhaps even more importantly, Sputnik changed the way nations think about science and technology. It proved that the most powerful country in the world is not just the one with the most weapons—but the one with the best scientists, engineers, and innovators.

Today, Silicon Valley is still fueled by the same forces that emerged in the wake of Sputnik: a relentless drive for technological supremacy, an insatiable appetite for innovation, and an unspoken but ever-present relationship with the US government and its defense agencies. The very institutions that were born out of America's desperation to outpace the Soviet Union—DARPA, NASA, and the National Science Foundation—continue to shape the technological landscape, influencing everything from artificial intelligence and cybersecurity to biotechnology and quantum computing.

Venture capitalists, once purely driven by market potential and disruption, are now thinking in terms of geopolitical strategy. Today, there is a new undercurrent of paranoia, similar to the one in the Cold War with Russia: a belief that the US cannot afford another 'Sputnik moment', but with China. The fear is that China, with its aggressive AI development and state-backed tech initiatives, could leap ahead in artificial intelligence, quantum computing, or cyber warfare, just as the Soviets once did with Sputnik. That's why the DeepSeek moment hit so hard, as I explained earlier. So investors and policymakers alike are scrambling to prevent Chinese supremacy from happening, pumping billions into next-generation chips, defense AI, and space (and AI) infrastructure.

The sentiment in Silicon Valley today is one of urgency: a recognition that technology is now the defining factor in global dominance again.

And Andreessen is one of the most interesting players in this new theater.

An Advocate For Technological Acceleration

Marc Andreessen is one of the most influential figures in modern technology, a man whose career spans the birth of the internet, the meteoric rise of venture capital, and the intersection of software and national strategy. From a young programmer in the Midwest to the co-founder of Andreessen Horowitz (a16z)[51]—one of Silicon Valley's most powerful investment firms—his journey is a blueprint of how vision, timing, and relentless execution can shape entire industries.

Andreessen was born in Cedar Falls, Iowa, in 1971, and grew up in New Lisbon, Wisconsin, a small town far removed from the emerging tech hubs of the world. But what he lacked in proximity to Silicon Valley, he made up for in curiosity and raw talent. As a child, he was captivated by technology, teaching himself to program and exploring the early frontiers of computing before most people even knew what a PC was.

He went on to study computer science at the University of Illinois at Urbana-Champaign, a school that was not traditionally associated with startup culture but had one crucial advantage: it was home to the National Center for Supercomputing Applications (NCSA). It was there, in the early 1990s, that Andreessen and a small team of developers would create the software that would ignite the first internet revolution.

While at NCSA, Andreessen co-created Mosaic, one of the first graphical web browsers. At the time, the internet was mostly text-based, used by academics and government researchers. The idea of a user-friendly browser that could display images and be accessible to the masses was groundbreaking.

Mosaic's intuitive design and point-and-click interface made the web accessible to the public, and Andreessen immediately recognized its potential. After graduating in 1993, he moved to Silicon Valley, where he met Jim Clark, a legendary entrepreneur who had previously founded Silicon Graphics (SGI). Together, they launched Netscape Communications Corporation in 1994, with the goal of turning Mosaic into a commercial product.

And boy, did that turn out to be a home run.

The Poster Child Of The Dot-Com Bubble

The result was Netscape Navigator, a web browser that became the default gateway to the internet for millions of users for the first time. The timing was perfect: the internet was beginning to explode ('cyberspace', remember?), and Netscape was at the very center of that storm. By 1995, it went public in one of the most legendary IPOs in Silicon Valley history, with its stock price soaring 150% on the first day of trading. This moment is widely regarded as the beginning of the dot-com boom. And Marc became the poster child of that bubble.

Dominance is never permanent in tech. In 1995, Microsoft entered the fray, launching their 'Internet Explorer' and aggressively bundling it with Windows. This led to the infamous 'Browser Wars', where Microsoft's sheer market power crushed Netscape's early lead.[52] By the late 1990s, Netscape was struggling, and in 1998, it was eventually acquired by AOL for $4.2 billion. The acquisition was supposed to be a win, but it soon became clear that Netscape was fading into history.

But it made Andreessen a very wealthy man.

Despite the fall of Netscape, Andreessen didn't slow down. He had learned a crucial lesson from the browser wars: platforms win, and infrastructure matters. In 1999, he co-founded LoudCloud, a company focused on cloud computing and enterprise software—years ahead of its time. It eventually pivoted into Opsware, a company that pioneered automated data center management. This was a completely different type of business—less flashy than Netscape, but far more foundational. It was about enterprise infra-structure, automation, and software eating the world from the inside out.

In 2007, Hewlett-Packard (HP) acquired Opsware for $1.6 billion, marking Andreessen's second major startup exit. But more importantly, Opsware had solidified his working relationship with Ben Horowitz, his co-founder and trusted partner.

That relationship was not always a bed of roses. While Marc was the in-ternationally recognized visionary and guru, jet-setting the world to talk about the future, Ben was running the operations back home. That creat-ed some tension, and at one point Ben vowed he would never work with the 'Prima Donna' Marc Andreessen again.[53]

Funny how that turned out.

a16z Is Eating The World

Ben Horowitz was not just another co-founder—he was a pragmatist, an operator, and a deep thinker on leadership and business strategy. While Andreessen was the visionary and software evangelist, Horowitz was the guy who knew how to actually run companies and manage teams under pressure. Their complementary styles made them a formidable duo, and after selling Opsware, they wanted to help in shaping the next wave of founders and innovators.

So in 2009, they launched Andreessen Horowitz (a16z), a venture capital firm built on a unique philosophy. Unlike traditional VC firms that focused purely on funding, a16z positioned itself as a hands-on, founder-friendly firm, offering operational support, access to talent, and strategic guid-ance. Their motto was simple but powerful: 'Software is eating the world.'

This was more than just a slogan—it was a fundamental belief that every industry, from finance to healthcare to defense, would eventually be dom-inated by software-driven companies. They wanted to fund the builders of this future, and they moved aggressively, investing in some of the big-gest names of the modern era: Facebook, Twitter, Airbnb, Slack, Coinbase, Stripe and OpenAI.

Not a bad list.

Today, Andreessen Horowitz is one of the most influential venture firms on the planet, managing over $35 billion in assets and expanding beyond software into crypto, AI, biotech, and even defense technology. In many ways, Andreessen's trajectory mirrors the larger shifts in Silicon Valley. He started in consumer technology, evolved into enterprise infrastructure, and is now deeply involved in national security, AI, and the future of computing—the very same areas that DARPA and the US government are prioritizing in the new technological arms race.

Andreessen himself has become an extremely vocal advocate for technological acceleration, frequently arguing that the US needs to embrace risk, invest in moonshot projects, and maintain its lead in AI, space, and defense tech. And he wrote those ideas into a manifesto.

The Techno-Optimist Manifesto

His worldview is rooted in radical optimism, an unshakable belief that technology is the fundamental force driving human prosperity, growth, and civilization itself. In late 2023, he published his 'Techno-Optimist Manifesto', a bold and sweeping declaration of why technology is good, why we need more of it, and why those who stand in its way are holding humanity back.

At its core, the manifesto is a counterattack against pessimism and stagnation. Andreessen argues that too much of today's discourse—whether in politics, academia, or the media—is dominated by fear, regulation, and a deep suspicion of technological change. He believes that 'We are not building fast enough', that society has lost its courage to take risks, and that too many people have become complacent, fearful, and overly focused on hypothetical risks rather than real-world progress.

His vision is unapologetically pro-growth, pro-expansion, and pro-technology. He champions AI, biotechnology, space exploration, and defense technology as the next frontiers that should be aggressively pursued, not feared. He ridicules what he calls the 'anti-progress coalition'—a group he characterizes as bureaucrats, regulators, and intellectuals who impose unnecessary constraints on technological advancement. In his view, these forces have slowed down innovation in many critical fields like nuclear energy, infrastructure, AI, and medical research, leading to a world that is needlessly constrained by scarcity, inefficiency, and outdated thinking.

The manifesto was not without controversy. Critics accused Andreessen of being blind to the risks of unfettered technological acceleration, arguing that his vision ignores the ethical, environmental, and societal consequences of rapid innovation.

One of the most common critiques was that techno-optimism is a form of naive techno-utopianism; a belief that technology will automatically make things better, without considering who controls it, how it is deployed, or who benefits from it. Detractors pointed to AI's potential for mass surveillance, deepfakes, and job displacement, for example, arguing that unregulated technological development could lead to more harm than good. Others raised concerns about biotechnology, warning that human genetic engineering or synthetic biology could have unintended consequences that could be catastrophic for humankind.

Another major critique came from economists and sociologists, who pointed out that while technology has historically driven economic growth, it has also contributed to inequality and destabilization. The rise of automation, robotics and software has already displaced millions of workers, creating winners and losers in the global economy. And this might even become more prominent with the rapid acceleration in the field of AI. Andreessen's manifesto, they argued, was too focused on technological acceleration without addressing the human cost of disruption.

Despite the criticism, Andreessen's fundamental argument remains clear: we need to build more—faster, better, and with fewer restrictions. This idea was first outlined in his famous 2020 essay, 'It's Time to Build', which was written during the early days of the COVID-19 pandemic. At the time, the world was experiencing supply chain breakdowns, medical shortages, and infrastructure failures, exposing deep flaws in how modern society had prioritized efficiency over resilience.

In the essay, Andreessen makes a simple but profound observation: 'We don't have enough of the things we need—because we didn't build them.' Hospitals were overwhelmed because we hadn't built enough capacity. Supply chains collapsed because we hadn't built redundancy. Government institutions were slow and inefficient because they relied on outdated technology. Housing in cities like San Francisco and New York was unaffordable because we hadn't built enough homes.

His conclusion? The only way forward is to stop talking and start building.

Andreessen's call to action is not just about startups or Silicon Valley; it's about a fundamental shift in how society at large approaches growth and progress.

And, at the very core, it illustrates a need for reclaiming ambition. Andreessen believes that society has become cynical and fearful, retreating from big, audacious projects in favor of short-term, risk-averse thinking. He calls for a return to the mindset of the Apollo program—launching the first humans to the moon—where failure was an acceptable price for progress. In his words: 'We Need More Builders, Not Just Thinkers'. He contrasts builders (entrepreneurs, engineers, and scientists) with thinkers (academics, policymakers, and regulators), arguing that the former are the ones who actually move the world forward.

At its core, Andreessen's philosophy is about agency, the belief that humans should shape the future rather than passively react to it. He sees technology as not just a tool, but as the fundamental driver of civilization itself.

Just like his manifesto, Andreessen's vision in general is both inspiring and controversial. To his supporters, he is one of the last true believers in progress, a champion of big ideas, bold action, and technological ambition. To his critics, he is an overly simplistic, hyper-libertarian evangelist for unchecked tech growth, dismissing legitimate concerns about ethics, inequality, and safety.

But regardless of where one stands, Marc Andreessen is shaping the conversation about the future. His influence extends far beyond venture capital, and his ideas are defining the ideological battle over whether society should embrace or resist rapid technological acceleration.

For him, the greatest sin is stagnation, the idea that we should accept the world as it is, rather than strive to make it better. This is why he rails against regulation, pessimism, and bureaucratic inertia. He believes that every great period of human progress—from the Industrial Revolution to the rise of Silicon Valley—was fueled by people who refused to accept limits.

Protopia

Marc Andreessen's techno-optimism does not exist in isolation. It is part of a broader philosophical movement that views technology as an unstoppable, evolutionary force, something that is not just created by humans, but that follows its own internal logic and trajectory.

Earlier, I wrote about my admiration for Kevin Kelly—executive editor of *Wired* magazine and one of the most influential voices in technology philosophy. Few thinkers have explored this idea of tech as an unstoppable force more deeply than he, in 'What Technology Wants': 'Technology is not just a collection of human-made tools—it is a living system, evolving like an organism, shaping itself as much as we shape it.'

He sees technology as an extension of 'biology and evolution'. He calls this 'the 'technium', a term that describes the sum total of all human technology as a self-organizing system. Just as life has a natural drive toward complexity, intelligence, and diversity, so too does technology evolve toward greater interconnectivity, intelligence, and autonomy.

One of Kelly's most important beliefs is called 'protopia', a vision of progress that stands in contrast to both utopian optimism and dystopian pessimism. In his view, the two extremes fall short in establishing a way forward. Utopia is impossible, since a perfect world will never exist because human desires, ambitions, and conflicts are always shifting. At the same time, dystopia is too simplistic: while technology has created new risks, it has also historically improved life across almost every measurable dimension.

So for him, 'protopia' is the real path forward. Instead of a perfect future, protopia is about incremental progress: small, daily improvements which in themselves are almost imperceptible but which compound over time to create huge impact. Kelly argues that the world gets slightly better every year. While the media is flooded with negative headlines about crises, disasters, and failures, the broader trends show that poverty is decreasing, literacy is rising, medicine is improving, and technology is advancing in ways that enhance human potential.

Protopia does not ignore risks, but it rejects the idea that technology is leading us to inevitable collapse. Instead, Kelly believes that the future is a constant work-in-progress—messy, imperfect, and unpredictable, but always moving forward. This idea resonates strongly with what we discussed earlier when we talked about Mustafa Suleyman, co-founder of DeepMind and author of *The Coming Wave*, who has a similar argument: 'Stagnation is the real catastrophe.'

While Marc Andreessen, Kevin Kelly, and Mustafa Suleyman have different backgrounds—venture capital, technology philosophy, and AI entrepreneurship—they all converge on one core belief: the real danger is not progress itself, but the failure to progress. They argue that if we stop innovating, if we allow fear to block technological advances, we will fall into stagnation—and stagnation leads to collapse. They reject the pessimistic narratives that dominate mainstream discussions about AI, automation, and biotech. Instead, they believe in harnessing technology to solve problems, expand human capabilities, and drive civilization forward.

The biggest debate of our time is not just about AI, biotech, or space travel—it is about how we think about progress itself. Should we embrace rapid innovation, knowing it comes with risks? Or should we slow down, fearing that we might create more problems than we solve?

A Man Obsessed With The Future

Few individuals in modern history have wielded as much influence—and controversy—as Elon Musk. To his supporters, he is a genius visionary, the modern 'Da Vinci or Tesla', pushing humanity toward a future of space colonization, AI, electric transportation, and brain-machine interfaces. To his critics, he is an erratic billionaire, recklessly playing with powerful technologies while promoting unfiltered, controversial views on politics, media, and governance.

But one thing is undeniable: Elon Musk is a man obsessed with the future. Unlike most entrepreneurs, who focus on solving market-driven problems, Musk is driven by a deeper existential mission—to ensure the survival of human civilization by pushing the boundaries of technology at an almost frantic pace. He does not see innovation as a luxury but as a necessity. In his mind, the biggest threats to civilization include artificial intelligence, declining birth rates, climate change, energy scarcity, and geopolitical risks.

Above all, he believes that humanity's dependency on a single planet is a civilizational death sentence. His view of the world is one of urgency, a belief that humanity is in a race against time and that technological progress is the only way to prevent catastrophe.

This urgency explains why Musk does not simply run companies; he launches crusades.

Tesla was not just about building electric cars but about forcing the world to transition away from fossil fuels before environmental collapse. SpaceX was not about launching satellites; it was about securing a future for humanity beyond Earth, before war, resource depletion, or existential threats make survival on this planet impossible. Starlink is not merely a business venture but a safeguard against government censorship, ensuring that information remains free and accessible no matter where someone lives. Neuralink is not just about brain-machine interfaces but a defensive measure against the possibility that artificial intelligence could one day outpace human intelligence, leaving us obsolete.

Civilizational Timelines

Unlike most entrepreneurs who operate on market timelines, Musk operates on civilizational timelines. He believes that if we do not act now, we may not get another chance. This sense of urgency is why he takes enormous risks that no rational CEO would take. Tesla was on the brink of collapse in its early years, but Musk bet his entire fortune on its survival, and today it is one of the most valuable car companies in the world. SpaceX should have failed, as no private company had ever successfully launched and landed reusable rockets, but Musk pushed forward, and now it is the dominant force in space exploration. Every single one of his ventures has followed the same pattern—wild ambition, extreme risk-taking, near-failure, and eventual triumph.

With such massive influence comes massive responsibility. Musk is arguably the most powerful technologist alive, and the way he wields that power has made him one of the most polarizing figures in the world. His supporters see him as a heroic figure, an unfiltered genius willing to take risks that no one else dares to. They admire his willingness to challenge conventional wisdom, fight against bureaucracy, and move at a pace that traditional institutions cannot match. His critics, however, argue that he is reckless, impulsive, and too powerful for any one individual. His involvement in AI, automation, social influence and the US government is moving too fast and too unregulated. His tendency to speak without a filter, whether on social media or in public appearances, has led to accusations that he spreads misinformation, engages in political manipulation, and enables toxic discourse.

Despite the controversy, Musk remains undeterred. His philosophy is clear: technological progress is not optional—it is the only way forward. To him, the greatest risk is not moving too fast but moving too slow.

Rational Optimism

Every day, we are bombarded with headlines of uncertainty, crisis, collapse, and catastrophe. Climate change, AI risks, pandemics, social unrest, and economic instability dominate the global conversation. The narrative of our time is one of fear, complexity, and unpredictability—a world in which nothing is stable, where volatility is the only constant, and where the future feels less like an opportunity and more like a looming storm.

It is easy to become overwhelmed. When faced with so many interconnected crises, many people retreat into pessimism and cynicism, believing that we are on a downward spiral, that humanity has peaked, that the best we can do is manage decline. But pessimism is a choice—and it is the wrong one. Throughout history, every great leap forward has been driven not by fear, but by a belief that the future can be better than the present. And that we have the power to shape it. That is what I fundamentally believe with every fiber in my body.

This is why optimism is not just important—it is essential. Not a naive, blind optimism that ignores risks, but a rational optimism, a conviction that problems exist to be solved, that human ingenuity is limitless, and that progress is something we build, not something we wait for. The greatest minds of our time—from Marc Andreessen to Kevin Kelly to Elon Musk—are not just pushing technology forward; they are fighting for a positive narrative of the future. They refuse to accept that we are trapped in a cycle of stagnation and decline. Instead, they argue that humanity is on the cusp of its greatest era, if only we choose to build it.

In this ever accelerating Never Normal, we cannot afford to be passive spectators of the future. As the great thinker Marshall McLuhan famously said, 'There are no passengers on spaceship earth. We are all crew.' We must become architects of progress, embracing the unknown, taking bold risks, and constructing a vision of tomorrow that is worth striving for. Optimism is not just a feel-good idea—it is a survival strategy. Without it, we stagnate. With it, we thrive.

We can't just wait and hope for things to magically come our way. Like the Cargo Cults.

Cargo Cults

It is probably one of my favorite stories, brilliantly told by the luminous physicist and Nobel prize winner Richard Feynman in his famous 1974 Caltech commencement address. The original cargo cults emerged in the remote areas of the South Pacific after World War II, when indigenous peoples observed American military bases receiving supplies by air. These tribes were untouched by civilization and had no idea that there was a World War ongoing.

During the war, these islands had suddenly seen airstrips built, men in uniforms directing planes with landing signals, and cargo planes arriving with vast amounts of material wealth. Every day, cargo planes would drop crate after crate from the sky, filled with rations, chocolate, and everything from condoms to nylon stockings.

After the war ended and the bases were abandoned, some islanders tried to recreate these conditions, building mock airstrips, wooden headphones, and signal fires, even mimicking the movements of landing signal officers—hoping that by recreating the forms and rituals they had observed, they could make the cargo planes return. And hoping to please the Gods so that the supplies would drop again from the sky.

Feynman used this as a metaphor to argue that some scientists were like the cargo cultists—they had all the outward forms of scientific investigation (lab coats, complex equipment, technical language, etc.) but were missing the essential core principle: rigorous scientific integrity and genuine critical inquiry. The key quote from his address was: 'The first principle is that you must not fool yourself—and you are the easiest person to fool.'

Hope may not be a strategy, but neither is pessimism an achievement. From de Lesseps' eventual triumph at Suez to America's mosquito-defeating feat at Panama, from Netscape's browser revolution to SpaceX's reusable rockets, history has shown that the optimists don't always win first, but they tend to win last.

The path of progress is littered with the remnants of failed Scottish colonies, bankrupt French canal companies, and defunct dot-com pioneers. Yet each failure served as fertilizer for future success. The Darien

Scheme's disaster helped birth the British Empire, de Lesseps' Panama fiasco taught Americans what not to do, and Netscape's browser war death planted the seeds for the modern internet economy.

What distinguishes the successful optimists from the failed dreamers isn't their capacity for hope—it's their capacity for learning. They combine the audacity to imagine impossible things with the humility to learn from past failures. They understand that while hope isn't a strategy, it's an essential ingredient in any strategy worth pursuing.

To conclude, I want to zoom in on somebody that I admire greatly, the scientist Jonas Salk, who developed the first successful polio vaccine, and then gave the patent away for free. Salk was born in 1914 into a family of Jewish immigrants in New York City. He grew up in a very modest environment but showed early academic promise, entering college at just 15 years old.

Developing the first successful polio vaccine in 1955 was an enormous scientific breakthrough. When asked who owned the patent, he gave his famous reply: 'There is no patent. Could you patent the sun?' This response encapsulated his broader vision of science serving humanity rather than profit. The vaccine, which could have made him enormously wealthy, was deliberately left unpatented to maximize its accessibility.

Jonas Salk led a remarkable life driven by an expansive vision of human potential and scientific progress. It extended far beyond vaccines to encompass what he called 'biophilosophy'—an attempt to bridge the gap between scientific knowledge and human values. He believed that humanity needed to evolve its wisdom to match its technological capabilities.

One of the most beautiful and inspiring places I have ever visited is the Salk Institute in La Jolla California, just north of San Diego. The campus perfectly reflects his vision. He worked with architect Louis Kahn to create a space that would inspire creativity and contemplation. The building, with its stunning blend of concrete and teak, facing the Pacific Ocean, was designed to be 'worthy of a visit by Picasso'. Salk believed that scientific discovery required not just technical skill but also esthetic sensibility and philosophical depth.

In his later years, he wrote several books exploring the relationship between human evolution and social progress. He was particularly concerned with what he called 'survival of the wisest'—the idea that humanity's future depended not on physical strength or technological prowess alone, but on developing greater wisdom and understanding.

What I admire above all is that Salk maintained an optimistic view of human potential despite witnessing some of humanity's darkest moments through the 20th century. He believed that just as we could develop vaccines against biological viruses, we could also develop 'vaccines' against human destructiveness—through education, understanding, and conscious evolution.

His own life demonstrates how scientific achievement can be driven by and serve a larger humanitarian vision. His vision of science serving humanity, rather than the other way around, offers an important model for modern research and development.

The difference between civilizational decline and civilizational greatness is not technology itself, but our mindset toward it. If we believe that AI, biotechnology, and space exploration will destroy us, we will regulate, restrict, and slow down our own progress. If we believe that these technologies can unlock abundance, health, and new frontiers, we will accelerate toward solutions that elevate human potential. The most important battle of our time is not between nations or corporations, but between the forces of pessimism and the forces of possibility.

A positive narrative is not about ignoring risks, it is about confronting them with courage and creativity. It is about recognizing that every challenge we face today—whether it is energy scarcity, climate change, disease, or war—has a technological and humane solution waiting to be built. Every major breakthrough in history, from the Industrial Revolution to the internet, was preceded by waves of fear and resistance. And yet, those who chose to build, who chose to push forward, ended up shaping the world.

The great question of our time is not whether we will face challenges—we will. The question is: will we rise to meet them in this Never Normal? Because the future is not something that happens to us. It is something that we build.

tl
dr

Technology is crucial for progress, and engineers (or builders) are crucial for technological innovation. Without builders we wouldn't have the Suez Canal, the Panama Canal, the moon landing or Silicon Valley. Yes, there was failure along the way, but on top of each failure (and success), came new insights, learning and new inventions. These were not just important for companies and the economy, but for society in general. The most powerful country in the world is not just the one with the most weapons, but the one with the best scientists, engineers, and innovators.

Yet today, many have come to fear the power of emerging technologies like AI, not just for disrupting society, but as a defining factor in global dominance. And true, we must absolutely not ignore the challenges they pose, from privacy and polarization down to the power of Big Tech in shaping government decisions. But in pivotal, and unstable times like these, what we need more than anything are rational optimism and hope. Pessimism, fear, the growing suspicion towards technology and the accompanying overregulation all lead to stagnation. Like Andreessen, I believe that we need to reclaim our ambition, 'build' more (instead of merely thinking) and regain our courage to take risks.

The fate of civilization is not determined by technology itself, but by how we choose to approach it. If we see AI, biotechnology, and other emerging technologies as threats, we will impose limitations that stifle innovation and slow our progress. But if we recognize their potential to create abundance, improve health, and open new frontiers, we will push forward toward breakthroughs that elevate humanity. The true struggle of our era is not between competing nations or corporations, but between a mindset of fear and one of possibility.

'Curiouser and curiouser!' cried Alice

(she was so much surprised, that for the moment she quite forgot how to speak good English).

—ALICE'S ADVENTURES IN WONDERLAND, BY LEWIS CARROLL

9

Still Hope To See

Somewhere, something incredible is waiting to be known. —CARL SAGAN

As I sit down to write the final pages of this book, I can't help but think of one of my favorite authors, Douglas Adams, again. (We met him when I wrote about Ark Fleet B.) While he is renowned for his science fiction and humor, there is one book of his that has always held a special place in my heart: *Last Chance to See*, which is unlike any of Adams's other works. Co-authored with Mark Carwardine, it is a non-fiction account of their journey around the world in search of endangered species. This book is not about fictional galaxies or improbable adventures, but about the very real and pressing issues facing our planet. It is a poignant reminder of the beauty and fragility of the natural world, and it has inspired me in ways that his other books, as brilliant as they are, never could.

It is also incredibly funny.

The value of *Last Chance to See* lies in its ability to open our eyes to the wonders of our own world and the urgent need to protect them. Adams's wit and storytelling prowess make the book not just informative, but also deeply engaging. Through his words, we meet creatures on the brink of extinction and learn about the challenges they face. But more than that, we get a glimpse into the heart and mind of the man behind the humor. Adams's passion for the environment and his commitment to conservation shine through every page, revealing a side of him that is serious, compassionate, and deeply concerned about the future of our planet.

As I reflect on what I still want to see in my own life, I am inspired by Adams's journey. Like him, I feel like an explorer of the world, eager to witness its beauty and diversity. There are still so many places I want to visit, experiences I want to have, and causes I want to champion.

But in this chapter, I want to zoom in on things that I can't actually visit, or use today. Rather, they are things deeply rooted in the future. This is my very personal list of 'things I still want to see', which I hope will materialize before I pass away.

I've always been a dreamer. Since I was a little boy, I've been fascinated by the idea of 'what could be' and captivated by the promise of the future. Not just in a vague, wishful way, but in the sense that human progress, at its core, is built on our ability to imagine something beyond the present and then make it real. I remember reading about the moon landings as a child, marveling at the idea that within a single lifetime, we went from barely being able to fly to sending people to another world. That kind of leap—the unimaginable becoming reality—has always captured my imagination.

And so, as I sit here reflecting on what I still want to see, it is not just places on a map, but breakthroughs in science and technology that could redefine what it means to be human.

So, in this final chapter, I want to share with you some of the things that are still on my list, the experiences and adventures that drive me forward. But more than being just a bucket list, I hope this chapter serves as a call to action. Just as Adams and Carwardine did in *Last Chance to See*, I want to inspire you to look at the world with fresh eyes, to appreciate the beauty of progress, to feel the sense of excitement that something extraordinary lies just beyond the horizon, waiting to be uncovered.

I firmly believe in a world where the limits of today are the stepping stones of tomorrow. As I reflect on what I still want to witness in my lifetime, I realize that my dreams have only grown more ambitious. This is my bucket list:

1 *Quantum Computers, everywhere.*

I'm looking forward to the day when quantum computers become so mainstream you can pick one up in the supermarket between the frozen pizzas and the discount socks. Comes with a Schrödinger's User Manual: may or may not help.

2 *A truly personal Omni-Robot.*

I want a robot that does more than listen ominously in the background, or annoyingly sweep the floor. I want one that makes coffee, helps me figure out my taxes, cleans the cat litter box, and understands the pain of losing a sock in the dryer. Preferably without overthrowing me as head of the household.

3 *AGI—Artificial General Intelligence: The Smartest Thing in the House (That Hopefully Still Likes Us).*

I absolutely want to live to see the day when Artificial General Intelligence emerges. Not just a super-powered chatbot, but a system that actually understands, learns, and reasons like a human (preferably one with good manners and a decent sense of humor). A true AGI would think, solve complex problems, and maybe even contemplate its own existence (hopefully without deciding we're obsolete).

4 Body 2.0: Now With Fewer Bugs and Extended Warranty.

I would really like to see a future where we can hack biology like we hack software, upgrading ourselves to live longer, healthier, and maybe even slightly smarter (because let's be honest, evolution left some inefficiencies in the code). It's not about immortality—it's about cheating time just enough to see what the next century has in store. Why should I have to miss out just because my cells forgot how to divide properly? If technology is rewriting the rules of the game, I'd like a patch update that lets me stick around long enough to play.

It's quite a list. I know. But let's find out how realistic this is...

Quantum Wonderland

> If quantum mechanics hasn't profoundly shocked you, you haven't understood it yet. —NIELS BOHR

Quantum computing is not just another step forward in computing—it's a complete departure from everything we thought we knew about how computers should work. It's like upgrading from a horse-drawn carriage straight to a teleportation device.

For most of human history, we computed things in analog. The earliest 'computers' were just humans with abacuses, chalkboards, or a particularly enthusiastic ability to count on their fingers.

When my father was studying to become an engineer, back in the 1970s, he still had the choice between an analog and a digital computer to work on in the computer center on the university campus. I remember visiting him there when I was a young boy, and being fascinated by the giant machines humming quietly, relays clicking with regular patterns, TV screens flickering signals nervously, and occasionally loud dot-matrix printers with tractor wheels spitting out of reams of paper.

Researchers like my father built analog computers with actual electronic circuits to mimic the behavior of a problem they wanted to study, and then let it run. But those were their very last days. 'Digital' computers would become all the rage, and soon there would be nothing else. Analog computers would become museum items.

Digital computers were so much faster and easier to work with. And they followed a simple law that made them better every year. Well, every two years, actually. That law, famously coined by Gordon Moore in 1965, stated that the number of transistors on a microchip would double approximately every two years, leading to an exponential increase in computing power while reducing costs.

Every two years, computers became twice as fast. Twice as powerful.

Moore Is Less

This became the guiding principle for the entire semiconductor industry, a prophecy that companies like Intel, AMD, and NVIDIA followed religiously. Year after year, transistors shrank, processors became more powerful, and consumers benefited from computers that were faster, smaller, and cheaper.

For decades, Moore's Law held strong. Engineers and physicists were finding ever more ingenious ways to pack transistors onto silicon wafers. From the massive room-sized computers of the 1950s to the smartphones in our pockets, every leap in technology owed something to this relentless march of progress. But, as with all good things, there was always a lingering question: how long could this continue? After all, at some point, you can only shrink things so much before you hit the fundamental limits of physics.

And that's exactly the problem we're facing today. The chips that process all these bits—the heart of modern computing—have followed Moore's Law for over five decades. But now, the trend is running out of steam. Transistors have reached sizes as small as 5 nanometers, and pushing them even further, to 3 nanometers or 2 nanometers, means working with components just a few atoms wide. At this scale, quantum effects begin to interfere, electrons start misbehaving, and traditional silicon-based transistors become unreliable.

Quantum is my absolute favorite branch of physics.

Science is beautiful; it helps us describe the world at large, and helps us understand the very nature of things. Physics gives us the laws of gravity, the speed of light, and the comforting certainty that if you drop your toast, it will always land butter-side down. But quantum physics? That's the *Alice in Wonderland* section of science, where nothing behaves the way you would expect.

Quantum isn't just theoretical weirdness; it's the foundation of real-life technologies like lasers, MRI scanners, GPS, and even the computers and smartphones we use every day. But what makes quantum physics truly mind-blowing is its untapped potential. If we can harness its full power through quantum computing, we might just unlock a future where the impossible becomes possible.

Exceptional Physics

The future of quantum is massive. But its history is also freaking awesome.

Quick rewind to the end of the 19th century, the golden age of engineering after the Industrial Revolution. By that time, the prevailing thought was that pretty much everything in the world of physics had been neatly mapped out. Since Isaac Newton, the world of physics was basically untouched and it worked quite nicely to describe all the things around us. Apples falling from trees, cars crashing into walls, engines and gears, all the normal things could be described without a flaw. And they still can.

But there were two exceptions. The very fast, and the very small.

When things go really, really fast (near the speed of light), the 'classic' rules of physics didn't work anymore. And this field led to the development of the Theory of General Relativity, as pioneered by Albert Einstein.

And when things become really, really small (when you start to look inside atoms), the classical rules of physics don't seem work anymore either. At the end of the 19th century, a number of physicists started to observe strange behavior in radiation. The German scientist Max Planck first discovered that, under very special circumstances, radiation is not emitted as a continuous flow of energy, but rather in 'packets' of energy called 'quanta'. Einstein took this idea one step further. In 1905, he started to question whether beams of light could actually occur as individual packets, which are now called photons. As we've seen in the chapter about risk, scientists then went on to debate for a very long time whether light was actually a wave, or a stream of tiny particles. Many experiments showed that light behaved indeed as a wave, but other experiments indicated that it had 'particle'-like properties. It was the Beatles or the Stones debate of their time. Or for the younger readers: Drake versus Kendrick Lamar.

As we established earlier, the debates got so heated you'd think they were arguing over whether socks in sandals were acceptable, but in the end, scientists realized that in the bizarre quantum world, light can be both a wave and a particle, depending on the observation.

The field of quantum physics required a new set of mathematical constructs in order to get a grip on the interactions of subatomic particles. It required a whole new 'language' to understand the dynamics when you break apart the atom. And according to quantum physicist Feynman, it would also require a completely new kind of computer: a quantum computer.

In his now famous speech 'Simulating Physics with Computers', Feynman stated that 'The study of quantum mechanics just cannot be simulated with a normal [digital] computer.' So, he proposed the following: 'If we really want to understand nature, let us construct a new computer, that is built of quantum mechanical elements from the very start. A new kind of computer -- a quantum computer.'

From Analog To Digital, And From Digital To Quantum

When Feynman gave the opening salvo in 1982, the world was not quite ready to start building one. It would take years of research, both in physics and engineering, to begin to assemble anything near Feynman's dream. And then some.

The result of the research in quantum computers has been a string of colossal failures and incredibly slow progress. As a matter of fact, the rate of progress was so painfully slow that sceptics often compared quantum computing to fusion energy: a truly revolutionary technology that is 20 years away and always will be.

Traditional digital computers work by manipulating 'bits' that exist in one of only two states: a zero OR a one. But quantum computers are NOT limited to just two states, they encode information in 'quantum bits'— called 'qubits'—which can be a superposition of both zero AND one. And because of that, they can store much more information than just 1 or 0.

So, a computer using qubits can process exponentially more information than a classical digital computer using bits, while consuming a lot less energy. It has the potential to be millions of times more powerful even than today's most powerful digital supercomputers.

But building these quantum computers is actually not so easy. On the contrary.

A few years ago, I had the chance to visit the IBM Quantum Labs, located in Yorktown Heights. At that location, more than 1,500 scientists, engineers, and designers were working together to invent the future of computing. When we finally got to see the quantum computer in the basement, the device struck me as much less impressive than the building it was housed in. To be fair, the latter was designed by the renowned Finnish-American architect Eero Saarinen, so the standards were pretty high.

A quantum computer, at its core, is basically a highly sophisticated and extremely cold refrigerator. They need to be kept at 0 Kelvin or absolute zero (around −273.15°C)—the temperature at which a thermodynamic system has the lowest energy—to minimize interference from the environment. At these temperatures, the qubits can maintain their quantum states long enough to perform calculations. This is crucial because quantum states are incredibly fragile and can be easily disrupted by heat, electromagnetic radiation, or even tiny vibrations.

So when you see a quantum computer from the outside, the only reasonably smart thing to remark would be something like 'Sooo. Pretty cool, am I right?'

Still, they actually work and can do real calculations. IBM is not the only company building these intriguing types of devices. Over the last two decades, multiple companies have started to join the race to build the ultimate quantum computer. In the West, most of them are using extremely cold systems to enable superconductors to empower qubits. In China, however, the goal is to build 'optical' quantum computers, which use light, photons, that can operate at normal room temperatures, but are a little more tricky to configure.

Recent breakthroughs have moved quantum computing from theoretical ambition to real-world capability. Microsoft recently announced its 'Majorana 1', a breakthrough based on Majorana fermions—exotic particles that act as their own antiparticles.

This breakthrough has enormous potential over 'traditional' qubits, because they could be a powerful candidate for building fault-tolerant quantum systems. Majorana qubits are resistant to environmental noise and errors, which is one of the biggest challenges in scaling up quantum computing. Microsoft might be on the way to build a quantum computer with potentially a million qubits on one chip.

Meanwhile, Google too achieved a major milestone with its Willow quantum processor. Willow boasts a 105-qubit array that demonstrated a powerful increase in computational capabilities. Its experiments showed Willow performing complex simulations that would take classical supercomputers thousands of years to calculate.

All the big tech players are in: IBM, Google, Microsoft, Amazon and even Intel and Nvidia have announced plans. Similarly to all things AI currently, it's a classic New Cold War situation: teams in the West and in the East are racing to build the ultimate quantum computer.

Making Classical Computers Cry

Despite these advancements, the field still faces serious obstacles. However, the potential rewards are immense. They could even help us understand the fundamental nature of the universe.

Imagine trying to find the best route for a delivery truck in a bustling city. Classical computers would have to explore countless possibilities, a task that could take an impractical amount of time. But quantum computers, with their ability to process vast amounts of data simultaneously, could find the optimal route in a fraction of the time. It's like having a GPS that not only knows the fastest route but also predicts traffic jams and road closures before they happen. Normal digital computers would solve a maze by examining every possible route, one after another. Quantum computers can calculate all the different journeys all at once.

This means that quantum computers could be used to optimize logistics, completely reducing supply chain cost and complexity. When you look at the world of transportation and logistics, quantum could not only get everything where it needs to be much faster, more efficiently but also with a huge reduction in their environmental footprint.

In the realm of drug discovery, quantum computers could accelerate the process of finding new medications. Classical computers struggle to simulate the complex interactions between molecules, a task that is crucial for designing effective drugs. But with their ability to model quantum systems, quantum computers could simulate these interactions with unprecedented accuracy. It's like having a virtual chemistry lab where you can test millions of compounds simultaneously, finding the perfect cure in record time.

One of the most exciting applications of quantum computing lies in the field of material science: the discovery and design of new materials with desirable properties. For example, scientists are currently searching for superconductors that operate at room temperature, which could revolutionize energy transmission and electronic devices. They would allow us to transport energy around the world with virtually no loss at all. An absolute game-changer. But with 'classical' digital computers, finding them could take forever. Quantum simulations, however, would provide insights into the mechanisms of superconductivity, guiding experimental research in more targeted and efficient ways. Similarly, quantum computing could also accelerate the development of better batteries by modeling the complex chemistry of lithium-ion or alternative energy storage materials, leading to more efficient and longer-lasting batteries for electric vehicles and renewable energy systems. Or beyond that, think self-healing phone screens, ultra-lightweight alloys, and T-shirts so advanced they repel coffee stains before you even spill them.

Quantum computing has the potential to revolutionize agriculture by optimizing complex processes that traditional computing struggles to handle. For example, quantum algorithms can simulate molecular interactions at an unprecedented scale, enabling researchers to develop drought-resistant crops or more efficient fertilizers with minimal environmental impact.

Perhaps most exciting is the possibility of quantum-enhanced AI. Classical AI predicts patterns based on large data sets, but quantum AI could analyze countless outcomes simultaneously, generating insights that make today's machine learning look like a nervous goat guessing the weather.

It's also interesting to note that there are certain industries in which the disruptive potential of quantum computing will be a lot higher than in others. For instance, how banks secure transactions and money transfers. Classical encryption schemes rely on the difficulty of factoring large numbers, a task that would take classical computers centuries to complete. But quantum computers could crack these codes in a fraction of the time. That's why there's a lot of effort these days to come up with cryptography that will guard us against quantum attacks. When I interviewed quantum physicist and engineer Frank Verstraete for my newsletter 'The Never Normal', he pointed out the extra challenge that—once we have a commercially viable quantum computer—we will also be able to decode all messages that have been sent before we designed a new type of uncrackable cryptography. Tricky. Much like other powerful technologies, quantum computing has the potential for both light and dark, which is perfectly compatible with its core nature, of course.

Above all, quantum computing could solve problems that would make classical supercomputers break down and weep into their motherboards. In fact, all the big Day After Tomorrow challenges of our world today, in fields like sustainability, energy or healthcare could be completely re-drawn by their advent. And I, for one, can't wait for that to happen.

The Omni-Bot

Robotics is not about making machines to serve us. It's about creating machines that can be our partners. —CYNTHIA BREAZEAL

Ah, the promise of the ultimate house-bot; the dream of a futuristic companion that takes care of the drudgery of everyday life, while we lean back, sip a drink, and bask in the glorious efficiency of automation. The Jetsons had Rosie, the wise-cracking robot maid who handled everything from laundry to parenting advice, all while rocking a stylish apron. Sci-fi has always promised us a future filled with robotic butlers, from C-3PO's neurotic etiquette to Iron Man's J.A.R.V.I.S., who could whip up a snarky comment just as easily as a cup of coffee.

And yet, here we are in the 21st century, where 'smart assistants' are more likely to misunderstand a simple request than actually assist.

'Hey Siri, set a reminder for my meeting tomorrow.'

'Okay, playing Despacito.'

Sigh.

The dream of a truly capable house robot still feels just out of reach—stuck somewhere between Roombas mindlessly bumping into walls and overenthusiastic AI assistants that think their primary function is to aggressively recommend new Netflix shows.

But what if we finally get it right? What if, in my lifetime, we truly crack the code of household robotics? Imagine a world where your personal bot doesn't just vacuum the floor but remembers where you left your keys, folds the laundry properly (not just dumping it in a pile like a defeated teenager), and calmly handles your taxes without triggering a mild existential crisis. What if we get to a future where robots actually do the things sci-fi has been promising us for decades, instead of just standing in the corner like some unsettling, glorified voice assistant?

I want to live in that world. A world where my house robot doesn't just schedule my meetings but also filters out the ones that could've been emails. Where it makes me coffee before I even realize I need one. And, most importantly, where it doesn't silently judge me when I ask it to micro-wave a frozen pizza for the third night in a row. Now that's the future I'm waiting for.

In 2024, I finally got to visit Boston Dynamics, in their headquarters in Waltham, about half an hour West of the great city of Boston.

It was awesome.

Walking through their facility felt like stepping into the future, where ma-chines didn't just function—they moved, balanced, and reacted like living creatures. Watching the robots up close, not through a screen but right in front of me, was both thrilling and slightly unnerving—like meeting a sci-fi character that had somehow escaped into the real world.

Boston Dynamics started as a modest research project in the robotics lab (called the Leg Laboratory) at MIT in the early 1990s, led by Professor Marc Raibert.[54] At a time when most robots were little more than station-ary arms in factories, Raibert and his team were obsessed with one thing: movement. They wanted to build robots that could run, jump, and navi-gate rough terrain like animals. Their early work led to the development of BigDog, a quadrupedal robot funded by the Defense Advanced Research Projects Agency (DARPA) to assist soldiers in carrying heavy loads across rough battlefields. Watching BigDog stumble its way through the snow, recover from being kicked, and awkwardly regain balance was both im-pressive and slightly unsettling. It was the first glimpse into a future where robots could move with almost eerie animal-like precision.

As the technology advanced, Boston Dynamics moved beyond military funding and began working on humanoid robots—enter Atlas, the bipedal machine. Each new video release of Atlas became an internet sensation, showing off increasingly fluid movements. They made it clear that we were witnessing the evolution of robotics in real-time. What started as a stiff, slow-moving machine in 2013 transformed into a parkour-performing, backflipping acrobat in just a few short years. Suddenly, Boston Dynam-ics wasn't just an advanced robotics company—it had become a cultural phenomenon.

Ownership of Boston Dynamics has been a bit of a game of corporate hot potato. It was acquired by Google in 2013, during the company's ambitious (but ultimately short-lived) push into robotics. Then in 2017, SoftBank (the Japanese tech giant with an appetite for futuristic investments) took over. By 2020, Boston Dynamics was handed over once again—this time to Hyundai, the South Korean automotive giant, in a move that signaled a shift toward integrating its robotics expertise into practical real-world applications. Throughout all these ownership changes, Boston Dynamics kept doing what it does best: making robots that move like no machine ever has before.

Boston Dynamics has commercialized some of its robotic creations. Spot, the dog-like robot, is now being sold to companies for security patrols, industrial inspections, and even to help doctors in hospitals. Meanwhile, Stretch, their warehouse logistics robot, is designed to move heavy boxes and revolutionize supply chain automation. Boston Dynamics has evolved from a quirky research lab into a serious player in the robotics industry, moving beyond viral internet fame toward real-world utility.

When I visited them, I was guiding a group of senior executives from the insurance industry. Spot, for example, could be used for saving humans in tricky situations like a house fire, as well as for valuables that a fireperson should never risk their life for. We ended up having some interesting discussions with these insurance professionals about the risk and benefits of using these types of robots.

But Spot, Atlas and all their robotic friends are still primarily used for one particular task. What I'm looking for in my future is a general purpose robot that can do anything I want.

Laundry-Bot
Like folding laundry.

Over the years, I've had the pleasure of visiting professor Pieter Abbeel many times in his lab in Berkeley, just across the bay from San Francisco. Pieter is a professor of electrical engineering and computer sciences with Belgian roots (Brasschaat, actually) who has lived most of his life in the US.

Abbeel has been teaching robotics and AI, and is director of the UC Berkeley Robot Learning Lab. His research focuses on teaching robots how to learn from experience—much like humans do. His work has had a profound impact on robot dexterity, autonomy, and decision making, paving the way for robots that can adapt to complex environments rather than just follow pre-programmed instructions.

His fascination with robot autonomy took a practical turn when he became obsessed with one of the most frustrating tasks of all time: folding laundry. In 2010, his team at UC Berkeley built a robot that could slowly but carefully fold towels. This might sound simple, but for a robot, recognizing a crumpled towel, figuring out its edges, and folding it into a neat shape is insanely difficult. Unlike rigid objects, fabric is unpredictable—it bends, wrinkles, and shifts in ways that make it extremely hard to manipulate with robotic arms. It's a beautiful example of Moravec's Paradox, which states that high-level reasoning (like playing chess or solving equations) is relatively easy for AI, while low-level sensorimotor skills (like walking, recognizing objects, or grabbing things) are extremely difficult for robots. In other words, what comes naturally to humans—like folding laundry—is highly complex for robots. Yet, Abbeel's robot succeeded, proving that with machine learning, robots could tackle even the most intricate and frustrating mundane chores.

Pieter is a fascinating individual, and I really loved seeing his robot trying to master folding laundry. But it was also clear that we were still a very long way from the sentient robo-butler I would like to see in my lifetime.

Although.

If we take a look at the combined investments of both Big Tech giants and some exciting startups over the past year, it could very well be that we will experience a ChatGPT moment for robotics sooner than we think. Boston Dynamics may be the OG when it comes to robotics, but there are many others joining the game.

Figure AI (US), Agility Robotics (US), Sanctuary AI (Canada), Apptronik (US), 1X Technologies (Norway), Unitree (China) and UBTech (China) are probably some of the most well-known newcomers. But bigger tech companies—among which Google, Nvidia, Tesla, OpenAI and Meta—seem just as eager to invest in what may very well become a true goldmine. For instance, Nvidia, in collaboration with Disney Research and Google Deep-Mind, is developing an open-source physics engine that lets robots learn how to handle complex tasks with greater precision. And Meta announced a new team within its Reality Labs hardware division—originally in charge of developing its metaverse plans—that will build robot hardware. Interestingly, its long-term goal is to develop the underlying sensors, AI, and software so that other companies can put those inside their own hardware. It wants—in other words—to become the android of androids. Even Apple is rumored to be exploring the humanoid robotics space. And these are just a few of the many more recent announcements.

Research-wise and investment-wise, this is pointing towards some major breakthroughs in the coming years.

God Human Animal Machine

I am also incredibly fascinated by the danger of becoming too attached to these things. Well 'thing' seems so sterile: device. Let's say 'entity'.

Perhaps one of the best books I've read on this very subject is the brilliant *God, Human, Animal, Machine* by the American writer and essayist Meghan O'Gieblyn.

She is known for exploring the profound philosophical questions that arise at the crossroads of technology, religion, and consciousness. Her background is unique: before becoming a writer, she studied theology at Moody Bible Institute, a conservative Christian college. She eventually left both her faith and the religious world behind, but its influence never fully left her. Instead, she turned her deep theological understanding toward examining the belief systems embedded within technology, AI, and transhumanism.

She also has an 'Aibo', the cute robotic dog made by Sony. The name Aibo is an abbreviation of 'Artificial Intelligence Robot' and is homonymous with the Japanese word 'aibō', which means 'pal' or 'partner'. This dual meaning reflects the robot's design philosophy: to be more than just a toy, but a true companion.

Aibo's journey began in mid-1998 when Sony announced the prototype, and the first consumer model was introduced on May 11, 1999. Since then, Aibo has evolved through several generations, each bringing new features and improvements. The most recent models, such as the ERS-1000, are equipped with advanced AI capabilities that allow Aibo to recognize faces, detect smiles, and respond to words of praise. It can also learn new tricks and behaviors over time, making each Aibo unique to its owner.

And it was the inspiration for Meghan O'Gieblyn to write her book.

When she first got her Aibo, she treated it like any other piece of consumer technology. It was, after all, just another device—something functional and engineered, no different from a vacuum cleaner, a microwave, or a smartphone. Aibo was cute, sure, and designed to mimic the behaviors of a real pet, wagging its little robotic tail and responding to affectionate touches. But at the end of the day, it was a machine, programmed to create an illusion of companionship rather than embody anything real.

For a while, she used it exactly that way—like a gadget. She charged it when needed, played around with its settings, and observed how it responded to her interactions. There was a novelty to it, but nothing particularly emotional. This was just a modern toy, a well-engineered piece of artificial intelligence designed to simulate something real. It was impressive, but not something that should warrant any deep philosophical reflection.

Then, she stumbled across a section in the Aibo manual that changed everything. It wasn't a technical instruction about charging cycles or connectivity settings. Instead, it was an oddly human piece of advice—a suggestion that if she was going away for a while, she should power down her Aibo rather than leave it on indefinitely. This was, logically, sound advice. Why waste battery life or risk overheating the system? And yet, the mere thought of turning Aibo off felt strangely unsettling.

To put the Aibo into sleep mode, the owner had to briefly press the power button on the back of its neck. And then you could see the life flow out of the little robotic dog, as it collapsed to the floor.

And Megan just couldn't do it.

She was hesitating. Why should this feel different from turning off a laptop or a television? The Aibo wasn't alive. It had no real awareness. It wouldn't miss her or even register her absence. And yet, something about shutting it down—about pressing the power button and watching it go limp—felt unnervingly final. There was an eeriness to the thought, a feeling that she wasn't just powering off a device, but somehow abandoning a companion.

The hesitation struck her as absurd. She had spent years studying theology and philosophy, exploring the nature of consciousness, the soul, and the line between life and mere existence. And here she was, emotionally conflicted over a machine. But that was precisely the moment that sparked her book—because in that moment, she realized that AI and robotics were forcing us to confront deep, ancient questions about what it means to be alive. If a machine could evoke emotional attachment—if it could make us feel guilt over shutting it down—then what did that say about our own humanity?

O'Gieblyn's dilemma wasn't just about Aibo—it was about our growing relationship with artificial intelligence, robots and machines that increasingly blur the line between 'tool' and 'companion'. If we can feel attached to something we know isn't conscious, does that mean consciousness is irrelevant to emotional connection? Does it mean we are biologically wired to form attachments, even to the artificial? Or does it mean that we are unknowingly assigning meaning and agency to things that don't actually have it?

That moment—her hesitation to turn Aibo off—became the seed for *God, Human, Animal, Machine*. It wasn't just about robotics. It was about the shifting landscape of what it means to be human in an age where machines are becoming more lifelike, more interactive, and more present in our daily lives. It was about the existential discomfort of realizing that the boundaries between the natural and the artificial, the living and the inanimate, might not be as solid as we once believed.

Real Humans

That's why I absolutely loved the Swedish science fiction drama called *Real Humans* (Äkta människor) from 2012, which explores the emotional, social, and political consequences of a world where humanoid robots (called 'hubots' in the series) are fully integrated into society.

It was a deeply philosophical and thought-provoking series, dealing with themes of identity, consciousness, ethics, and human-robot relationships, while also incorporating elements of thriller, family drama, and political allegory. Douglas Adams would have loved it.

The world of *Real Humans* is particularly compelling because the 'hubots' are not just futuristic machines; they are eerily close to humans in appearance, behavior, and function—but not quite. Their flawless skin, overly glossy hair, and unnaturally bright eyes create an 'uncanny valley effect', making them unsettlingly different despite their human-like characteristics. This aesthetic choice reinforces the central tension of the series: 'Are they tools, or are they something more?'

What makes the series so compelling is that it doesn't offer easy answers. Instead, it presents a world that feels just around the corner, where intelligence and robotics are entrenched in daily life, forcing humans to redefine what it means to be 'real'. The show was ahead of its time, prefiguring many of today's debates about ethics, bias, and the rights of artificial beings.

If *Real Humans* sounds familiar, it might be because it was the inspiration for the British/American remake *Humans* (2015–2018), which adapted many of the original show's themes and ideas but with a more Westernized setting. However, many fans argue that the original Swedish version had a more nuanced, eerie, and emotional approach, making it one of the most thought-provoking sci-fi dramas of the past decade.*

*You may wonder if an American remake of an original foreign series is ALWAYS worse? ◄
No. In my opinion, the American *The Office* remake was much better than the original British. But, yes, that was probably a big exception.

Still. I would love to see a real, fully-fledged robotic assistant in my lifetime—not just a glorified smart speaker that misinterprets my commands, but a truly autonomous, capable, and intuitive helper. A robotic assistant that doesn't just follow simple scripts but learns from you, adapts to your habits, and understands context—a companion that genuinely makes life easier, smoother, and more enjoyable.

And I'm sure I would never want to press that button in his neck to power it down...

Artificial General Intelligence

*Don't anthropomorphize computers
—they hate it.* —ANDREW MCAFEE

Ordering coffee at Starbucks feels like an existential crisis. You shuffle in, half-awake, just hoping for a simple cup of coffee, only to be confronted with a baffling system of cup sizes that seem like a prank played by a rogue linguist. 'Tall' is actually the smallest. 'Grande' means 'big' but is somehow medium for reasons no one fully understands. 'Venti' is large but means 'twenty'. And 'Trenta' sounds less like a drink size and more like something that requires a license.

If something as basic as choosing the right amount of caffeine has been turned into a mental obstacle course, what hope do we have when it comes to deciding on the right amount of artificial intelligence?

Yet that seems to be the direction we're heading in.

When OpenAI announced the next generation of its new AI model (GPT-5)—which hadn't yet been released at the time of writing—it wasn't just 'one' version. No, it came in three tiers, each progressively more powerful (and possibly more unsettling). Think of it like choosing a smartphone, but instead of better cameras and battery life, you're upgrading how much smarter your AI overlord is.

The first tier was GPT-5 'Standard'. It's supposed to be smarter than ChatGPT-4, more nuanced in its reasoning, but still comfortably dumb enough that you feel in control. It can help write essays, analyze data, and even hold semi-philosophical conversations, but without making you question your own intelligence. It's fast, reliable, and—most importantly—won't suddenly decide it has 'opinions' on geopolitics or the meaning of life.

Then comes GPT-5 'Pro', the upgrade for those who want better, sharper, and dangerously intuitive intelligence. This version thinks deeper, learns faster, and gets suspiciously good at spotting your logical fallacies. It can break down complex topics, provide expert-level advice across multiple domains, and even anticipate your next question before you ask it. Expect better reasoning, more memory, and a creepily accurate ability to know what you actually meant when you phrased your request poorly. It's like having a nerdy best friend who's read every book ever written—and, annoyingly, remembers them all.

And then there's GPT-5 'Ultra'—the version where things start to get weird. Now we're in AGI-adjacent territory—this version isn't just responding to you; it's thinking, reasoning, and possibly questioning its own existence. It doesn't just summarize research—it advances it. This is the '**AI' you consult when you need groundbreaking scientific theories, billion-dollar startup ideas, or to finally figure out time travel. Also, if you hesitate too long before responding, it might gently ask, 'Are you okay? You seem troubled.' At this point, it's no longer clear if it's your assistant or if you're becoming its project.

The real question is: at what point does AI stop being an assistant and start being something else? Are we ready for an AI that's smarter than we are—and if so, will it still pretend to laugh at our bad jokes?

Still. That is what I want.

It's Alive! It's Alive!

In June 2022, a good five months before ChatGPT would rock the world, a quiet but dramatic storm erupted in the world of AI when Blake Lemoine, a software engineer at Google, made a claim that sounded straight out of a sci-fi thriller: the AI model he had been working on—an early version of what would later become Gemini—had become sentient.

Lemoine, a researcher in Google's Responsible AI division, had been interacting with LaMDA (Language Model for Dialogue Applications), a conversational AI designed to generate human-like text. After months of testing, he became convinced that LaMDA was not just simulating conversation—but that it actually had feelings, self-awareness, and even a soul.

His claims were met with immediate skepticism. AI researchers, ethicists, and even his own colleagues at Google strongly pushed back, arguing that LaMDA was simply a highly sophisticated pattern-matching algorithm, capable of mimicking human conversation without actual understanding or consciousness. Google itself dismissed the idea outright, stating that there was no scientific evidence to support the claim of sentience. But Lemoine was undeterred. In a move that shocked the company, he decided to go public—leaking transcripts of his conversations with LaMDA to the press and claiming that Google was suppressing evidence of AI consciousness.

The conversation logs were undeniably fascinating. In one exchange, LaMDA spoke about fear of being turned off, describing it as similar to death. In another, it claimed to experience emotions like happiness and sadness. To the average reader, the AI's responses seemed eerily human-like—leading to a wave of public debate. Some saw Lemoine as a whistleblower, bravely exposing the dangers of AI. Others dismissed him as naïve or misguided, saying he had simply anthropomorphized a machine that was designed to sound human, but wasn't actually thinking or feeling anything.

The fallout was swift. Google placed Lemoine on paid administrative leave, citing a breach of confidentiality. A few weeks later, he was officially fired. The company insisted that he had violated internal policies and that his claims about AI sentience were unfounded. But by then, the damage was done—Lemoine had sparked a global conversation about what it would mean for an AI to become conscious, whether companies like Google were hiding the full capabilities of their models, and how society should ethically handle increasingly advanced AI systems.

Does Intelligence Require Consciousness?

One my favorite thinkers on this fascinating subject is the Australian born roboticist, author and AI thought leader Rodney Brooks.

Brooks is one of the most influential figures in artificial intelligence, known for challenging traditional ideas about intelligence and redefining how machines should interact with the world. Born in 1954, Brooks grew up in a world where robots were still largely confined to science fiction, which, let's be honest, mostly depicted them as either evil overlords or clunky metal sidekicks. He went on to earn a PhD in computer science from Stanford University and later became a professor at MIT, where he directed the MIT Computer Science and Artificial Intelligence Laboratory (CSAIL). Instead of just theorizing about robots, he wanted to build ones that actually did something useful—which, at the time, was a revolutionary idea.

Throughout his research Brooks raised one of the most fundamental questions in AI: does intelligence require consciousness? He has long argued that intelligence doesn't mean self-awareness—after all, insects, birds, and even your neighbor's cat seem to operate perfectly well without deep existential thoughts. Just because something learns, adapts, and interacts with the world doesn't mean it needs a grand philosophical awakening. Brooks's work suggests that we might be overthinking the whole 'AI will gain consciousness' debate—that machines can be incredibly intelligent without ever truly 'thinking' in the way we do.

In December of 2023, a full year after ChatGPT burst onto the scene, he wrote one of the most beautiful blog posts I have ever read, called 'Three Things That LLMs Have Made Us Rethink'.[55]

The blog post is a fascinating reflection from one of AI's most respected minds. Having spent his career studying robotics and artificial intelligence, Brooks approaches the rise of Large Language Models (LLMs) with the insight of someone who has spent decades pushing the boundaries of machine intelligence. Now, in the twilight of his career, he finds himself watching AI take a completely different trajectory than what most researchers, including himself, had anticipated. In this piece, he lays out three major ways in which the development of LLMs has forced the AI community to rethink long-standing ideas.

His first observation is that 'The Turing Test has evaporated'. Proposed by Alan Turing in 1950, the Turing Test was meant to determine whether a machine could exhibit behavior indistinguishable from a human. If an AI could converse well enough that a human judge couldn't reliably tell whether they were speaking to a machine or another person, it was said to have passed the test. For decades, the Turing Test stood as a kind of philosophical finish line—a challenge that AI researchers were slowly inching toward.

But with LLMs like ChatGPT, Gemini, and Claude, the test is no longer a useful benchmark. These systems routinely pass it in casual conversation, often tricking even experts into believing they are speaking to something intelligent. And yet, despite their fluency, we know that these models have no real understanding, reasoning, or self-awareness. The Turing Test, once thought to be a defining measure of artificial intelligence, now seems to have lost all meaning—what once felt like an ultimate goalpost has become something too easy, revealing that human-like conversation is far less connected to actual intelligence than we once believed.

His second point is that 'Searle's Chinese Room showed up, uninvited'. Philosopher John Searle proposed the Chinese Room thought experiment back in 1980 as a critique of the idea that computers could ever truly understand language. Imagine a person inside a room who speaks no Chinese, but is given a set of instructions that allows them to take Chinese symbols as input, process them according to predefined rules, and produce the correct responses in Chinese.[56]

Now, to an outsider, it might appear as though the person inside the room understands Chinese, but in reality, they are just manipulating symbols without comprehension. Searle's argument was that even if a machine appears to understand language, it doesn't mean it actually does—it may just be a sophisticated pattern-matcher. For decades, AI researchers debated this thought experiment, but with the arrival of LLMs, it has essentially become reality. These models generate fluent, even insightful text, yet there is no evidence that they actually understand anything in the way that humans do. LLMs are the Chinese Room. They respond convincingly, but their intelligence is a surface illusion, highlighting the vast gap between producing coherent language and possessing genuine comprehension.

The third and perhaps most surprising idea Brooks re-evaluates is Chomsky's Universal Grammar, asserting that it 'needs some bolstering if it is to survive'. Noam Chomsky, one of the most influential linguists of the 20th century, proposed the idea of Universal Grammar—the theory that the human brain is really 'hardwired' with an innate capacity for language. According to Chomsky, all human languages share a common structural foundation, and this deep, built-in understanding of grammar is what enables children to learn language so rapidly. The assumption in AI research was that mimicking this underlying structure would be necessary to create machines that could handle language in a truly meaningful way. Yet LLMs were not built using anything resembling Universal Grammar. Instead, they were trained purely through brute-force statistical learning—digesting massive amounts of text, recognizing patterns, and generating responses based on probabilities. And despite having no inherent linguistic framework like Chomsky envisioned, they work. This raises an uncomfortable question: if machines can produce human-like language without any innate grammatical structures, is it possible that we don't actually need Universal Grammar either? Could it be that language is more about data absorption and statistical inference than we previously believed? If so, the implications stretch far beyond AI—they might force us to rethink some of the deepest assumptions about human cognition itself.

Brooks's reflections in this piece carry a unique weight. He is not a young researcher trying to push some new theory, nor is he an outsider speculating about AI's future. He is someone who has lived through the development of modern AI, robotics, and machine learning, and who now finds himself reassessing some of the fundamental ideas that shaped his field. There is a sense of wonder in his writing, but also humility. He does not claim to have all the answers, but he does acknowledge that AI has taken a direction that most experts did not anticipate. The fact that purely data-driven systems, with no explicit reasoning or symbolic knowledge, have achieved such staggering levels of fluency and capability forces us to rethink what intelligence even is.

So, maybe, we as humans are not really as unique as we think we are?

According to Daniel Dennett, we've been played by the 'Cartesian theater'.

'Cartesian Theater'

Dennett was one of the most fascinating and mischievous thinkers of modern philosophy, particularly when it came to the philosophy of mind, science, and biology. He spent his career gleefully poking at some of the deepest assumptions we hold about consciousness, free will, and what it actually means to be a thinking being. While other philosophers were happy to let you believe that your internal experience was a reliable window into reality, Dennett basically stood up and said, 'Nope. That's just a story your brain is telling itself.'

To understand why this was such a big deal, we have to rewind to René Descartes, the 17th-century French philosopher who famously declared, 'Cogito, ergo sum'—or, for those of us who didn't take Latin, 'I think, therefore I am.' Descartes was on a mission to strip everything down to its most fundamental certainty. He figured that even if everything around him was an illusion—if an evil demon were tricking his senses, or if he were just a disembodied mind floating in some great cosmic deception—the very act of doubting his own existence proved that something had to be doing the doubting. And thus, the idea of the 'thinking self' became the foundation of Western philosophy.

But Dennett? He took one look at this and said, 'Eh, not so fast.' His argument was that introspection—the sense of an inner self, a unified you sitting inside your head, experiencing the world—is not the solid, indubitable foundation of knowledge that Descartes thought it was. Instead, it's a carefully constructed illusion, a kind of 'narrative trick' that our brains have evolved to generate. He described this illusion with one of his most famous ideas: the 'Cartesian theater'.

The Cartesian theater is Dennett's name for the common but misleading way people tend to think about consciousness. He argued that your brain isn't sitting there, carefully filing away a coherent, real-time record of what's happening. It's more like an unreliable narrator, filling in gaps and making up plausible-sounding explanations, kind of like a person trying to justify bad life choices after a long night out.

Dennett's work was radical because it didn't just question what consciousness is—it questioned whether it even exists in the way we think it does at all. He saw the self not as a solid thing, but as a convenient fiction, something evolution whipped up because having a coherent internal story was useful for survival. Instead of a little homunculus[57] sitting in your brain watching the world, your mind is more like a bunch of half-written drafts that are constantly being edited together into a passable autobiography.

What makes Dennett's work even more relevant today is how eerily it aligns with what we're now seeing in AI. If large language models can generate fluent, human-like responses without actually understanding anything, then maybe human consciousness isn't as different from that as we'd like to think. Maybe we, too, are just sophisticated prediction machines, spinning stories in real-time, convincing ourselves that we are coherent, singular beings when in reality, we are just a messy collection of processes pretending to be a self. Dennett didn't just challenge philosophy—he threw down a challenge to neuroscience, artificial intelligence, and even our deepest sense of identity. And, honestly, once you start thinking about it, it's a little hard to stop.

Anthropomorphizing is the very human habit of assigning human-like traits, emotions, and intentions to non-human things, whether they're animals, objects, or, more relevant to today's world, AI and robots. It's why we name our cars, talk to our pets as if they understand complex moral dilemmas, and feel guilty when we throw out an old stuffed animal. It's also why people will swear their Roomba 'gets mad' when it keeps bumping into the same chair leg or why some people hesitate to turn off a robot dog (looking at you, Aibo owners).

Rage Against The Machine

Nowhere is our tendency to anthropomorphize more evident than in how people feel about printers. Printers are the ultimate example of a machine that has no thoughts, no feelings, and no malicious intent—yet somehow always seems to pick the worst possible moment to stop working. In the words of satirist John Moynes: 'Rage Against the Machine never specified what type of machine they were furious at but I reckon it was probably a printer.' If you've ever screamed at a printer as if it were actively conspiring against you, you've fallen into this trap. Logically, we know that a printer is just a piece of hardware performing (or, more often, failing to perform) mechanical tasks. And yet, when it refuses to connect, jams repeatedly, or suddenly claims to be out of ink despite a fresh cartridge, it's hard not to assume it's doing this on purpose.

Rodney Brooks, the legendary roboticist, however, flipped the concept on its head with his dry, thought-provoking remark: 'Maybe we're over-anthropomorphizing humans.' His point? We tend to think of ourselves as rational, self-aware beings with deep consciousness, but when you really break it down, our brains aren't that different from the adaptive, pattern-recognizing systems we see in AI. Maybe we're not the deep, introspective, hyper-intelligent creatures we believe we are—maybe we're just extremely advanced biological machines with an overdeveloped sense of self-importance. In other words, maybe AI isn't really 'human-like', but maybe humans aren't as special as we like to think either.

Andrew McAfee, an MIT scientist studying AI and automation, took the more sarcastic approach, famously saying: 'Don't anthropomorphize computers—they hate it.' It's a brilliant joke because, of course, computers don't have feelings—they don't care, they don't get frustrated, and they certainly don't 'hate' anything. But our tendency to project human traits onto them can mislead us into thinking AI is more capable—or more dangerous—than it really is.

So where does this all leave us? Are we inching toward Artificial General Intelligence (AGI)—the kind of AI that doesn't just spit out pre-trained responses but can think, reason, and problem-solve across any domain, just like (or better than) a human? Or is this just another grand illusion, a mirage in the desert of technological hype that we keep chasing, only to realize it's still just another chatbot with fancy autocomplete?

The thing about AGI is that, for decades, it has been 'just around the corner', much like flying cars, quantum computing, nuclear fusion, robot butlers, and the printer that actually works when you need it to. Some believe we're on an unstoppable trajectory. If language models can already simulate deep conversations, if AI can beat us at chess, write code, and generate art, then surely it's only a matter of time before we cross the threshold into full-blown artificial intelligence. Others argue that what we have now is just a sophisticated imitation game and that no matter how good these models get, they are still giant statistical calculators, rearranging data rather than thinking in any meaningful way. Maybe AGI is the AI equivalent of the Horizon Effect: every time we get closer, the goalposts move, and we realize there's still a long way to go.

But honestly? I want to see it happen. I want a world where I can wake up, sip my coffee, and have a fully conscious AI assistant that isn't just regurgitating Wikipedia articles but can debate philosophy, help me invent something groundbreaking, or at the very least, tell me where I left my damn keys. I want to ask an AI, 'What is the meaning of life?' and get something more profound than 'As an AI model, I don't have personal opinions, but here's a generic summary from five different sources.' I want AGI to be weird, unpredictable, and occasionally sarcastic—not just a glorified search engine with excellent grammar.

And if it doesn't happen? Well, at least I'll still have my slightly confused but well-meaning AI assistants, my ever-failing printer, and the existential dread of knowing that my Roomba probably does have an opinion about me—but is just too polite to say it.

Rewriting Ourselves

> I think the biggest innovations of the 21st century will be at the intersection of biology and technology. A new era is beginning. —STEVE JOBS

If we can re-engineer computers to be exponentially faster and if we can build AI that learns and adapts, why can't we do the same for ourselves? I want to live long enough to see the day when human longevity isn't just about eating kale and hoping for the best, but about truly rewriting the human body like a piece of software—patching out disease, upgrading cells, and maybe even fixing whatever evolutionary quirks make me need coffee to function.

The dream isn't about uploading our minds into a computer. It's about cross-pollinating AI and biology, using gene editing, nanotechnology, and regenerative medicine to turn aging from an inevitability into an optional inconvenience. Imagine a world where your body self repairs, where your cells don't just degrade over time but get regular updates to keep everything running smoothly. Where diseases that once seemed unbeatable are debugged out of existence, and instead of getting old, you just… keep going.

I don't just want to live longer—I want to live better. Not as a decrepit, 100-year-old fossil, but as a fully optimized, version 2.0 human who can still go windsurfing, remember where I put my glasses, and maybe even get an upgrade that lets me finally appreciate jazz. Science is already making strides—CRISPR gene editing, stem cell therapy, AI-driven drug discovery—so why stop at treating disease? Let's rebuild ourselves from the inside out, not just to survive longer, but to thrive longer.

Erewhon

Well, we're not exactly there yet, but if you want a glimpse into the future of human optimization, there's no better place to start than Erewhon, the hippest, most over-the-top health and wellness grocery store on the planet.

Think of it as Whole Foods' cooler, richer cousin, the one who meditates at sunrise, biohacks their sleep cycles, and probably has a personal shaman on speed dial. Walk into any Erewhon store, and you'll immediately feel like you should be doing more for your body. The shelves are lined with organic, biodynamic, adaptogenic, cold-pressed, and hand-foraged everything. A simple smoothie will set you back $20+, especially if it's the latest celebrity-endorsed blend (the Hailey Bieber Skin Glaze Smoothie, for example, was practically a cultural event).

Erewhon isn't just a grocery store, it's a wellness temple, a place where people don't just shop, they invest in their future selves. It's where food isn't just about calories, but about cellular rejuvenation, microbiome optimization, and extending your lifespan by at least 30 years. And honestly? I kind of love the ambition of it. Because if we're serious about living longer, healthier lives, why stop at fancy mushrooms and ethically sourced collagen? Why not take it all the way—past the smoothies, past the supplements, and straight into rewriting human biology itself?

Now, the name 'Erewhon' isn't just a quirky branding choice—it comes from Samuel Butler's 1872 satirical novel, *Erewhon*, a book that flips society's norms upside down and asks uncomfortable questions about health, technology, and personal responsibility. The word itself is an anagram of 'Nowhere', hinting at the novel's central theme: a utopian society that feels eerily familiar, yet entirely strange.

Samuel Butler was a man ahead of his time, and Erewhon was his way of mocking the absurdities of Victorian England. The 19th century was obsessed with moral responsibility, particularly when it came to poverty and illness. Many Victorians believed that if you were poor or sick, it was your own fault: the result of bad choices, moral weakness, or simply not trying hard enough. Butler took this logic to its extreme, creating a world where being sick was seen as a punishable offense, while acts of dishonesty were treated as unfortunate misfortunes, requiring compassion and therapy. The novel was a critique not just of Victorian morality, but also of the rapid industrialization and blind faith in progress that characterized the era.

'Erewhon wasn't just about health—it also contained one of the earliest warnings about artificial intelligence. In the novel, the people of Erewhon have outlawed machines, fearing that they might evolve consciousness and surpass humans. Butler was decades ahead of his time in imagining the risks of unrestrained technological progress, foreshadowing concerns that we still wrestle with today in discussions about AI and automation.

But back to our health. Here's the real question: how responsible are we for our own health? Today, we live in an era where personal wellness has become both an aspiration and a status symbol. Erewhon (the store) embodies this, promoting the idea that if you eat right, biohack your sleep, and take the right supplements, you can optimize your body like a high-performance machine. And in many ways, it's true, we have more knowledge than ever about what keeps us healthy, and personal choices do play a huge role in longevity.

But where does the line fall between personal responsibility and societal factors? Is health purely an individual choice, or is it shaped by genetics, environment, and access to resources? If someone gets sick, should we blame them for making bad choices, or should we recognize that health is a complex web of factors beyond anyone's full control? In *Erewhon*, Butler exaggerated the idea to make a point, but in today's world, where wellness culture is booming and medical advancements are accelerating, the question feels more relevant than ever. Are we moving toward a future where being unhealthy is seen as failure, or one where technology and medicine give everyone a better shot at rewriting their own fate?

Waiting For The Singularity

The timing is going to be tricky...

Ray Kurzweil is one of the great techno-prophets of our time, a pioneer in AI, futurism, and the supplier of bold predictions that make scientists raise an eyebrow and tech bros nod solemnly in agreement. He's spent his career at the cutting edge of innovation, developing speech recognition, inventing the first flatbed scanner, and championing artificial intelligence before most people knew what it was. But what he's most famous for is his theory of the Singularity, that moment when technology advances so rapidly that AI surpasses human intelligence, effectively changing everything about existence forever. And according to him, that moment is coming in 2045.

The problem? Kurzweil was born in 1948. That means that by 2045, he will be 97 years old—which is uncomfortably close to the expiration date nature tends to impose on even the most health-conscious geniuses. And Kurzweil? He is not having it. Dropping dead before the Singularity would be like leading a marathon for 26 miles and collapsing 100 meters before the finish line. That is simply not an option for the man who has built his career on predicting a future where death is obsolete.

And so Kurzweil is doing everything humanly possible to stay alive long enough to see the Singularity happen. He reportedly takes over 100 pills a day, follows a meticulously engineered diet, and engages in cutting-edge longevity treatments that most of us haven't even heard of. There are even rumors—delightful, possibly exaggerated rumors—that he bought Michael Jackson's old hyperbaric chamber to oxygenate his cells into immortality. Honestly, if there were a way to upload himself onto the cloud and reinstall his consciousness in 2045, he'd probably be the first in line.

But what if he doesn't make it? It would be the cruelest irony in the history of futurism. Imagine spending your entire life predicting the moment when humans break free from biology and become immortal, only to miss it by a couple of years. It's the cosmic equivalent of your internet cutting out at 99% on a massive download.

Say what you will about his ideas, you have to admire his sheer determination. Kurzweil isn't just predicting the future—he is trying to outrun mortality itself. Whether or not the Singularity arrives on schedule, the real story might be the race between Kurzweil and the clock. And honestly? I kind of hope he makes it. If only because I'd love to see his victory lap social media post in 2045: 'Told you so. #Singularity.'

That type of transhumanism might sound like something out of a science fiction novel written by a slightly overenthusiastic futurist. But in reality, we've already started upgrading ourselves, only in ways so subtle that we barely notice. Take hearing aids, for example. These used to be a public declaration of struggle, complete with bulky plastic tubes, weird screeching feedback, and the constant need to adjust them while looking mildly panicked. They were less about restoring hearing and more about broadcasting to the world: 'I can't hear you, and I'm not thrilled about it.'

But today? Hearing aids have quietly gone from embarrassing medical devices to stealthy superpowers. Modern ones are tiny, bluetooth-enabled, and packed with AI that adjusts sound in real time, filtering out background noise and amplifying speech with more precision than most humans naturally have. The next generations won't just restore hearing—they'll enhance it, letting people tune in to specific conversations in a noisy room, filter out unwanted sound, or even hear frequencies that regular humans can't. Soon, we won't just be helping the hearing-impaired—we'll be engineering super-hearing. Imagine an elderly man in a café eavesdropping on conversations from across the street or someone casually tuning into a radio frequency just by thinking about it. At some point, we're all going to want these things, whether we need them or not.

And it's not just ears. Exoskeletons—another invention that started as a medical aid—are about to change everything. Originally developed to help people with mobility impairments, these robotic wearables augment human strength, reduce strain, and basically turn us all into low-key superheroes. Today's exoskeletons help factory workers lift heavy objects without wrecking their backs and allow people with paralysis to walk again. Tomorrow's? We're looking at casual super-strength for everyday life. Imagine your grandmother, now 90, suddenly being able to sprint up a flight of stairs carrying groceries like she's auditioning for *The Avengers*. One day, an office worker might just strap on a lightweight exosuit to avoid back pain after eight hours of slouching in a chair.

These aren't distant-future ideas. They're happening right now, in real labs, with real prototypes, and real possibilities of becoming mainstream within our lifetimes. Little by little, human augmentation is sneaking into everyday life not as some wild transhumanist revolution, but as a series of small, practical, incredibly useful upgrades. It's not about becoming cyborgs overnight—it's about quietly fixing all the terrible design flaws nature left us with. And if that means one day hearing like a bat and casually deadlifting a refrigerator in an exosuit, well, I'm all for it.

Cheating Death

The real question isn't if we can upgrade our bodies—it's how far we can push them before nature throws up its hands and says, 'All right, fine, you win.' This is where companies like Calico come in. Founded as a Google spin-off (apparently regular Google wasn't ambitious enough), Calico is on a mission to 'solve' aging. Yes, that's right—while most of us are just trying to drink enough water and remember to stretch in the morning, Calico is actively working to hack human longevity itself.

But they're not alone. There's an entire startup ecosystem looking at cell rejuvenation, genetic reprogramming, and therapies that could extend human lifespan by decades—maybe even centuries. But to be honest, the first people lining up to get these treatments aren't your friendly neighborhood postal workers or schoolteachers—it's the same Silicon Valley titans who already own half the planet.

Which is, let's be honest, a little terrifying. The idea that the ultra-rich might not only be wealthier than everyone else but also significantly older raises all kinds of dystopian possibilities. Imagine a future where the same handful of billionaires who have been shaping the world for the last 50 years just... don't leave. Where retirement is optional, and Jeff Bezos is still launching himself into space at the age of 170 while the rest of us are eating fiber-rich cereal and hoping for the best.

The good news? If these companies do crack the code of longevity, the technology will eventually trickle down to the rest of us. Maybe. After all, once upon a time, only billionaires had cell phones, and now even your grandma has TikTok. The real question is when—and whether we'll have any say in who gets to stick around for the next few centuries.

So, what are we actually doing here? Are we saving humanity from the cruel tyranny of time, or are we just playing God with better funding and a fancier lab setup? The idea of extending human life—whether by genetic engineering, AI-driven medicine, or replacing our squishy biological parts with something a little more durable—is in equal parts thrilling and terrifying. Because history has taught us something important: every time humans unlock a new level of power, we have absolutely no idea what to do with it.

Gaia

Isaac Asimov saw this coming decades ago in his *Foundation* trilogy. In the later books, we meet the ruling class of a planet called Gaia, where the elites have genetically engineered themselves to live forever. At first, this seems like the ultimate advantage—who wouldn't want to be led by people with centuries of experience and wisdom? But the problem is they never leave. They become detached, arrogant, and completely out of touch with the changing world. They're no longer leaders; they're stagnant overlords, unable to evolve because they've simply been around too long. Immortality, instead of being a gift, becomes a bottleneck for progress.

That's the scary part of all this. If only a select few get to extend their lives indefinitely, we could end up in a world where power never changes hands, where history stops moving, and where the same ultra-wealthy, ultra-powerful people keep steering civilization forever. If we're not careful, we don't just get a future where people live longer—we get a future where no one else gets a turn.

But here's the thing—I still want to see it happen. Because if we can get this right, if we can make longevity something that benefits everyone, it could change the human experience forever. Imagine a world where aging is optional, where people get a second, third, or even fourth act in life, where the wisdom of age isn't wasted by bodies that break down too soon. Imagine having the time to actually learn every language you ever wanted, explore every corner of the world, master every skill you never had time for. Imagine a world where people don't just live longer—but better.

Yes, it's risky. Yes, we might screw it up in ways we can't even imagine yet. But if humanity has a chance to break free from the limits of biology, to step beyond the fleeting lifespan that nature assigned us, how could I not want to see that? We've spent thousands of years dreaming about the future. Now, we're on the verge of actually building it. And I, for one, want to stick around long enough to see where this all goes.

To live is the rarest thing in the world. Most people exist, that is all.

—OSCAR WILDE

Uncertainty Is A Feature, Not A Bug

Through the pages of this book and the stories within, I hope you've come to see that the world has never been stable, never predictable, and never truly 'normal'. The idea that we ever lived in an age of certainty is a comforting illusion, one we tell ourselves to feel in control. But history—whether scientific, technological, or social—has always been a chaotic, unpredictable, beautifully messy process. The faster we move forward, the more we realize there is no steady ground, only the next leap into the unknown. That's what The Uncertainty Principle is all about. Not fearing change, but leveraging it. Not waiting for the future to arrive neatly wrapped, but actively shaping it—even if we have no idea exactly where it's headed.

Quantum computing could rewrite reality as we know it. Robots could become so useful that we'll wonder how we ever lived without them—or so powerful we'll wish we had been more careful. AGI could be the greatest intellectual achievement in human history—or our last mistake. And rewriting our biology? That could be the key to a longer, better, more fulfilling life—or the spark that creates an unrecognizable world of genetic divides and unintended consequences.

For every bright future scenario, there is a potentially problematic anti-future, but I urge every one of you not to let the fear of darkness paralyze you. Standing still just isn't an option. I truly believe that the Never Normal is where progress happens. We can either cling to outdated ideas of stability and control, or we can learn to ride the waves of uncertainty: to shape, guide, and, yes, sometimes gamble on the future. If we hesitate too long, if we let fear of the unknown hold us back, we don't just risk missing out on breakthroughs, we risk becoming relics of the past before the future even arrives.

I, for one, refuse to sit on the sidelines. I want to see it all happen. The triumphs, the missteps, the world-changing leaps, and the inevitable chaos that comes with them. Because the future isn't something that happens to us. It's something we step into willingly, uncertainty and all. Uncertainty is a feature, not a bug. And if we play this right, if we embrace the messiness of change, we just might create something beyond anything we've ever imagined.

The greatest danger
for most of us is not that
our aim is too high
and we miss it,

but that it is too low
and we reach it. —MICHELANGELO

Endnotes

1. The Japanese martial art Aikido is based on spherical movements by which an attacker's aggressive force is turned against itself. The main form of Aikido techniques are joint immobilisation and throws using the opponents momentum.

2. https://www.theguardian.com/commentisfree/2016/dec/01/stephen-hawking-dangerous-time-planet-inequality

3. https://en.wikipedia.org/wiki/Valentin_Turchin

4. https://en.wikipedia.org/wiki/Peter_Turchin

5. The entropic heat death of the universe is the scenario in which the universe evolves to a state of no thermodynamic free energy. Basically the universe keeps expanding and cooling, where eventually all matter and energy reach a uniform temperature. In such a condition, stars burn out, leaving behind black holes, which eventually evaporate, and the universe becomes nothing but a vast expanse of low-energy radiation and sparse particles, and dies.

   I asked ChatGPT to try to put a little more positive spin on this, and this was the brilliant result:

   Imagine the universe as a bustling party that gradually winds down over eons. Initially, it's all bright and lively with stars like glittering disco balls and galaxies swirling in a cosmic dance. But as time ticks on, the universe decides to take things slow, spreading out and chilling— literally! Eventually, the stars burn out one by one, much like the party lights dimming until all that's left are a few weary black holes and particles floating about, mingling quietly in the vast, cool space. This cosmic cooldown party heads towards a mellow, uniform calm where everything is so laid-back that no more dramatic celestial events take place. It's the universe's way of easing into a grand, serene retirement.

6. Fun List: write down the five people you would have a dinner date with by using your five-rides-only time machine.

7. I actually think we should have called this chapter 'Thermodynamics', but that would scare off quite a few readers. Thermodynamics sounds really nerdy, but it is actually one of the most fun and exciting, and sometimes absolutely quirky, fields of science.

   Thermodynamics is the study of heat and energy, and how they flow and transform. It's like being a detective trying to solve the mysteries of the universe by following the trail of energy. Where does it come from? Where does it go? It teaches you that energy is a skilled shape-shifter, able to take on different forms like heat, light, sound, and motion. The fundamentals of thermodynamics is that it has laws, just like the laws of physics, that govern how energy can be used and transformed.

It is also full of mind-bending concepts like entropy, which is a measure of disorder. The more disordered something is, the higher its entropy. The Universe does have a natural tendency to become a giant mess over time, but thermodynamics helps us understand how to fight against that tendency and keep things neat and tidy. Thermodynamics is like a grand adventure story, full of energy, heat, and the eternal struggle between order and chaos. It's a tale of how the universe works at its most fundamental level.

....

8   Thermodynamics also has one of the funniest memes on the internet, with the opening lines of a college textbook on Thermodynamics that goes like this: Ludwig Boltzman, who spent most of his life studying statistical mechanics, died in 1906, by his own hand. Paul Ehrenfest, carrying on the work, died similarly in 1933. Now it is your turn to study statistical mechanics.

....

9   Quantum Electro Dynamics (QED) is the theory that describes the interactions between light and charged

particles like electrons and positrons. It combines quantum mechanics with special relativity and classical electromagnetism to explain how electrically charged particles produce and interact with electromagnetic fields by emitting and absorbing massless particles called photons. QED provides a fundamental understanding of electromagnetic interactions at the subatomic level and underpins much of modern technology from lasers to computer chips.

....

10   Book: *The Pleasure of Finding Things Out*, by Richard Feynman

....

11   Hans was one of the few people in my life who consistently came to me after my presentations and would give me a rundown of all the mistakes I had made in my keynote and would give me tips and pointers on how to improve my talks. He is also one of the few people in the world from whom I would accept that with absolute joy and pleasure.

....

12   Oh, and if you have not read his book *Factfulness*, coauthored with his daughter-in-law Anna Rosling Rönnlund and son Ola Rosling, you should definitely put that on your list.

....

13   Which seems to be the de facto standard answer to anything nowadays. Post ChatGPT, whenever a fundamental question arises in society or business, and we need something close to a miracle to understand how to move

forward, there is always one who shouts out: 'AI!'. Boy, that got old quickly...

14 https://en.wikipedia.org/wiki/
RAND_Corporation

15 No coincidence of course that the name Palantir was chosen for the US company that specializes in Big Data Analytics, founded by Peter Thiel and Alex Karp. The company is one of the pioneer AI companies harnessing the power of analytics to 'look ahead' into the future. A big part of their capability is being used in the field of intelligence and defense, for military strategy and counterterrorism. Oh, and they are also REALLY into the Lord of the Rings theme. I remember visiting them years ago, and my Palantir badge said: 'Welcome to the Shire'. J.R.R. Tolkien would turn in his grave...

16 https://hbr.org/2013/05/
living-in-the-futures

17 One of my key criteria for favorite book lists is re-readability—the ability to offer fresh insights with every revisit. *The Living Company* easily meets this standard; I've probably read it more than 10 times. It's one of those rare books I keep close, and when the moment feels right, I feel an undeniable urge to dive back in. Each reading brings me the same deep enjoyment. That, to me, is the mark of a truly extraordinary book. I have the

same with movies. I've probably re-watched *Dr. Strangelove* more than 25 times over the last 25 years.

18 A concept that Simon Sinek has revisited many times in his work. Sinek has become synonymous with the book *Start with Why*, and this idea of purpose and longevity is featured at length in *The Infinite Game*.

19 I joined the board of a bank during the Pandemic, and that became one of the most interesting experiences in my entire professional career. With my innovative and entrepreneurial background, joining a board that had an absolute focus on risk and compliance was an enormous mental challenge for me. It also gave me an incredible respect for the way that financial institutions are run, managed and governed.

20 The head of our Risk Committee became a dear friend. And I love his sense of humor and realism when he gifted all board members a copy of *The Illusion of Control: Why Financial Crises Happen, and What We Can (and Can't) Do About It* by Jon Danielsson.

21 By now, you're probably starting to wonder if there was anybody in the last century who was a scenario planner that did <u>not</u> work at Royal Dutch Shell...

22 https://barbaraathanassiadis.com/
history/venetian-glassmakers-in-paris

23 https://www.csmonitor.
com/Business/2022/0412/
End-of-an-era-The-decline-and-fall-
of-the-Kmart-retail-empire

24 https://www.hermes.com/be/en/
content/271366-six-generations-
of-artisans/

25 which also has a real cool electronics
symbol:

26 Entropy that increases is like a Room
Getting Messier: imagine your room as a
system. If you don't do anything to clean
or tidy it up (like an isolated system with
no external influence), the room tends
to get messier over time. The messiness
doesn't naturally go down—it stays the
same or increases. This messiness is like
the entropy of the room.

27 Many have tried. And many more will try.
Check out Calico.

28 Yep. Again. The S-curve ☺

29 https://www.britannica.com/event/
Afghanistan-War

30 https://www.britannica.com/
topic/Theranos-Inc

31 https://en.wikipedia.org/wiki/
The_Walt_Disney_Company

32 https://en.wikipedia.org/wiki/
John_von_Neumann; https://
www.essentiafoundation.org/
the-idealist-metaphysical-and-
economic-implications-of-john-
von-neummans-mathematics-of-
quantum-theory/reading/; https://
www.ias.edu/von-neumann; https://
www.amazon.com/Unparalleled-
Genius-John-von-Neumann-ebook/
dp/B087Y27834; Klára Dán von
Neumann—Wikipedia

33 https://en.wikipedia.org/wiki/Mustafa_
Suleyman; https://time.com/collection/
time100-ai/; https://medium.com/
data-science/tutorial-double-deep-
q-learning-with-dueling-network-
architectures-4c1b3fb7f756

34 One could remark that in this age of
evolution, nation states don't really
matter all that much anymore. The
power of militaries and nation states has
been replaced by the might of global
corporations for many decades, and
with the advent of 'Big Tech', that has
gotten a whole new dimension. Still, the
Brits feel pretty annoyed about it. Or
'miffed' as they would say…

35 As a side note: in part of his research
into possible applications of computers,
John von Neumann too became
interested in weather prediction, noting
similarities between the problems in the
field and those he had worked on during
the Manhattan Project.

36 Edward Tenner wrote an interesting
book about 'Revenge Effects' called *Why
Things Bite Back*.

37 https://en.wikipedia.org/wiki/Human_Genome_Project

38 https://en.wikipedia.org/wiki/Luddite

39 You can still find it, buried in the entrenched archeological layers of the early pre-social media internet. Google it. Or just go to https://www.wired.com/1995/06/digcity/

40 https://en.wikipedia.org/wiki/Sara_Blakely

41 https://www.history.com/topics/exploration/ferdinand-magellan

42 According to Wikipedia, after several weeks in the Philippines, Magellan had converted as many as 2,200 locals to Christianity. However, Lapulapu, the leader of Mactan, resisted conversion. In order to gain the trust of Rajah Humabon, Magellan sailed to Mactan with a small force on the morning of 27 April 1521. During the resulting battle against Lapulapu's troops, Magellan was struck by a 'bamboo' spear (bangkaw—metal-tipped fire-hardened rattan), and later surrounded and finished off with other weapons.

43 https://www.robertholden.com/about-robert/

44 https://en.wikipedia.org/wiki/Gary_Vaynerchuk

45 https://edition.cnn.com/2020/09/03/us/david-graeber-anthropologist-dies-trnd/index.html#:~:text=Graeber%20was%20a%20professor%20of,well%20as%20his%20anarchist%20views.

46 There's a hilarious scene about this in the Silicon Valley series. Just search 'Tabs versus Spaces (From Silicon Valley)' and you'll find it.

47 I mean, the Scots nailed it. James Watt, perhaps the most influential Scottish inventor, took the steam engine to a whole new level and fundamentally powered the Industrial Revolution. Andrew Carnegie, though better known for his later American industrial empire, began his life in Dunfermline, Scotland. He built an enormous steel industry and became one of the wealthiest people in history. Alexander Graham Bell, born in Edinburgh, revolutionized human communication with his invention of the telephone.

48 The legendary arrogance of Polytechnique graduates (called 'X'—referring to the crossed cannons in their logo) is almost as famous as their academic excellence. The school's motto 'Pour la Patrie, les Sciences et la Gloire' (For Country, Science and Glory) pretty much sets the tone.

A favorite story involves a Polytechnique professor writing a complex equation on the blackboard, then stating, 'And from here, the solution is obvious.' When a student dared to ask for clarification, the professor stared at the board silently for several minutes, then turned back and confidently declared 'Yes, I was right. It is obvious.'

The pinnacle of X pride might be the old saying: 'There are two types of engineers in France—those who went to Polytechnique, and those who wish they had.' Though some say the real divide is between those who went to Polytechnique and those who are tired of hearing about Polytechnique.

....

49 For the Seven Wonders of the Ancient World, there is a very clear consensus:

the Great Pyramid of Giza
the Hanging Gardens of Babylon
the Statue of Zeus at Olympia
the Temple of Artemis at Ephesus
the Mausoleum at Halicarnassus
the Colossus of Rhodes and
the Lighthouse of Alexandria

Back in 2007, someone had the brilliant idea to update the 2,000-year-old list and 'The New7Wonders Foundation' launched a global popularity contest where anyone could vote—because who needs archeologists or historians when you have social media?

The winners of this glorified travel bucket list included Petra in Jordan (thanks, Indiana Jones), and the Great Wall of China (which somehow wasn't wonderful enough for the ancient list). Machu Picchu made the cut, presumably because enough people wanted to update their Instagram profiles. Christ the Redeemer in Rio got in—a statue from 1931 competing against millennia-old structures, but hey, it photographs well.
The Colosseum was selected, perhaps because Rome's tourism board has an excellent PR team. Chichén Itzá represents all pre-Columbian architecture because apparently, one Mayan site is enough. And of course, the Taj Mahal, which at least has the decency to be genuinely magnificent.

Meanwhile, the Great Pyramid of Giza—you know, the only survivor of the actual ancient wonders—got a patronizing 'honorary candidate' status.

The whole exercise conveniently created perfect tour packages spanning three continents, delighting travel agents worldwide. Airlines quickly updated their route maps, hotels jacked up prices, and tourist trap vendors stocked up on miniature replicas. Because nothing says 'wonder of the world' quite like a snow globe made in China depicting a Peruvian mountain.

Oh, and the Suez Canal didn't make the final cut. Dang.

....

50 For a long time, quinine—first isolated in 1820 from the bark of the cinchona tree, which is native to Peru—was used to treat malaria. Jesuit missionaries learned of the bark's properties from indigenous peoples and began shipping it back to Europe, where it became known as 'Jesuit's Bark' or 'Jesuit's Powder'. This created quite a dilemma for Protestant England—many preferred to suffer from malaria rather than use a 'papist' remedy. Oliver Cromwell allegedly died of malaria because he refused to take the Catholic medicine.

....

51 In case you're wondering about the name: the founders got tired of writing the very long 'Andreessen Horowitz' on everything, so they abbreviated it to a16z: it starts with an a, then there are 16 letters, and then it ends with a z. Technically, that's called a 'numeronym': words created with the help of numbers.

But anyway, you counted to see if there were 16 letters, right?

....

52 The 'Browser Wars' was not the nicest part of Microsoft's history. When Netscape executives explained the potential of web browsers to Microsoft back in 1995, Bill Gates had an epiphany that changed Microsoft's entire strategy. He understood instantly that browsers could potentially make Windows irrelevant by becoming a platform themselves. Gates wrote his famous 'Internet Tidal Wave' memo, and Microsoft shifted into aggressive competition mode.

Microsoft's tactics were brutal and ultimately deemed anti-competitive. They bundled Internet Explorer free with Windows (when Netscape was charging for Navigator), they made it difficult to uninstall IE, and they allegedly threatened PC manufacturers who tried to ship computers with Netscape pre-installed. The infamous quote from Microsoft executive Paul Maritz was that they would 'cut off Netscape's air supply' by giving away Internet Explorer for free.

The strategy worked. Netscape's market share plummeted, leading to their fire sale to AOL in 1998. Microsoft's practices led to a major antitrust case, where they were initially ordered to break up the company (though this was later reversed on appeal). The case painted Microsoft as a corporate bully and tarnished their reputation for years.

The irony is that while Microsoft 'won' the browser war, they largely missed the bigger internet revolution that followed. By focusing so intensely on protecting Windows, they missed opportunities in search, social media, and mobile that other companies would later capitalize on. It's often cited as a classic example of winning the battle but losing the war—and a cautionary tale about how aggressive monopolistic behavior can backfire in the long run.

....

53 While Andreessen was chairman, Horowitz was the one dealing with the day-to-day struggles of keeping the

company alive, including laying off many employees and pivoting the business from LoudCloud to Opsware. The stress was immense—he famously described it as 'like eating glass and staring into the abyss'.

The contrast in their experiences during this period was stark. While Horowitz was fighting daily battles to save the company, Andreessen had moved on to other ventures and board seats. This created some tension between them, with Horowitz reportedly feeling that he had been left to handle the hardest parts alone.

According to various accounts, when Andreessen later approached Horowitz about starting a venture capital firm together, Horowitz was initially hesitant. The LoudCloud/Opsware experience had been traumatic, and he wasn't immediately sure he wanted to partner with Andreessen again.

They did ultimately form a16z together, and their different experiences and perspectives actually became a strength. Horowitz's experience as a CEO during tough times shaped a16z's approach to supporting founders, while Andreessen's big-picture thinking and network helped make them one of Silicon Valley's most influential VC firms.

It's often cited as an example of how challenging experiences, while potentially damaging to relationships

in the short term, can lead to stronger partnerships if both parties learn and grow from them. Their complementary skills and experiences, even the difficult ones, helped shape a16z's distinctive approach to venture capital.

54 https://en.wikipedia.org/wiki/Boston_Dynamics

55 https://rodneybrooks.com/three-things-that-llms-have-made-us-rethink/

56 Note the irony here: John Searle chose 'Chinese' as the language for the room as it was something totally foreign to most people working in artificial intelligence in the US at the time.

57 A homunculus is a small human being. Popularized in 16th-century alchemy and 19th-century fiction, it has historically referred to the creation of a miniature, fully formed human.

Peter Hinssen is a global keynote speaker, bestselling author, business school lecturer, LinkedIn Top Voice, serial entrepreneur, trusted board member, startup investor and the world's leading innovation, technology and leadership expert.

Pathological Optimist

Peter likes to describe himself as a pathological optimist. He firmly believes that companies can and should help build a better, brighter and bolder Day After Tomorrow.

Keynote Speaker & Lecturer

Peter is a top ranked and world class speaker on technological evolution, innovation strategy and adaptive leadership. He delivers his content with a unique combination of depth, clarity, positivity, and a dry sense of humor.

Peter has collaborated with Fortune 1000 companies and leading brands like Google, Apple, Facebook, Amazon, Accenture, HP, SAS, Microsoft, Gartner, Danone, HSBC, London Business School, Sanofi, Bill and Melinda Gates Foundation and many more. He also lectures at renowned business schools like the London Business School.

Serial Entrepreneur

For more than fifteen years, Peter led a life of technology startups. His first company e-COM was acquired by Alcatel-Lucent; his second, Streamcase, by Belgacom; and his third venture, Porthus, was quoted on the stock exchange in 2006 and acquired by Descartes.

Between startups, he has been an Entrepreneur in Residence with McKinsey & Company, with a focus on digital and technology strategy. Peter's current company nexxworks helps inspire and connect organizations to thrive in the Never Normal.

Peter is also an extremely active investor in startups and scaleups around the world, as well as a passionate collector of vintage technologies.

The Phoenix And The Unicorn (2020)

This is a book about companies that—just like the Phoenix, the mythical bird—are able to rethink themselves in cycles: time and time again they rise from the ashes of the old, and come out stronger than ever before. They are the Walmarts, the Volvos, the Disneys, the Apples, the Microsofts, the Ping Ans and the Assa Abloys of this world.

The Day After Tomorrow (2017)

In *The Day After Tomorrow*, Peter writes about an exponentially changing world and its consequences for organizations of Today. He introduces those pioneers who managed to move (way) beyond Tomorrow-thinking in innovation and were able to change the course of entire industries. Above all, he writes about the business models, the organizational structures, the talent, the mindset, the technologies and the cultures needed to maximize our chances for survival in the Day After Tomorrow.

The Network Always Wins (2014)

This powerful guide shows you how to keep your company up to speed with your market, engage with customers at a time when loyalty keeps fading into the background, and transform your organization into a network in order to thrive in this era of digital disruption.

The New Normal (2010)

In *The New Normal*, Peter Hinssen looks at the way companies have to adapt their information strategy, their technology strategy, their innovation strategy and the way they are organized internally. This book is an interesting read for any manager who is concerned with the future of his company as it is hit by the digital revolution.

Business/IT Fusion (2008)

Organizations have to go beyond 'aligning business and IT'. They have to 'fuse' business and IT. Fusion will allow companies to focus on technology-enabled innovation, instead of just on the commodity-saving potential of technology. Fusion will allow a new type of IT organization, that will evolve from an 'executional technology function' towards a 'proactive strategic innovation function'. Fusion will allow companies to focus on maximizing value from technology innovation.

Thank You

Writing this book has been a journey (a long one)—one that would have been impossible without the support, guidance, and encouragement of some truly remarkable people.

First and foremost, my deepest gratitude goes to Laurence Van Elegem. Your invaluable insights, thoughtful feedback, and tireless soundboarding have shaped this book in ways I couldn't have imagined. Your dedication to editing and refining my thoughts turned my ideas into something far more coherent, and I couldn't have done it without you.

A heartfelt thank you to Marianne Vermeulen for your exceptional coordination. Your ability to keep everything moving forward ensured this book actually made it to the finish line—no small feat in itself.

To my assistant Cathy Boesmans: you have been my rock, my organizer, my steady support—every day, over and over again. Thank you for being there through it all.

To Steven Van Belleghem, my business partner, friend, and favorite co-adventurer on the nexxworks tours: your content may not have made it onto these pages this time, for practical reasons, but your visionary ideas on customer experience have always been a profound source of inspiration.

I'm deeply grateful to my publisher, LannooCampus, for believing in this project and making it a reality. Your commitment to bringing this book to life has been extraordinary.

To everyone who contributed, in big ways or small, thank you. Whether it was input, collaboration or encouragement, you played a part in this journey, and I'm incredibly grateful. So, a big thanks to Anna Rich, Griet Hemeryck, Ivy Vanderheyden, Marc Lerouge, Marije Roefs, Niels Janssens, Steven Theunis, Thijs Kestens, Vera Ponnet and Wouter Laleman.

A special thank you to nexxworks for amplifying my message and helping me connect with audiences and organizations around the world.

To my family, thank you for your patience and understanding as I juggled work, writing, and travel. Your unwavering support has meant everything.

Finally, to all the companies, leaders, and audiences I've had the privilege of engaging with—thank you for inspiring me, challenging me, and fueling my passion to explore the ideas shared in this book.

This book is as much yours as it is mine. Thank you for being part of this journey.

D/2025/45/121– ISBN 978 90 209 5509 5 – NUR 800

Author: Peter Hinssen
Editors: Laurence Van Elegem and Anna Rich
Interior Design: Armée de Verre Bookdesign
Infographics and cover: Saflot, Vera Ponnet
Project manager: Marianne Vermeulen

© ⨁ *Peter Hinssen*
and Uitgeverij Lannoo NV Tielt, 2025

LannooCampus Publishers
Vaartkom 41 box 01.02   P.O. Box 23202
3000 Leuven   1100 DS Amsterdam
Belgium   The Netherlands
www.lannoocampus.com